W9-AGC-182

Acknowledgments

Grateful acknowledgment is made to the following for permission to reprint and use copyrighted material:

Lynne Rienner Publishers: Sam C. Sarkesian, *US National Security: Policy-makers, Processes, and Politics*, 2nd edn (Boulder, CO: Lynne Rienner Publishers, 1995).

Stephen J. Cimbala (ed.), *Clinton and Post-Cold War Defense* (Westport, CT: Praeger, 1996).

Sam C. Sarkesian and Robert E. Connor, Jr (eds), *America's Armed Forces: A Handbook of Current and Future Capabilities* (Westport, CT: Greenwood Press, 1996).

THE
US MILITARY PROFESSION
INTO THE
TWENTY-FIRST CENTURY

For if the trumpet give an uncertain sound, who shall prepare himself to battle?

I Corinthians 14, 8

THE
US MILITARY PROFESSION
INTO THE
TWENTY-FIRST CENTURY

War, Peace and Politics

Sam C. Sarkesian and
Robert E. Connor, Jr

FRANK CASS
LONDON • PORTLAND OR.

First published in 1999 in Great Britain by
FRANK CASS PUBLISHERS
Newbury House, 900 Eastern Avenue
London, IG2 7HH

and in the United States of America by
FRANK CASS PUBLISHERS
c/o ISBS, 5804 N.E. Hassalo Street
Portland, Oregon, 97213-3644

Website: www.frankcass.com

British Library Cataloguing in Publication Data

Sarkesian, Sam C. (Sam Charles)
The US military profession into the twenty-first century:
war, peace and politics
1. Civil–military relations – United States 2. National
security – United States 3. United States – Armed Forces
4. United States – Military policy 5. United States – Armed
Forces – Political activity
I. Title II. Connor, Robert E.
355'.033'0073

ISBN 0-7146-4919-8 (cloth)
ISBN 0-7146-4472-2 (paper)

Library of Congress Cataloging-in-Publication Data

Sarkesian, Sam Charles.
The US military profession into the twenty-first century: war,
peace and politics: Sam C. Sarkesian and Robert E. Connor, Jr.
p. cm.
Includes bibliographical references and index.
ISBN 0-7146-4919-8 (cloth). – ISBN 0-7146-4472-2 (paper)
1. United States–Armed Forces. 2. World politics–1989–
I. Connor, Robert E. II. Title.
UA23.S2745 1999
355' .00973' 0905–dc21   99-32176
                                                          CIP

Typeset by Vitaset, Paddock Wood, Kent
Printed in Great Britain by
MPG Books Ltd, Bodmin, Cornwall

Contents

List of Figures and Tables

Preface

The suspicion of large standing armies is deeply rooted in the American psyche. As is well known, this has its origins in the American revolution and the cautions expressed by the Founding Fathers. From this evolved civilian supremacy over the military – an indisputable constitutional principle. In turn this has led to the notion of a 'wall' between the military and politics. For the most part, the wall has prevailed as a dominant theme in the relationship between them. Most civilians and many military professionals have accepted this wall as a fact of life. While military men have been periodically involved in political disputes, the general view has been that politics and the military are clearly separate spheres. The central thesis of this book is that not only is the notion of such a wall historically inaccurate but it distorts the relationship between the military and the political system. The use of military force has always been shaped by political considerations, as has military strategy. This is particularly the case today. The American domestic landscape and the international strategic landscape in the remainder of the twentieth century and into the next are politically and militarily inextricable.

To respond effectively to these landscapes, the concept of military professionalism must be philosophically broadened and intellectually nurtured to encompass a more prominent political dimension. The military must adopt the doctrine of constructive political engagement, framing and building a judicious and artful involvement in the policy arena. This is the fundamental theme of this book. The military profession cannot remain silent in the context of the American political process if its views are to be known. The goal is to ensure that military concerns and perspectives are properly integrated into the policies that have an impact on military life; and that political perspectives are integrated into the military dimension.

A brief glance at the past 50 years shows that the difficulties facing the US military are not new phenomena. Since the end of World War II, the US military has passed through difficult times. These have included trying to come to grips with atomic/nuclear warfare, the Korean War, the Vietnam War, and adjusting to a volunteer military system. To be sure, much of this was experienced in the context of the Cold War and the possibility of a US–USSR conflict. There was a clear adversary, major ideological differences, and efforts at creating two distinct worlds between East and West. All of this gave the US military a clear focus and purpose.

In the post-Cold War era the US military is struggling with particularly difficult and complex issues. The new world order (or disorder) has created strategic uncertainty and operational ambiguity, which is likely to continue well into the twenty-first century, the Gulf War in 1991 notwithstanding. As a result, combined with the changing domestic landscape, broader notions of national security, encompassing values as well as interests, the US military has been plunged into a variety of missions and contingencies that appear peripheral to its raison d'être. These operations other than war include a variety of humanitarian missions, peacekeeping, peace enforcement, unconventional conflicts, and domestic missions as well as a host of drug-abatement activities. At the same time, the military is engaged in serious efforts to prepare for information-age warfare.

Compounding these challenges is that the US political–social system is changing, with the rise of issues such as multiculturalism, diversity, gender, race, and homosexuality, and debate over the meaning of Americanism. The spillover of such issues into the military domain raises serious questions regarding the degree to which the military reflects (or should reflect) society.

At one level, the US military is faced with the issues of the post-Cold War era and the new world order, while trying to come to grips with transition into the twenty-first century and the new millennium. In more specific terms, the US and its military are not seriously threatened by major conventional wars, even though there is much concern about weapons of mass destruction, particularly after the nuclear tests by India and Pakistan in 1998, and possible renegade behavior of some elements of the Russian military. Also in the late 1990s, most Americans seem to accept the peace and prosperity claims of the Clinton Administration, regardless of the 1999 Kosovo conflict.

At another level, the US military is trying to come to terms with democratization, civil–military relations, and operations other than war, while retaining its raison d'être. While the general public expects the military to conform to basic principles of democratic society, within the military there is discomfort and concern about how to do this and still maintain military cohesion and prepare for future conflicts. As a consequence, the military profession is faced with rethinking the implications of the new strategic and domestic landscapes on its primary purpose – success in battle and winning the nation's wars; and doing this with reduced resources and manpower.

To repeat, the US military is faced with two broad challenges: coming to grips with the new international security landscape and responding to the American domestic environment. While there are a number of political–social actors and considerations, it is our firm belief that the military profession is the *critical* actor in responding to these challenges. It is the military profession that shapes military culture, the military image, and sets the guidelines and parameters for the military system to function within the US political system. It is the military profession that must ensure that its moral and ethical principles, and standards of military conduct maintain the legitimacy and credibility of the US political system. And it is the military profession that is the primary actor in designing military strategy and operational doctrine, and maintaining military effectiveness. This view of the military profession is the organizing concept and philosophical underpinning of this book.

This volume partly evolves from what was written in 1981. 'The fundamental issue for the military in the post Vietnam era is how to revise the professional ethos and adapt it to the new international security environment and the nature of liberal democratic society.'[1] Until recently, we felt that the fundamental issue had been resolved or was being resolved. President Reagan's affirmation of the Vietnam War as a 'noble cause', the end of the Cold War, and the success in the Persian Gulf War offered solid support for our view.

We were wrong. The theme in this volume is that US military professionalism, as it is presently conceived of and followed, will find it difficult to meet the challenges of the remainder of the twentieth century and into the next. Not only is this true with respect to the international-security landscape, but the existing military professional posture will make it extremely difficult to respond to domestic political–social issues and to interact harmoniously with the American political system. Moreover, the new generation of political leaders, and much of the population, in general, have little, if any, military experience. This also is characteristic of many in the media. While this may not necessarily lead to an inappropriate national strategy, it does create a gray area in understanding and responding to the military.

This volume examines military professionalism and the revisions, modifications, and/or changes necessary to respond to the changed domestic and strategic environments. While particular attention is given to the US Army, the study applies to the military profession, in general. Nonetheless, it is the US Army that faces the most difficult problems.

There are four parts to the book: The US Military Profession in a Changing World; American Society and the Military; The New World Order and the Utility of Military Force; and Conclusions. Parts II and III are the primary focus of this study. The book begins with an introduction of two chapters: an overview of the volume and the concept of military profession. This is followed by the two major parts of this work: American society and the military; and the new world order and utility of military force. The first major part is a study of the relationships between American society and the military. This includes a historical introduction to politics and the military that serves as a background for the subsequent chapters in this part. A discussion of American culture and its changing dimensions follows with a comparison with military culture. The next chapter is on the national security system, providing a portrait of the role of the military in the decision-making process. And finally, all of these matters are put into the context of civil–military relations and how these relations have changed and are changing. In the broader framework, this part stresses the changes in the American political–social system and the way in which domestic political–social forces are spilling over from society into the military, and the military's efforts to respond appropriately.

The second major part is a study of the new world order and the utility of military force. This begins with a discussion of the characteristics of the new world and the strategic landscape, including a comparison of the Cold War and post-Cold War periods and the legacy of the superpower era. Subsequently, there is a study of US strategy and conflict characteristics, addressing the relationship between strategy and conflict and how these are likely to evolve into the next century. The next chapter examines the effectiveness of US military force across the conflict spectrum. The final chapter in this part is a study of conflict characteristics, military doctrine and force structures, and how all of this affects military capability.

In both major parts, the key questions focus on the military professional perspective, how this relates to prevailing views of the national leadership, the National Command Authority, and the American public. From this the military professional need for involvement in the political realm is addressed.

Part IV focuses on the new military professionalism and the need for constructive political engagement. This begins with a broad summary and conclusion of the substance of the book and ends with a review of what the military profession needs to do to respond effectively to the major challenges it faces in the new domestic and strategic environments. This leads to a 'new' military professionalism challenging the traditional view of a 'wall' between the military and politics and a military profession disengaged from the political realm. Constructive political engagement is the key for the military profession.

The last chapter in Part IV is an Afterword. This re-examines civilian and military cultures as it is affected by the commander-in-chief. The impeachment of President Clinton in late 1998 and the Senate verdict in 1999 had some impact on the military and military profession. For many in the military, the character and conduct of President Clinton raised issues of double standards and crystallized the notion of a 'gap' between the civilian and military cultures. This is examined and related to the earlier chapter on civilian and military cultures.

There is necessarily a degree of overlap from chapter to chapter. A particular issue or subject may have multiple dimensions beyond the focus of any one chapter. Further, chapters vary in length. This is not intended to privilege one subject over another; rather, it reflects our view of the scope of understanding of one subject in comparison with another. Thus, for example, Chapter 3, 'Politics and The Military: A Historical Introduction', is longer than several other chapters. This is because we believe that the political dimension of the military from the founding of the republic to the end of the nineteenth century has generally been neglected or subsumed under other matters; or, to some degree, placed on the periphery of military and politics. Yet, the roots of modern-day intermingling of politics and the military are in this earlier period.

Some of the subjects included in this study are likely to be undergoing research in other quarters that may lead to new formulations or differing interpretations. The intent here, however, is not to delve comprehensively into any particular subject, even if it could be done in one volume; many of these subjects and issues require separate volumes. It is not intended to provide answers to all of the issues and questions raised in this study. Rather, the purpose is to provide a guide to the primary issue – constructive political engagement. Regardless of what new formulations or research will uncover and the comprehensive factual basis of the subjects examined here, the primary focus is to examine and show the need for a political voice for the military profession. What we have attempted to do is to clarify what has been and what appears to be the position of the military and what should be the role of the military profession in ensuring its voice is heard.

Further, we acknowledge that projecting into the twenty-first century is replete with conjectures. It is unlikely that any observer can predict with any sense of certainty what the twenty-first century will bring in terms of domestic and international landscapes. Nonetheless, we have tried to identify the directions and possible events that may reinforce or change such directions, and how this may play in the next century. Again, the focus is on the political dimension of military professionalism.

This volume is not intended to serve as an operational manual to implement programs and training designed to correct professional shortcomings. One will not find, for example, what changes of curricula are needed in senior service schools to develop the dimensions of professionalism advocated here. Nor will one find extensive analysis of force structure and doctrine. While the last part addresses the problem of 'what needs to be done', this is viewed from a broad perspective aimed at the philosophical and political underpinnings of the military-professional ethos.

At this writing, it remains to be seen how the 1999 impeachment of President Clinton and his capacity to lead in the Kosovo crisis will affect the military and the military profession. We are convinced that the moral authority of the Commander-in-Chief is critical for effective response to the international landscape. We are equally convinced that such moral authority is essential in maintaining the trust and honor of the military. To be sure, the military profession will continue to function professionally and the military will respond as effectively as possible. But the intransigence of the Commander-in-Chief over matters revealed and alleged in 1998 will surely place a dark cloud over the entire military establishment. We address this matter briefly in the first chapter, then glance at it in Chapter 11, and revisit it in the last chapter in the context of civilian and military cultures. We believe that such a troubling issue is beyond the military establishment and is in the broader realm of the US political system and the American people. This is not to deny the impact that such a matter will have on the military profession and the military, in general.

We have attempted to combine our experience as military professionals with our years in academia. That is, we have tried to follow the guidelines of scholarly research with participant–observer insights. At the same time, we have tried to be sensitive to the views of colleagues in academia and military professionals and former professionals, discussing with a number of them a variety of subjects mentioned in this volume. We have also studied assessments from appropriate literature. One hopes that all of this has led to a book that is reasonably balanced and not one of classroom theoreticians lecturing the military profession. Nonetheless, what is written here is likely to challenge a number of views of military professionalism that exist in both military and civilian circles. Of course, some will read this volume with an eye towards placing our views into a particular part of the political spectrum. This is to be expected given the book's political dimensions. And some will be critical of this volume because what is presented differs considerably from their own views.

To be clear, this is a book of reflection. It is not organized around an extensive research effort, nor on quantitative analysis. It mainly consists of reflections on what we have written before and our views of the international strategic landscape and American domestic directions in the final years of the 1990s and into the twenty-first century. The primary focus is on the role of the military profession in responding to these domestic and international issues. The book does not purport to provide some magic formula for solving all of the problems of the military and the military profession.

This is fundamentally an effort to define a reasonable starting point for the military profession in responding to the challenges of the next millennium. In the process we have tried to assess as fairly as possible, what many others have written about the US armed forces and the military profession. In any case, we are solely responsible for the analysis and conclusions.

PART I

THE US MILITARY PROFESSION IN A CHANGING WORLD

1

War, Peace, Politics, and the US Military

In the transition to the twenty-first century, the US military faces challenging and troubling issues. The strategic landscape remains unsettled, American society is changing, military contingencies have become embroiled in what many call non-traditional missions, while the military is struggling to respond to a variety of internal travails and at the same time prepare for the new century. All of this is taking place as budgetary constraints and societal expectations seem to dominate the political landscape. Thus, the US military faces a dilemma: how to respond to the uncertainties of the new domestic and strategic landscapes, nurture a proper relationship with society, and yet retain its raison d'être. In trying to cope with this dilemma, much attention has been given to civil–military relations in the post-Cold War period.[1] But the study of military professionalism in the same period has been generally subsumed under other matters, although it is the military profession that holds the key to how the US military will respond to this dilemma.

While the dilemma encompasses a number of considerations, the most critical is the military professional ethos into the twenty-first century. This has its roots in two important issues: the relationship of the military to American society and the utility of military force in the new world order. The troubling dimensions of such issues have revealed the need for a more assertive military profession within the political sphere, an assertion that is clearly necessary to clarify the military perspective to the American public and elected officials. Although the military profession is not the only actor in shaping and affecting these matters, it is the view here that it is *the* critical actor by virtue of its unique purpose.

It is the thesis here that the necessary step in resolving this dilemma is for the military profession to develop a more comprehensive view of the meaning of politics and the driving force underpinning the US political system, and adapt doctrine based on constructive political engagement.[2] This may trigger criticism from segments within the profession and in civilian circles. However, prudent political involvement by the military profession will reinforce the notion of civilian control, provide a more incisive concept of military professionalism, and place the military profession in a position to respond more effectively to the twenty-first century's domestic and strategic landscapes.

The remainder of this chapter offers an overview of the issues examined in the two major parts of this book: the relationship of the military to American society and the utility of military force in the new strategic landscape. Subsequent chapters examine these issues in more detail, focusing primarily on constructive political engagement and the military profession in America's political–social system. But first it is important to place these issues in a historical context.

HISTORICAL CONTEXT

The problems facing the military and the military profession are not new phenomena. Troubling times have been part and parcel of military history.[3] And this has not been confined to the US military. In the post-Napoleonic period in France, for example, Alfred de Vigny, of noble birth and a one-time soldier, lamented the fate of the Army.

> It is cut off from the main body of the nation, and trails behind like a child, undeveloped in mind and forbidden to grow up. When a modern Army ceases to be at war, it becomes a kind of constabulary. It feels ashamed and knows neither what it is nor what it is supposed to do, whether it rules the state or is its slave. It is a body searching high and low for its soul and unable to find it.[4]

While the historical periods may differ, the reasons for troubling times for the military usually evolve from generally similar circumstances. These periods need to be studied and the appropriate lessons drawn to serve as reference points for the current period. Here, we limit our overview to reference points from the founding of the American Republic to the end of the nineteenth century. It was during this period that much of the groundwork was laid for the political–military intermix of later years.

From the Revolution to the Post-Civil War Period

The notion of civil supremacy over the military was established in the views of the Founding Fathers and spelled out in the Constitution. The role of George Washington in expressing the subordinate role of the military to civilian leadership seemed to settle the notion of civilian supremacy. But this did not mean that there was a distinct wall between civilian and military life. The concept of the military profession had not developed into one sharply distinct from civilian life. Indeed, it was a common practice for individuals to move directly from civilian life into senior military positions.

Senior military officers were embroiled in politics before and during the Civil War. Their activities ranged from trying to assert their authority over the president and various members of Congress to setting themselves up to run for political office. This was seen in the Mexican War, with President Polk asserting his authority to select one general over another, driven by political motives. The political entanglements of Generals Winfield Scott and George McClellan are well known. The point is that the period from the American Revolution through the Civil War era was replete with political involvement in one form or another by senior military officers.

During the post-Civil War period, 1870–90, the US military went through a difficult period trying to adjust to the new domestic landscape. The Army went through what has been termed the 'dark ages' and the Navy a 'period of naval stagnation'.[5]

> The postbellum era has been tagged by military historians as 'the dark ages' of the United States Army. Considering political–military relations, there is little wonder. Criticisms from business apologists, labor antagonists, and rededicated pacifists converged on Washington; and what one finds in the Congressional records is a conglomerate of unappealing sketches of the Army and its leaders.[6]

Also during this period Congress passed the First Reconstruction Act, setting the stage for Army personnel to become governors, police, and judges throughout much of the old Confederacy.[7] There was no external threat to the United States, and the Army was relegated primarily to coastal defense, Indian wars, expansion to the west, and taming the old Confederacy. During the same period, the Army was also involved in domestic labor strife. The raison d'être of the Army seemed out of fashion.

According to Kemble,

> Prior to the 70s regular Army units had rarely been called upon to quell civil disorders. But between the first great wave of protests in 1877 and the Pullman strike of 1894, they were used repeatedly – in more than three hundred separate labor disputes, according to most accounts. State militias, immediately available to the governors, were employed even more.[8]

However, the Navy emerged out of the stagnation of the post-Civil War period as the United States evolved into a world power in the aftermath of the Spanish–American War. In the late nineteenth and into the twentieth century the Navy became the prominent service as the notion of 'Island America' became the security posture. The Navy's purpose was to keep the seas open for maritime commerce and to keep potential adversaries far from America's shores. In the process, naval officers remained distant from society. This external mission (included the Marines Corps) relegated the Army to a coastal defense mission. With the Spanish–American War and into World War I, the Army's role shifted to external considerations. Indeed, with the acquisition of territories resulting from the Spanish–American War, the United States acquired the trappings of empire.

The United States as a World Power

The revitalization of the US military in defeating Spain and in developing into a major world power led to a new dimension of US military policy. This 'represented a fundamental change'.[9] It also led to a new dimension in civil–military relations, with the US military gaining a more professional status and respect from the American political elite.

But shortly following World War I, the United States returned to its 'island nation' concept and isolation. President Harding's call for 'normalcy' resonated throughout the American people. Disillusioned with the 'old world' in the aftermath of World War I, the United States turned inward.[10] When the war ended, one historian wrote, 'The army was hastily demobilized, pouring millions of bored trainees and battle-shaken veterans into the job market without plan.'[11]

In between the two world wars, the Navy was seen as the first line or defense, while the Army Air Force was a fledgling service arm. For the most part this changed little until the 1930s and into World War II.[12] In the main, during periods of US strategic withdrawal the military profession became more distant from society, turned inwards, and found it difficult to gain a respectable place in the American political–social system. Clearly, World War II changed all of that.

Immediately following World War II, the draft was abolished, albeit for only a short time, and again America looked to a return to normalcy. The assumption was that the military would revert to a prewar posture. But the Cold War changed the strategic landscape. With its onset and the rise of a superpower world, the military gained a highly respectable place in the American domestic scene as well as in most international circles. Involvement in Korea was one watershed, marking the change from World War II euphoria to a more conflict-ridden world. A variety of lesser conflicts engaged the US military. The Vietnam War created another watershed – one that lingers today.

The Vietnam Era

In the late 1960s and into the early 1970s, the Vietnam War created a particularly troubling time for the military establishment. The ambiguities of the war and the 'Age of Aquarius' created an anti-military sentiment in the United States among very vocal groups, spilling over into society, in general.

> The Age of Aquarius is not a happy time for the US military establishment.
> Flower children are in the streets. Wars are unfashionable.

In circles of the New Left, men in uniform have come to symbolize the corruption of American life, the distortion of national priorities, the darker impulses of the American soul.

In colleges and high schools, new heroes have emerged whose battle cry is, 'Resist!' Politicians decry militarism, priests and doctors and lawyers encourage draft evasion, military recruiters are driven from college campuses, ROTC buildings are stoned and burned.[13]

During the same period, a number of books and articles reflected suspicion of and concern about the military establishment, pinpointing waste and mismanagement, and portraying inflexible and immature military perspectives.[14] All of these matters tarnished the military image and that of military professionals. This was also the case within the military, where distinctions were made between draftees and 'lifers' – career military men.

A paper delivered in 1970 stated:

> The anti-military sentiments that have surfaced during the past few years have created in the minds of many, a rather distorted image as to the relationships of the military to the problems of US society ... From the sociological viewpoint, one can point to a number of indicators with respect to the diminished military image ... The My Lai massacres, the alleged graft and corruption associated with the highest circles of senior enlisted men, the charge of military–industrial collusion, and the stress of the mass media on military activities within Vietnam, create the type of image which makes duty, honor, country sound hollow.[15]

Looking back at Vietnam, General Norman Schwarzkopf, commander of coalition forces in the 1991 Gulf War, who served two tours of duty in Vietnam, wrote, 'We in the military hadn't chosen the enemy or written the order – our elected leaders had. Nevertheless, we were taking much of the blame ... I couldn't shake the feeling that America had betrayed the South Vietnamese.'[16]

Contrary to the material published during the Vietnam War period, the General Schwarzkopf view is seen in later studies of America and Vietnam. One of the most poignant statements is by Lieutenant-General Hal Moore and Joseph Galloway.

> The class of 1965 came out of the old America, a nation that disappeared forever in the smoke that billowed off the jungle battlegrounds where we fought and bled. The country that sent us off to war was not there to welcome us home. It no longer existed. We answered the call of one President who was now dead; we followed the orders of another who would be hounded out of office, and haunted, by the war he mismanaged so badly.[17]

While the reality of Vietnam may recede into the background, the Vietnam Veterans Memorial in the nation's capital will be a constant reminder to every generation of Americans of the sacrifices and calamity of this war. Moreover, because of the divisive nature of the war and the withdrawal of the United States from Vietnam, leaving its ally to face the enemy with little material backing from the United States, this war is likely to remain an enduring memory particularly to those who served in the US military and to military professionals in general.

The Vietnam War had a marked negative impact on civil–military relations and on the military profession. 'It convinced the officer corps of the need to politicize military interests. It helped to ... foster greater "separation" of the military from certain segments of society.'[18] Yet other military professionals felt that 'politics' had subordinated military considerations, leading them to argue for a continuing wall between the military and politics.

The issue of speaking out and in providing a realistic military perspective was a major issue in the Vietnam War. The role of the Chiefs of Staff in the decision to go to war and in its conduct was aptly portrayed by McMaster as 'five silent men'.[19]

> The war in Vietnam was not lost in the field, nor was it lost on the front pages of the *New York Times* or on college campuses. It was lost in Washington, DC ... The disaster in Vietnam was not the result of impersonal forces but a uniquely human failure, the responsibility for which was shared by President Johnson and his principal military and civilian advisers. The failings were many and reinforcing: arrogance, weakness, lying in the pursuit of self-interest, and, above all, the abdication of responsibility to the American people.[20]

This view is shared by Jeffrey Record, who concludes that in the Vietnam War, 'The military, by virtue of its constitutional role as an instrument of civilian authority, was relegated to the role of accomplice in what amounted to the most strategically reckless American enterprise of the twentieth century.'[21] He concludes that 'If the country was poorly served in Southeast Asia in the 1960s by its civilian leaders, those leaders were in turn poorly served by the professional military.'[22]

One cannot help but wonder how the American involvement in the war might have changed or the conduct of the war differed if the Joint Chiefs had, indeed, engaged in constructive political engagement and aired their concerns about the Vietnam War. That is, if the Joint Chiefs had pressed such views on President Johnson and Secretary of Defense McNamara, as well as on the American public and elected officials.[23]

The Cold War and Beyond

The withdrawal from Vietnam in the 1970s began a revitalization of the US military. The refocusing of US security efforts on the Soviet Union and renewed efforts to 'win' the Cold War did much to alleviate military problems and reconcile issues of civil–military relations. Military professional bitterness about politics and political leaders in the Vietnam War faded and was dissipated to a great degree by President Reagan's labeling of the US involvement as a 'noble cause' and by the honor given to the Vietnam Veterans Memorial in Washington. Later, this was reinforced by the US success in the Gulf War. Yet the Vietnam War remains part of the military professional psyche.

During the Cold War the United States was primarily focused on deterring the communist 'Evil Empire', including nuclear deterrence, and in responding to the two 'hot wars' of Korea and Vietnam. The world seemed to be divided into two camps: the West and its allies and the East and its 'satellites'. At the same time, Third World states were undergoing political–social changes, with China, for example, transformed into a communist state and other states emerging from colonial rule. The collapse of the Soviet Union and the dismantling of much of the communist empire changed the strategic landscape and ushered in a new world order. Most of these changes have been extensively studied in a variety of publications.[24]

The US involvement and success in the Gulf War in 1991 seemed to confirm the capability and effectiveness of the US military. In a ground war that lasted 100 hours, the conventional military system defeated Iraqi forces. This engagement was preceded by an extensive air campaign. For many this became the 'model' for future wars.

The post-Cold War period and the transition to the twenty-first century has not diminished the problems facing the US military. Many are analogous to earlier periods. While some of the problems of the Cold War have continued into the new period, new ones have emerged as a result of the changed international environment. In the current period, the military profession is struggling with questions such as how to reconfigure military force structure, design strategy and operational doctrine for a new world order that does not appear to have serious short-term threats to American security. Complicating this is the fact that the national leadership has yet to design a clear strategic vision for the new strategic landscape. Adding to this difficult and muddled period, the military's internal problems have led to questions regarding military leadership.[25] However, many who point to these issues seem to have overlooked the deep troubles and confusing times the military passed through in earlier years. But the more compelling question is: has anything been learned from the past?

At least one lesson should be clear: the US military profession cannot withdraw into an ethical cocoon and take on a defensive posture. Prudent and positive response to these issues, publicly aired and articulated, with the senior leaders of the military profession leading the way, is the most important lesson to be learned. Equally important, this demands a positive political role for the military profession. Further, it requires a broad knowledge of politics and political realities, and a realization that the military profession is both a military and a political institution. This overview sets the stage for the study of the military profession and constructive political engagement.

AMERICAN SOCIETY AND THE MILITARY

There are two dimensions to the military's relationship with society: the political–social expectations of society (democratization), and the role of the military in the political process or more pointedly civil–military relations. While these two dimensions are separate, they are closely related and each is affected by the other.

Democratization

In the linkage between the military and political–social expectations of society, the primary question is to what degree does the military reflect society, or to what degree should the military reflect society? Or in more specific terms, what should be the degree of 'democratization' of the military? While this encompasses a variety of issues, the military's policies regarding the role of women in the military, homosexuals, and race are of particular importance. In turn, these trigger a number of other issues, such as fairness of the military justice system, sexual harassment, and equality in career opportunities.

Incidents such as Tailhook, the Lieutenant Kelly Flinn and Command Sergeant-Major Gene McKinney affairs, sexual harassment issues at the Aberdeen Proving Grounds, and debates over the role of women in the military reinforced what some in society saw as the need for the military to reform.[26] Moreover, the storm of silent outrage in the military precipitated by the efforts of President Clinton immediately upon taking office in 1993 to lift the ban on gays in the military underscored the divisiveness of such issues and signaled the difficult social issues facing the military.

From another perspective, American demographics and their reshaping of the domestic environment have an impact on the US military. Not only has this to do with military age youth and qualifications for military service, but also with the changing face of America. The possible shift to an American majority made up of minorities in the next century may also cause a reshaping of the Judeo–Christian heritage and the Anglo–Saxon orientation, as new interpretations of these legacies and heritages take hold in American society.

The changing domestic environment and its effect on the American military was well expressed by one military author who wrote, 'The societal trends indicate a fundamental change in national values. The country's primary value-influencing institutions are promoting altered values for future recruits. These altered values are significantly different than the Army's values.'[27] Yet, it is the case that the values inherent in the US military and the military profession must be compatible with American democratic values and remain within the orbit of the American political–social system.

Civil–Military Relations

Civilian control of the military is a basic tenet of American society. That the military is subordinate to civilian leadership is also fundamental to the military profession. But such relations are also shaped by the political tone of the national leadership and political–military linkages between the military institution and society. Moreover, how society and national leaders perceive the characteristics of the military shapes their view of the degree to which the military reflects society.

With, perhaps, the general exception of major conflicts, military professionals usually have been suspicious of political leaders. (Interestingly enough, the United States has not declared war since World War II.) At times, this has resulted in outright disdain. The Vietnam War is a case in point. For any number of military professionals, the role of President Lyndon Johnson and other officials in the conduct of the Vietnam War seemed to confirm their negative perceptions of politics and political leaders. The attempt to 'micro-manage' the war from the Oval Office and the contradictory political signals and confusing command structure did little to bolster the military's view of the political leadership. As noted earlier, part of the disenchantment may well have been caused by the role played by the Joint Chiefs during the Vietnam War as well as the role of President Johnson and Secretary McNamara.[28]

In the 1980s and through the end of the Gulf War, civil–military relations were based on a relatively comfortable relationship between military and society. This was in stark contrast to the difficulties during the latter part of the Vietnam War and extending through the Carter administration. In the post-Gulf War era, however, the civil–military equation is undergoing change; partly brought about by the redeployment of most of the US military to the continental United States, the reduction of forces, a furious operational tempo, and the revolution in military affairs, the 1999 Kosovo conflict notwithstanding.

More important in the long term, the confidence of the military in itself and in the political leadership throughout the 1980s and through the Gulf War eroded as the Clinton administration took office and plans for the military became public. Equally disturbing to the military, the tone set by the Clinton administration in coming to office in 1993 regarding the military did little to restore or maintain trust between the military and the political leadership in the Oval Office.

While a more harmonious relationship was later established between President Clinton and the presidential hierarchy with the military, it was shattered by the publication of the report of Independent Counsel Kenneth Starr listing '11 acts that may constitute grounds for impeachment of the president'.[29] Published in many newspapers as well as placed on the Internet, the lurid details of the sexual involvement of the president with a White House intern raised a storm of controversy in the United States. 'Throughout the controversy this year ... the nation's military leaders have had little to say in public about the crisis embroiling their commander-in-chief.' As of September 1998, no official survey of military personnel had been taken. Secretary of Defense William Cohen stated he believed that 'the president is capable of carrying out his responsibilities as commander-in-chief'. But senior military professionals acknowledged 'privately ... that the president's adulterous affairs and misleading statements may cause a devastating and irrecoverable erosion in his standing among service members and further damage sagging morale in the ranks'.[30]

Col. Harry Summers's critical response to the president's affair, 'Clinton betrayal imperils us all', appeared in the *Army Times* and was likely to reach any number of military personnel.[31] Writing that 'moral authority is the very engine of war', Summers concluded that the diminished moral authority of the president will surely affect American ability to respond effectively in conflict.

According to George Melloan, the president 'is not only an embarrassment to America's fighting men, but to the nation as a whole ...'. His transgressions are:

> fundamentally about honor, something that American military officers have always striven hard to teach and preserve. Today they are caught between their loyalty to that tradition and their duty to salute their civilian masters, including a commander in chief who has demonstrated a lack of character sufficient to get a second lieutenant cashiered.[32]

At the time of writing, it is unclear where all this will lead. Nonetheless, it seems fair to say that the impact on the military, while perhaps primarily subdued within the profession and the military system as a whole, has been one of consternation bordering on disgust. One hopes that this will not have a deleterious effect on civil–military relations and that the military profession accepts the fact that there are many honest and trustworthy individuals in positions of power who are committed to military readiness, effective military response, and acknowledge the importance of honor, duty, and country.

New Civil–Military Relations?

For a great many Americans, the Clinton administration represented a new generation of baby-boomers. Some in this generation had reacted against the Vietnam War, as illustrated by the activities of Bill Clinton during the latter part of the war: his avoidance of military service and the part he played in demonstrating against the war. Further, a new generation of elected officials has taken office at the national level: a generation of the post-Vietnam era, few of whom may have had any military service and whose claim of leadership includes breaking from the old generation. This has spilled over into the public realm.[33]

A new generation of military leaders has also emerged with the passing of the Vietnam generation. This new generation reflects the experience in the Gulf War and a variety of peacetime engagements, such as those in Bosnia and Somalia, as a United Nations instrument, and hurricane assistance (Hurricane Andrew in Florida). Equally important, this generation is linked more closely to social issues emanating from society, forcing a rethinking of the degree to which the military should reflect society and still maintain its combat effectiveness. This is complicated by the troubling questions regarding the proper use of the military in a variety of operations that are not initially seen as clear issues of war and peace.

Combined with the dynamics of domestic social issues, civil–military relations are likely to evolve into an equation reflecting the 'fog of peace', a relationship which parallels that which existed during the period 1946–50.[34] As noted earlier this was a period in which the US military reverted to a peace posture and which Americans turned back to as the 'good old days'.

Further, the use of the military in operations other than war has had an impact on civil–military relations, exacerbated by what some call the 'demilitarization of the military' and the issue of overstretching of US forces.[35] While concluding that there was no crisis in civil–military relations, a special task force studying the issue,

> agreed that deep and pervasive difficulties plague American civil–military relations ... The three core problems discussed at length were the politicization of the military, the growing divide between civil society and those who wear the uniform, and the centralization of military power in the Joint Staff and in the chairman of the Joint Chiefs of Staff (JCS).[36]

Whether one agrees or disagrees with this view, it is clear that changes have taken place, and are taking place, in the relationship between society and the military. This is not something that has just emerged; but democratization, the utility of military force, and the presumed 'wall' between the military profession and politics in the new strategic landscape have crystallized matters.

As Cohen observes,

> Throughout much of its history, the US military was remarkably politicized by contemporary standards. One commander of the Army, Winfield Scott, even ran for president while in uniform, and others (Leonard Wood, for example) have made no secret of their political views and aspirations. But until 1940, and with the exception of periods of outright warfare, the military was a negligible force in American life, and America was not a central force in international politics. That has changed ... civil–military relations in the United States now no longer affect

merely the closet-room politics of Washington, but the relations of countries around the world.[37]

THE NEW WORLD ORDER AND MILITARY PURPOSE

The shape of the new world order emerging from the end of the Cold War remains unclear. Indeed, some call it the new world disorder. There are continuities from the Cold War era as well as fundamental changes. Information technology, globalization, transnational challenges, and concerns about the new millennium have made fundamental changes in the world order of the twentieth century. In turn, these have changed the strategic landscape and, according to many, changed the nature of warfare. Indeed, for the foreseeable future, there seems to be little fear of major conventional conflicts. To be sure, the India–Pakistan nuclear issues in 1998 heightened the concern over nuclear proliferation and the possibility of nuclear confrontation and regional conventional conflict. The serious political and economic troubles in Russia in 1999 added to this concern because of the number of nuclear warheads and missiles within Russia. Also, the bombing of US embassies in Kenya and Tanzania rekindled questions about the US response to international and domestic terrorism. Nonetheless, what seems to be emerging is a strategic landscape characterized by any number of limited regional conflicts and military operations short of war (or lesser conflicts), rather than major wars of a conventional character.

Throughout American history, US armed forces have been involved in operations that have little connection to success in battle. Lessons from such experiences, however, seem to have been ignored or lost in the focus on external adversaries and application of traditional strategies. And, as one observer notes, 'Our defense policy no longer designates a specific enemy but nonetheless prepares for large-scale war anywhere in the world on short notice. We have yet to recognize that today's most urgent security problems cannot be handled by traditional methods of confrontation.'[38]

Earlier reference to the post-Civil War period is a case in point. The military role during that period falls within the current terminology of operations other than war. As one late nineteenth-century observer was reported, '"In reality, the Army is now a gendarmery – a national police," wrote a colonel in 1895.'[39]

Moreover, immediately following World War II, a number of US Army armored units in Germany were reorganized into constabulary squadrons whose purpose was to function as a national gendarmery taking the place of German police in the American Zone of Occupation. This continued for about a three year period until German police forces were able to function. The constabulary units were trained and equipped to maintain law and order, and to deal with the German civilian populace and displaced persons. But they were hardly prepared for actual combat. The point is that, historically, the US military has been involved in a variety of what are now called operations other than war. Yet it appears that the wrong lessons or no lessons have been drawn from such experience.

The Current Period

As noted earlier, currently the US military is being tasked to undertake peace-keeping, peace enforcement and a variety of operations other than wars. According to one source the US military is increasingly being shaped as an international constabulary equivalent to an international gendarmery.[40] Even so, a number within the military profession insist that the military can still retain its capability to conduct combat operations.[41] Others in the profession, however, are convinced that such missions undercut readiness and have a negative impact on morale and quality of life.

The response to date to these various peace operations and operations other than war has mainly been ad hoc and driven by conventional military structures and operational doctrine. All the military services are in the process of designing doctrine and forces for the next century. Indeed, the services seem to be going to great lengths to prove the validity of their roles in future warfare. Nonetheless, it appears that military doctrinal and force structure are versions of those of the Cold War era.

For some, however, operations other than war (OOTW) must be seen as war and can include unconventional conflicts.[42] Regardless of the efforts at preparing for war in the twenty-first century, operations other than war have become a continuing problem for all the services. This has led to debates about the role of each military service, and questions about the meaning of national interests. Others argue that when military involvement in operations other than war is deemed *absolutely* necessary, then it should be strictly limited to a support function. If there is a clear possibility that operations other than war will encompass unconventional conflict, then the strategy should be based on an American version of Sun Tzu, whose writings on *The Art of War*, written in China over a thousand years ago, argued that the center of gravity of conflict is the social–political milieu. From this, the US special forces become the main instrument.[43] If mainstream military forces are necessary as a follow-on in such contingencies and the commitment is deemed to be in the *vital* interests of the United States, then the military must be prepared to function as an Army of occupation, with all that that entails in terms of the length of the commitment and rules of engagement.

In any case, US military involvement in operations other than war requires a sophisticated command and control structure and a realistic political–military intermix, with political objectives being the driving force. These are major conclusions in an excellent study of civil–military operations by John Fishel.[44] 'Political, rather than military, objectives dominate. Where this was under-emphasized, the United States had difficulty in attaining its goals. Where this was given its due, the operations tended to be more successful.'[45]

Regardless of the various views about military doctrine and operations other than war, a fundamental criticism from many within military professional circles is that such operations tend to decrease military readiness and undermine combat efficiency. Nonetheless, there are indications that the military profession is being driven to incorporate doctrines addressing operations other than war as part of the military's major missions now and into the twenty-first century.

The Information Age

The US military is seriously engaged in preparing for information-age/third-wave warfare. Such efforts involve the development of hi-tech weaponry and the creation of a 'warrior' armed with information age sensors, communications, and electronic equipment. Conventional and nuclear war categories are where such efforts will probably have the most impact. Those least affected by information-age/third-wave warfare are operations other than war.[46]

The effort of the military services to respond to the information age is spelled out in *Joint Vision 2010*, 'the conceptual template for how we will channel the vitality of our people and leverage technological opportunities to achieve new levels of effectiveness in joint warfighting'.[47] Each service has published guidelines to implement *Joint Vision 2010*.[48]

But for some the battlefields of the next century are more likely to be variations of Chechnya and Somalia, and modern versions of Vietnam. Such conflicts are least vulnerable to hi-tech military systems. The acquisition and use of modern military technology is often seen as a solution to the problems of warfare in the late twentieth century, with information warfare the latest example. Unconventional conflicts, or irregular warfare, however, remains for some unaffected by changes in technology.[49] In such conflicts, sociology, psychology, and history will have more to say about the nature of the conflict, including its persistence and intensity, than technology and Western doctrine. 'Westerners, with their superior technology and organization, have been killed for a long time by primitives or "savages" whose style of warfare the Westerners misunderstood and whose skills exceeded those of the West in irregular warfare.'[50]

Finally, modern military forces, driven by information-age warfare, based on the principles of Clausewitz, Jomini, Douhet, Mitchell, and Mahan, have yet to develop a strategic umbrella to respond successfully to operations other than war. While the strategies driving conventional and nuclear warfare remain rooted in traditional notions, those for operations other than war remain elusive. The strategies for the twenty-first century seem to resemble the past.[51]

CONCLUSIONS

It is clear that there are a host of uncertainties surrounding the role of the military in the new world order and in its response to the domestic political–social system. These are compounded by the surge in information technologies and the efforts of the US military to move into the twenty-first century. The shape, capability, and posture of the military rest primarily with the military profession. Equally important, civilian leaders need to develop a thorough understanding of the use of force and its effect on the US military, the American public, and in the international world. This need applies equally to those in the media.

What does all of this have to do with the role of the military profession and the notion of constructive political engagement? The military profession must ensure that its voice is clearly heard throughout the American political system. Yet it is clear that given the strategic landscape, the changing domestic environment, and the use of the military in operations other than war, conditions will develop that will create friction between military and society. Indeed, cries of an 'out of control' military have already been heard from some. These are likely to increase if the military profession adopts the notion of constructive political engagement.

The domestic environment and diminished fears of major wars have placed the military in a complex relationship with society. The changing domestic landscape, with debates over the meaning of Americanism and American culture, has raised a number of social issues spilling over into the military institution. Democratization, civilization of the military, and notions of demilitarization, have become almost commonplace concerns. These matters, combined with the tendency to see the military in constabulary-type missions, pose serious challenges to the military profession. How can the military reconcile its need to prepare for war successfully, conduct operations other than war, and respond to the changing domestic landscape?

The military professionals' continuing concern about the military culture will always result in their casting a suspicious eye on attempts to change the military's structure and make its value system closer to that of society as a whole. Further, the use of the military for operations other than war is also likely to be seen by many professionals as a threat to its prime purpose. The very nature of such operations is shaped by political and diplomatic factors limiting the scope of military operations, often with no end game or specific rules for withdrawal. Yet, the military professional sees the use of the military as a decisive force to be inserted to achieve a clear and specific political–military goal.

Once a decision for military action has been made, half-measures and confused objectives may exact a heavy price in the form of a protracted conflict or uncertain goals. These consequences are not in accord with the traditional military perspective and are peripheral to the essential elements of US national military strategy: the ability rapidly to assemble the forces needed to win, and espousal of the concept of applying decisive force to overwhelm adversaries and thereby terminate conflicts swiftly with a minimum loss of life. Regardless of the efforts to reconcile operations other than war with the primary purpose of the military, considerable friction remains.

The issues presented in this introductory chapter point out the need for the military profession to ensure that its voice is heard not only by those in the executive and legislative branches but also by the American public. In the prevailing strategic and domestic environments, there are increasing differences between the National Command Authority and Congress over the military's primary role and its involvement in operations other than war. Indeed, the military is likely to be used as a political instrument more often than not, in operations other than war. As a result, the military is faced with trying to reconcile operations short of war with success in battle. This problem permeates virtually every level of the military system.

It is important, therefore, that military professionals and those in the civilian sector understand the need for constructive political engagement. This not only means that the limits of political engagement be recognized, but that an acceptable equilibrium between military and society be sustained, an equilibrium that ensures that the military profession recognizes the limits of political involvement and civilians recognize the need for military involvement in appropriate political arenas.

The military has a legitimate role in the political sphere. The primary role is to provide clear and unequivocal estimates and recommendations to civilian policy makers when the use of force is considered. There will always be differences between the requirements of policy and the brutal realities of the battlefield. There is no way around this tension.

It needs to be added that the same holds true with respect to the need to inform the executive and legislative branches as well as the American public about military culture and the issues which create (and can create) problems within the ranks of the military. This also requires awareness of the fundamental difference between the purpose of the military establishment and those of civilian establishments, the fundamental differences between military personnel and civilians, and the fundamental difference between the nature of leadership in military and in civilian life. Thus, military advice and the need to inform the public go beyond the decision to use military force. In any case, the United States and the military profession cannot afford another 'five silent men'.[52]

2

The Military Profession

The term 'military profession' refers primarily to the armed forces' officer corps but includes enlisted military professionals, particularly those of the highest ranks. In an official capacity, however, it is the officer corps that is involved with any number of civilian groups and institutions affecting civil–military relations. The officer corps sets the reference points in the military community and shapes the environment in which military families exist. It is the officer corps that is accountable and responsible for military effectiveness and institutional character. Thus, the military profession and the officer corps become virtually synonymous.

The attitude of the American people regarding the integrity and the professional competence of the corps of officers of the armed forces has vast national importance. While American civilian leaders make the war and peace decisions, it is the officers of the armed forces who provide the military leadership required for successful military operations.[1]

The period of the emergence of the military profession is the subject of differing views. In a personal account of the profession of arms, British General Sir John Hackett writes,

> The function of the profession of arms is the ordered application of force in the resolution of a social problem ... The bearing of arms among men for the purpose of fighting other men is found as far back as we can see. Service under arms has been seen at some times and in some places as a calling resembling that of a priesthood in its dedication. This view has never wholly disappeared.[2]

Samuel Huntington, however, states that 'Prior to 1800 there was no such thing as a professional officers corps. In 1900 such bodies existed in virtually all major countries.'[3] He further notes that prior to 1800, those who led armies and navies 'were either mercenaries or aristocrats. Neither viewed officership as a profession'.[4] While it is difficult to identify specifically the period in which the military profession as we know it today emerged, it is generally the case that it relates to the emergence of modern society and primarily a concept of Western culture, emerging out of the European state system and European wars. In this respect the military profession has many of the characteristics of other professions in modern societies.

As noted earlier, many of the issues currently facing the military profession were present in 1981, primarily in the aftermath of the Vietnam War.[5] Looking back will help in establishing the historical roots of current issues and help dissipate some of the criticism aimed at the military profession in its efforts to respond to the new domestic and international landscapes.

Earlier studies provided a background for the larger study in 1981.

> The profile that emerges from these studies is that of a profession that is generally conservative ... While there does not appear to be a visible divergence between military and civilian values in the abstract – i.e., in the broader sense of democracy and domestic policies – there is a distinctly different perspective on matters relating to war, military policy, and influence of military leaders. This difference is exacerbated by the professional perception of society's negative and deprecative attitudes regarding the military and military lifestyles.[6]

The conclusion regarding the gap between the military profession and civilian society was described as follows:

> This separateness between society and the military is crystallized into a more perceptible form by the homogeneity of professional views on specific matters dealing with the military, views of the institutional context, and self-depreciation. Indeed, one can see evidence of the existence of a type of 'military mind' which insists upon professional autonomy, separateness from society, and greater influence in policy decisions affecting the military.[7]

And as Hackett points out, 'The essential basis of the military life is the ordered application of force under an unlimited liability. It is unlimited liability which sets the man who embraces this life somewhat apart.'[8] He concludes that the professional soldier 'will be (or should be) always a citizen. So long as he serves he will never be a civilian.'

The differences between the military and society has created a 'gap'. Although there have been periods of political involvement, in general a gap has been characteristic of the US military since the founding of the Republic. In the current period this has led to a pervasive debate about the meaning of the gap and the required response. This is highlighted by three general perspectives. First, is the view that the gap reflects a qualitative difference between the US military and society, which is a result of differing values and differing cultures. This gap must be maintained to ensure that the military is capable of performing its primary purpose. Second, there exists a view that the gap must be considerably narrowed by designing a military that is a close reflection of society in terms of its culture and social composition. This must be done to ensure that the military not become an institution unto itself, separate from society and virtually isolated from the system it is supposed to serve. Third, the gap can be accommodated as long as the military accepts its subordination to civilian authority and makes an effort to understand its political role within the political system, while maintaining its political passivity. This matter is discussed in more detail in Chapter 4, 'Civilian and Military Cultures'.

For some, the notion of a distinct gap appears to be diminishing, reinforced by the view that military professionalism has been declining. This is a result of the changes taking place within the military in coming to terms with technological demands and downsizing. In addition the notion of 'occupation' seems to be undermining that of 'profession', with all that that suggests regarding commitment or the lack thereof. The net effect is a challenge to the traditional concept of military professionalism. To examine the new professionalism or de-professionalism, we need first to review military professionalism as it has been said to exist for the past several decades.[9]

?#2

CHARACTERISTICS OF THE MILITARY PROFESSION

Part of what it means to be a member of a profession is having a deep commitment to a set of abstract values and principles that define the profession. This means that members of a profession accept certain values that are specific to their profession as being more fundamental than other values.[10]

Six elements are paramount in shaping the character of the military profession: (1) the profession has a defined area of competence based on expert knowledge; (2) there is a system of continuing education designed to maintain professional competence; (3) the profession has an obligation to society and must serve it without concern for remuneration; (4) it has a system of values that perpetuate professional character and establish and maintain legitimate relationships with society; (5) there is an institutional framework within which the profession functions; and (6) the profession has control over the system of rewards and punishments and is in a position to determine the quality of those entering the profession.

Particularly important is that the military profession holds the view that it is a unique profession and further distinguished by ultimate liability and by the state as sole client. These characteristics distinguish the military profession from other professions and society in general.

As Millis noted,

> Military service stands by itself. It has some of the qualities of a priesthood, of a professional civil servant, of a great bureaucratized business organization and of an academic order ... it has something of each of these in it but it corresponds exactly to none ... [it] is set apart, therefore, from those who have followed other walks of life.[11]

With respect to the sole client, military professionalism must be placed in the context of the political system from which it evolves. Thus, while there are certain universal principles applicable to all modern military systems, these are tempered by the values and attitudes of the political system. In brief, the military profession functions within the orbit of the political system in which it serves.[12]

> These special characteristics separate the military profession not only from society but also from other professions. In brief, military professionals are expected to be prepared to give their lives to serve the profession and the state. Their services can be legitimately offered only to the state. Although these characteristics and self-perceptions are often imperfectly reflected in the military profession, they are critical in shaping professional mind-sets and behavior, in formally articulating the meaning of military profession, and in determining the professional's relationship to the state.[13]

While these are the broad principles of military professionalism, the ways in which they are interpreted and translated into the institutional system and individual behavior have varied over the years. 'Each of these are both self-evident and elusive – elusive because the application of any of these qualities to a particular situation is difficult to define.'[14] This may well be a result of the complex ingredients that go into the totality of the concept of the military profession. These characteristics make it difficult to examine military professionalism. Adding to this difficulty is the fact that there is no clear line of demarcation regarding the meaning of professionalism with respect to its status within the American political system. While civilian supremacy is a clearly established constitutional framework, how that is translated into specific military professional behavior falls into a gray area. There is a hint of this according to the views of one authority on the US Army.

> All officers of the armed forces, and all soldiers, too, are bound by their oath to do their utmost to achieve the prompt and successful completion of the mission assigned, even at the risk of their lives when necessity requires, and without regard to their personal views as to the correctness of the national policy or the wisdom of the orders under which they act.*[15]

The asterisk at the end of the quote is explained in a footnote as follows: 'Still, experienced military leaders know that officers and soldiers fight more courageously and sacrifice more willingly when they hold a deep conviction as to the worthwhileness and the justice for which they fight.'[16]

Military Professional Tiers

In examining the military profession, we need to identify the various tiers that comprise the totality of military professionalism. The first tier is the military professional orbit at the highest levels and relationships to the national leadership and to society in general. The second tier is military professionalism as it is viewed and practiced within the military system. The third tier is military professionalism as it functions within the immediate local unit and as reflected within the local command structure and immediate military community. It is the aggregate of these relationships and tiers that is the totality of the military profession. It is also clear that the concept of military professionalism becomes more complex when viewed from this three-tier framework.

The interpretation of military professionalism may differ from tier to tier, but the core professional principles of integrity, loyalty, and service permeate every tier. This also means that the totality of the profession evolves from 'trust' between and within each tier. In political terms, it is the first tier that has the greatest impact on the political process. But it is important to note that problems involving other tiers can be of such proportions that they envelop all of the tiers. Occurrences of sexual misconduct at the lowest tiers, for example, have engaged the totality of the military profession. Similarly misconduct of some in the first tier reverberate throughout all of the tiers. The fact is that although there is some difference in the way the professional ethos may function within the various tiers, the tiers may be separate but they are inextricable. The impact of one tier on others and their relationships preclude any simple explanation of military professionalism. For example, in 1998 and into 1999 it was not clear what impact there would be on the top tier because of some disenchantment by those in lower tiers with senior military professionals.

SCHOLARLY PERSPECTIVES

Scholars studying the military profession seem to agree that the core of military professionalism rests in the notions of duty, honor, country. These encompass professional values of integrity, obedience, loyalty, commitment, trust, honor, and service. The professional value system – the professional ethos – is a critical factor. 'Ethos' refers to universal characteristics and values passed on from one generation of officers to the next.[17]

The study of civil–military relations in the United States gained some impetus in the 1950s, highlighted by the work of political scientist Samuel P. Huntington, followed several years later by the work of sociologist Morris Janowitz.[18] This is not to suggest that earlier scholars ignored the subject.[19] What seems to distinguish Huntington and Janowitz, however, is that they expanded the analysis of military professionalism and civil–military relations to encompass a variety of political and sociological components.

Most scholars and those interested in the study of the military profession are familiar with the works of Huntington and Janowitz, and little needs to be said here regarding the substance of these works. The concern here is the applicability of several major themes in these works that focus primarily on politics and the convergence and/or divergence between the military and society. These include the concept of military professionalism in the context of the post-Cold War security environment. The purpose is not to offer another comparative perspective identifying similarities and differences in the themes of Huntington and Janowitz, or to offer analyses of subsequent studies evolving from their works. Rather it is to identify reference points from their studies and the starting point for further analyses with respect to politics and the military profession.

Although the works of Huntington and Janowitz were published more than three decades ago, they still provide fundamental themes of military professionalism. These works also reveal the difficulties in coming to grips with specific guidelines for the military profession in terms of political dimensions. This problem also exists in translating and interpreting the professional value system throughout the military establishment and in relationship to the civilian sector.

The political-science perspective of Huntington deals with civil–military relations and control of the military, that is, state control of the coercive instruments, legitimacy, and the proper functioning of the instruments of the political system. The fundamental military-professional principle, according to Huntington, is 'the direction, operation, and control of a human organization whose primary function is the application of violence'.[20] Moreover, the skills required of the military professional is 'an extraordinary complex intellectual skill requiring comprehensive study and training'.[21]

Huntington has much to say regarding politics and the military profession. The military profession must disdain political involvement. Concerned about a balance between the military profession and civilian society, he argued that: 'A strong, integrated, highly professional officer corps ... immune to politics and respected for its military character, would be a steadying balance wheel in the conduct of policy.'[22]

The military profession must remain distant from society. It is conservative and has a 'realistic' set of values that drive the military establishment – an establishment that must function within a liberal society. Society's control rests on both objective and subjective factors. To maintain military character and integrity, the military profession must remain distant from society, while still operating within the orbit of the nation-state: an apolitical military profession, well entrenched in the specifics of military skills, and military perspectives. This raised the issues of convergence, divergence, or fusion of the military and society, issues that remain the basis of much of the debate today.

Huntington reiterated his major themes in a 1978 publication.[23] He also noted that the 'professional military ethic tends to be one of conservative realism'.[24] He concluded: 'In the end, the dilemma of military institutions in a liberal society can only be resolved satisfactorily by a military establishment that is *different but not distant from* the society it serves.'

Stating that the military was basically a conservative oriented organization functioning within a liberal society, Huntington argued for a politically neutral military, isolated from society, and focused primarily on its raison d'être – victory in war.[25] This required a shift from subjective to objective civil control – that is a shift from responsiveness to civilian political control mechanisms to responsiveness to perceived military threats. This has been labeled the traditional approach to military professionalism.

Janowitz's sociological approach focuses on attitudes and values, the political–social system within the military, the socioeconomic characteristics of military professionals, and the impact these have on military professionalism. The results are the well-known 'absolutist–pragmatist' categories and the constabulary view of military professionalism. The absolutist approach rests on the belief of the permanency of war and the concern with victory. The pragmatist emphasizes 'the discontinuity of the military past with the future ... the distinction between "absolute" and "pragmatic" codes is roughly equivalent to that which obtains between conservative and liberal doctrine ...'.[26]

In the constabulary concept, Janowitz distinguishes between absolutists and pragmatists, where absolutists are those professionals whose views rest in traditional concepts of military victory and pragmatists are those who are more concerned with the measured application of force and its political consequences.[27] Janowitz's views placed the military profession much closer to societal values and as sensitive to the political–social expectations.

> The military establishment becomes a constabulary force when it is continuously prepared to act, committed to the minimum use of force, and seeks viable international relations, rather than victory, because it has incorporated a protective military posture. The constabulary outlook is grounded in, and extends, pragmatic doctrine.[28]

Janowitz affirms the need to maintain some differences between the military and the civilian: 'the constabulary force is designed to be compatible with the traditional goals of democratic political control'.[29] He concluded, 'To deny or destroy the difference between the military and civilian cannot produce genuine similarity, but runs the risk of creating new forms of tension and unanticipated militarism.'

Sociologist Charles C. Moskos added another perspective to military professionalism.[30] He concluded that the military is shaped by two themes – institution and occupation. The former was based on the view that as a 'calling' the military had essentially an institutional perspective. In the latter case, the individual military professional saw his or her role mainly as a job to be done – an occupational theme. He also concluded that both themes are encompassed within the profession, but saw the profession moving from the institutional to the occupational model.

Other scholars noted that the military is a political instrument. Accordingly, military professionals need to develop a sophisticated understanding of and sensitivity to the American political system and the political–social environment.[31] Some further argued that becoming involved in political decision making was an integral part of military professionalism. However, such involvement was to be driven primarily by military purpose and not political partisanship. Thus, military professionals had to study and understand the democratic political system and its social and economic underpinnings if they were to perform effectively. However, it is clear that political advocacy and dogmatic political activism by the military considerably diminishes the concept of military professionalism.

References to military professionalism in a recent study by Snider and Carlton-Carew attempt to come to grips with issues raised by Huntington and Janowitz.[32] An empirical study of education and the military profession by Sarkesian, Williams, and Bryant adds to the literature on the meaning of the military profession and its relationship to society.[33] These authors conclude, in part:

> The military professional mind-set concerning the concept of the military as a career is changing. The importance of higher education, the notion of second careers, dual professionalism, and military–social issues have become important parts of military professionalism. Although it is not clear where this will lead, it is clear that the old generation is passing and the traditional view of military professionalism and civil–military relations is changing.[34]

A recent study by Hoffman uses the concept of 'decisive force' to explore its implications for the military profession.[35] In the context of US military culture, the author identifies three major components of military professionalism: autonomy, apoliticism, and absolutism. He writes, for example, that 'An especially vital element of American military culture is found in its adherence to a strong sense of professionalism'.[36] He refers to Huntington's three distinct characteristics: expertise, corporateness, and social responsibility. Hoffman concludes that 'the American Way of War now includes extensive representation of the military in policy making circles, and the supporting contention that subjective control is the operative form of maintaining civilian control over the military today'.[37]

MULTI-PROFESSIONS AND CAREERISM

The military profession is not a monolith. As will be shown in Chapter 8 there is disagreement between the military professionals in each of the military services about strategy and doctrine. This extends to disagreements about the role of each service and indeed, the role of various units within each service as well as the National Guard and Federal Reserves. But such issues do not diminish the broader notion of military professionalism as detailed here. That is, military professionals, in the main, regardless of the military service, have a commitment and a professional ethos that binds them together in service to the country.

In the post-World War II period, there evolved the notion of multi-professionalism within the military. Doctors, lawyers, and engineers, for example, served as military officers. They served as military professionals and also as professionals in their particular discipline or training. Janowitz suggested such developments more than 25 years ago.[38] This notion of multi-professionalism is complicated by the persistent controversy regarding the role of managers, leaders, and technicians.

Those in the ground combat forces, for example, argue that military leadership is best expressed in the command of combat units where the human factor is important, in contrast to the managerial perspective characteristic of technical and support units. In the present climate, the managerial notion is reinforced by the need for skilled weapons technicians, information-age specialists, logisticians, and administrators. Additionally, as more professionals increasingly view their military careers as only part of their working life span, they recognize the need to develop skills other than combat leadership as preparation for second careers in the civilian sector.

These differences have led to the re-emergence of a two-armies concept and with it a two-professions concept, one associated with the ground combat arms and the other with the military support system. These are not new themes. Distinctions between two armies were suggested earlier by Charles Moskos and William L. Hauser, as well as others.[39] But these were seen earlier by most as curiosities rather than realities. However, in the new era there are signs that such a division can emerge, if not in a distinct form, at least implicitly within the military. This is particularly the case with the US Army.

According to some, from the two-army concept, the most likely evolution will be a three-military system.

> The first component will be a mainstream military system containing primarily combat support and combat service support elements (i.e., the noncombat elements of the military). The second system will consist primarily of the ground combat arms, including the combat divisions of the army and the marine corps. The third system will be primarily the special operations forces, including Ranger units and Navy Seals, special air squadrons, and the Special Forces.[40]

In addition, there are various opinions within the profession on any number of issues, including, for example, the proper military role in the political system and the degree to which it must reflect society. Moreover, there are disagreements within and between the various armed services regarding proper roles, missions, and resources.[41] Competition for scarce resources, issues of missions and contingencies, modernization, preferential assignments, and career opportunities, among others, will perpetuate and sharpen competition between services. Similarly, inter-service competition stemming from these conditions are likely to spill over into the domestic political sphere, with services making alliances and seeking support from other political actors to serve particular service interests. These issues have also surfaced in debates over 'jointness', the definition of that term, and its impact on the various military services.[42] (See Chapter 8.)

This is not necessarily a new phenomenon. Immediately following World War II, the efforts to unify the military services and the organization of the Department of Defense led to rivalries among the various services, particularly between the Navy and the other services. This evolved into the 'Battle of the Potomac' and the 'Revolt of the Admirals'.[43] High-ranking officers of the US Navy railed at the efforts to unify the services and the efforts by the Army and newly created Air Force to co-opt roles and missions which they felt were the Navy's prerogatives. This led to an outright 'rebellion against authority'.

> The 'crew' was not rabble, but an elite group of decorated admirals who had devoted their lives to the Navy and their country. And the 'captain' was not a crazed despot; he was President Harry S. Truman, and his 'Executive Officer' was Secretary of Defense Louis A. Johnson ... [T]his event was a flagrant peacetime challenge hurled by top-ranking military men at the civilian leadership of the military.[44]

The revolt failed and cast a shadow on the examination of the issue of military professionals, politics, and civil control of the military. The point is that to presume that the profession is a monolith conveys the image that there is 'one' professional view on everything, a stereotype held by many Americans.

Further, the successor military generation will be a new breed. Those with Vietnam experience will have passed from the scene, to be replaced by the Gulf War generation. Although Vietnam is an indelible part of the military psyche, the Gulf War appears to be a new reference point for strategic perspectives and operational guidelines. At the same time, the humanitarian mission in Somalia in 1992–93 and peace-enforcement missions such as those in Bosnia in 1996 and Kosovo in 1999 and beyond serve as reference points at the other end of the spectrum. However, as stated earlier, the experience of Vietnam remains an indelible part of the US military ethos.

The military profession also has any number of troubling issues associated with officers' careers and military management. While these do not necessarily impinge upon the notion of professionalism, they do affect the structural and procedural environment within the profession, and may indeed have an impact on the notion of professionalism as time goes on. What some critics argue about the Army may well apply in various degrees across the other services.

For example, Ralph Peters has written:

> The Army is in trouble on many fronts ... Readiness continues to drop. Worthy experiments, such as the Army After Next, become political playthings. The Army's long neglect of the National Guard has collapsed into fratricide. The Air Force picks our pockets while we wallow in self-pity. And this is only the start of

the list ... Traditional approaches are accepted uncritically and, in the cut-throat competitiveness of today's force, officers avoid giving any sign that they might be, somehow, outside of the mainstream. Where is the creative thought in today's Army? Where is the spirit of daring and innovation?[45]

Similar concerns were voiced by McCormick. 'Most observers agree that the attitudes and behavior of the officer corps have changed dramatically in the post-Cold War era. At the root of these changes are three sources of anxiety and uncertainty that make an army career increasingly unattractive and stressful.'[46] The author goes on to discuss the sources of anxiety as erosion of benefits, downsizing, and uncertain career patterns for advancement.[47]

The point is that there are any number of issues within the military profession that seem to be contrary to the higher ideals of the profession. Furthermore, as most military professionals would acknowledge, there are a small number of professionals who place 'careerism' ahead of professional morals and ethics. And often it is these individuals who gain public notoriety and tarnish the entire profession in the public's eye. Yet the fact remains that the military profession has those special and unique characteristics that distinguish it from society in general. And it is this factor that is often misinterpreted or overlooked in the present environment.

CONCLUSIONS

Civil control and military professionalism are more complex issues in the post-Cold War period, complex for both society and the military profession. There are three fundamental issues: first, the degree to which the military profession should reflect society and yet maintain its professional integrity; second, the degree to which the military must adhere to its primary purpose, its raison d'être, and still successfully engage in operations other than war – or non-combat missions and contingencies; and third, and perhaps the most controversial, is to what degree, if any, the military profession should engage in politics within the American political system. All of these are placed in an uncertain strategic landscape and changing domestic political–social environment.

As one scholar concluded,

> The concept of professionalism seems to demand that professionals themselves be constantly aware of the delicate balance they must maintain in their own behavior between autonomy and fusion. They cannot be so totally separated as to become the proverbial 'society within a society', but neither can they afford total integration within the civilian overhead.[48]

The problem seems clear, but the answer elusive. The military must maintain its own culture and its raison d'être if it is to serve society effectively. At the same time, how does the military maintain the support of society and ensure that its values, culture, and raison d'être are within the 'orbit' of the American political system – that is, supportive of the values and culture of the American system? The direction seems clear: it must not only reinforce the traditional principles of military profession, closely connecting these to all tiers of the profession, but it must also become a political actor – embarking on prudent political involvement, primarily to maintain a strong linkage with the American public and civilian authorities, a linkage that is best described as equilibrium – one that is rarely ever static, and one that cannot be developed by political passivity or maintained by political activism. How can these be accomplished if the military profession avoids political engagement?

PART II
AMERICAN SOCIETY AND THE MILITARY

3

Politics and the Military: A Historical Introduction

Military involvement (or political engagement) in the political realm is an age-old phenomenon. The intrusion may be subtle and beneficial or violent and deadly. History records both and all the variations in between. This chapter is an historical overview of the political engagement of the US military covering the period from the creation of the regular Army to the creation in 1903 of the Chief of Staff and the General Staff. This period laid the groundwork for the military and politics through the twentieth century. The focus is on the members of that small fraternity who commanded the Army, variously referred to as commanders-in-chief, commanding generals, senior officers and generals-in-chief. These were the individuals closest to and, therefore, most influenced by and influential in national politics. Some attention is also focused on the role of the military academy at West Point in shaping the Army's military/political posture.

BACKGROUND

Traditionally, in most European countries, standing armies have been seen as a tool of government oppression. This was nowhere truer than England, where memories of the Stuart monarchs and the Protectorate were still fresh in the minds of many American colonists. The Founding Fathers were, after all, almost entirely transplanted Englishmen or their descendants. Navies, on the other hand were viewed, on the whole, in a more benign light, though taxes to maintain them could be burdensome. Navies were necessary to protect commerce and fend off invasion. Rarely could the Navy be used to coerce the citizenry or abridge their rights. It is for these very reasons that the Constitution of the United States charges Congress to 'raise and support Armies, but no appropriation of money to that use shall be for a longer term than two years', while it mandates that Congress shall 'provide and maintain a Navy'. The Army had, therefore, for a great portion of its history, a much more tenuous existence than the Navy, though this by no means exempted the Navy from neglect, even criticism, from officials in government. This situation and the fact that there really was little discernible difference between Army 'professionals' and their civilian counterparts, tended to make the codified relationship between the Army as an institution and the government less firm and, at times, more strained than that of its sister service.

Given its historical roots and its radical republican philosophy, it is small wonder that the relationship between the government of the new republic and its military was, for over a century, ill defined, strained, jealous at times and poorly legislated. Neither the Army nor the Navy had, during this period, attained that level of professionalism, described by Huntington in his seminal book *The Soldier and the State*, to which we in the late twentieth century have been accustomed.[1] Indeed, early in the nineteenth century the line between the professional officer and private gentleman was infinitely more blurred than it is today. This was especially true in the Army. The diminutive size of the Army, the lack of any major campaigns (after the war of 1812) for a great part of its existence, and the nature of garrison duty left abundant time for officers so inclined to devote a great deal of resources and energy to civilian pursuits. A line naval officer, on the other hand, spent a great deal of his career on station aboard ship, many miles from home for months or even years at a time. Andrew Jackson and Zachary Taylor were every bit as much 'professional' Army officers for their time as were Wellington or a young Napoleon, but each, regardless of their fame, had been at liberty while still in uniform to pursue political and other interests.

The command relationship between the commanding generals and the government that evolved during the Revolution and remained little changed throughout the nineteenth century also exerted influence on the development of the services. As Russell Weigley points out, before the Civil War 'the principle officers had moved back and forth between officership and politics. They did so without threatening civil supremacy because they were essentially civilians themselves, more than they were professional soldiers with any distinctively military outlook.'[2] Owing to this peculiar relationship with the civilian leadership, the personality and character of the senior officer of the Army was a crucial ingredient. With no term limits and no mandatory retirement age, high-ranking officers could exert a great deal of influence not only on the service but in other arenas as well. As Samuel Huntington points out, prior to the Civil War 'lateral entry directly from civilian life into the higher ranks of the officer corps was ... a common phenomenon ... Of the Army's thirty-seven generals from 1802 to 1861 not one was a West Pointer'.[3] Habits of a lifetime, including free and open exercise of partisan politics, especially politics that undoubtedly resulted in those very appointments, were not easily shed. Therefore the antebellum Army did not benefit from the professional socialization process created by an academy and the resultant corporate ethic that was so much a part of its character during the second half of the nineteenth century.

There was, then, no expectation in this young republic that 'professional' officers keep to themselves, or even curb their political interests. Huntington regards this as being the 'influence of popularism' which 'encouraged officers to be active in politics. The pattern was set by Commanding Generals of the Army.'[4] Many officers, regardless of their seniority, indulged such interests to the fullest. Appointments, even in time of war, were made, refused or delayed solely because of the candidate's political affiliations. The lack of any restriction on political activism, either codified or traditional, conspired to create a political climate between civil and military leadership far removed from today. However unfamiliar the role of politics in the civil–military relations of the nineteenth century may seem, the lines of continuity to our era are quite clear.

THE AMERICAN REVOLUTION: THE PRINCIPLE OF CIVILIAN CONTROL

The relationship between the new republic and its armed forces was forged in the crucible of the Revolutionary War. During the Revolution, the linkage between George Washington's Army and Congress evolved from a body of five legislators to a war office headed by a secretary.[5] Though there were some differences of opinion, the working association between Washington and Congress proved to be, for the most part, uncommonly smooth. 'Military business was conducted by correspondence and in personal visits to each other's headquarters, and cooperation, not competition, was the order of the day.'[6]

The general and the secretary were largely left to sort out their relationship on their own. A tradition of vague regulation was inaugurated which would affect the formal command relationship even beyond the creation of the general staff in 1903.

The Newburgh Incident

For all practical purposes, the American Revolution was over by March 1783. The American Army was in winter quarters in the remote New York town of Newburgh. It had withstood military reversals and undergone much suffering, but it prevailed, primarily because of the leadership of General George Washington. Yet it was to go through another challenge brought on by its own hand. Though he had sacrificed and suffered much, Washington's distress on that March day, even with the fruits of his perseverance so close at hand, had never been as acute.[7]

In his hand Washington held an anonymously written address to the Continental Army.[8] As Washington interpreted the address, it called for a desertion of Congress by the Army if the war continued and the establishment of 'a new state in the wilderness'. Additionally, the address called for an officers' meeting on 15 March.[9]

Complicating matters, and making them even more dangerous in Washington's opinion, was the fact that an Army delegation to Congress, led by Major-General Alexander McDougal, had fallen in with civilian political factions.[10] 'McDougal and the nationalists implied that if the officers' demands were not met, the army might defy congressional control over the military.'[11]

Washington took steps to counter those involved in the Newburgh effort.[12] He called his own meeting and confronted the disgruntled officers. While trying to read a letter from Congress Washington reached for his spectacles, apologizing to his brother officers that he had grown not only gray, but also blind in their service. 'Washington's virtuoso performance undermined whatever was afoot ... the crisis was over.'[13]

Washington was a dyed-in-the-wool believer in the supremacy of civilian control over the military. He came by this conviction honestly, for it was part of his English heritage. His mother country's history indicated clearly that it wasn't only monarchs who could use a standing Army to limit or even suppress the freedoms of the citizenry. The Remonstrance of the Army, Pride's Purge and the rule of the major generals, events of England's tumultuous seventeenth century, had taught that lesson very clearly.[14] He was determined that his Army would leave no such legacy. It is unclear just how dangerous the situation at Newburgh was or might have become, but it was an inauspicious start for the new republic and its Army.[15]

The Antebellum Army

After the Revolution the American government, under the Articles of Confederation, was as impotent an entity in dealing with military matters as it was in every other way. Shays' Rebellion (August 1787–February 1788) served to focus concern on a national standing Army and the centralized authority to command it and added 'impetus to a movement to convene a Constitutional Convention'.[16] The Constitution named the president commander-in-chief of the armed forces, causing a subtle yet important change in the chain of command. The military roles of the president and the secretary of war were legislated and clear.[17] That of the senior Army officers was not.

> During the century and a quarter from George Washington's installation as commander-in-chief to Samuel B. M. Young's induction as chief of staff, uncertainty, misunderstanding and controversy swirled around the office, involving from time to time some of the leading figures of their day.[18]

A large part of the problem was that the senior officer of the Army was not its institutional chief; that is, the entire entity did not 'belong' to him. Between 1813 and 1815 Congress, taking a lesson from the war of 1812, increased the size of the Army to 12,000 men (still minuscule but gargantuan compared with previous peacetime establishments) and effected other, bureaucratic reforms.[19]

Up to this time the Secretary of War tried to perform a host of duties for the Army, such as commissary and quartermaster, in addition to those of his office. Congress created a 'general staff' that actually consisted of 'a group of autonomous bureau chiefs, such as an adjutant general and inspector general and quartermaster general, with each chief reporting to the Secretary of War'.[20]

What this meant was that the commanding general actually commanded only the field army. He was almost completely cut off from the functions of personnel, logistics, ordinance, topographical engineering and supply, those areas of not a specifically military nature, which Huntington called technicism.[21] Secretary of War Elihu Root, whose reforms would create a more modern general staff in 1903, put it this way:

> The laws require all great departments [bureaus] which build the fortifications and furnish the arms, supplies and munitions of war and actually expend the money for those purposes ... to act under the direction of the Secretary [of War] and withhold from the officer who is called 'Commanding General of the Army' all control over those departments.[22]

The fact that once an officer was assigned to one of these departments, he would rarely be reassigned to a line unit was cause for distrust and animosity in all officer ranks between line and general staff.

The state of the United States Army's officer corps, from which any future commanding general would be chosen, was, during the years before and directly after the war of 1812, something less than inspiring. Part of the problem was political meddling.

> Although the authorized level of the Army was increased to almost ten thousand men during a war scare in 1808, Republican leaders used the expanded officer corps to reward the party faithful. Winfield Scott, who served with these officers in the war of 1812, claimed that most were 'imbeciles and ignoramuses'. Those from the Federalist states, he said, were mainly 'coarse and ignorant men, while those from the Republican states were swaggerers, decayed gentlemen and others – fit for nothing else'.[23]

Winfield Scott went on to say, 'The army of that day, including its general staff ... presented no pleasing aspect. The old officers had ... sunk into either sloth, ignorance or habits of intemperate drinking.' A young officer himself in 1809, Scott recalled some 55 years later that 'Party spirit of that day knew no bounds, and, of course, was blind to policy. Federalists were almost entirely excluded from selection ... Such were the results of Mr Jefferson's low estimate of ... the military character.'[24] While it was probably of no solace to the Army, the Navy suffered as well at the hands of Jefferson's Republicans. From the Republican perspective, even the Navy wasn't immune from contempt. Rather than being the necessary commerce-protecting guarantor of international respect, it was a costly, international trouble-maker.

Even the war of 1812 did not rapidly change the personnel profile of the Army officer corps, nor did the emergency suspend political favoritism.[25] Political appointments were by no means peculiar to the period before and during the war of 1812. They were well known during the Revolution, and would continue to be common in the future. While an officer like Scott was incensed by what he regarded as dangerous and unwarranted interference with military matters in the name of partisan politics, he would think nothing of acting on behalf of his own political party, or even of running for a national office, while still in uniform. The careers of the most influential antebellum Army commanding generals provide clear insights into the intermingling of politics and officership.

COMMANDING GENERALS: FROM WILKINSON TO SCOTT

Only two men hold the distinction of having been commanding general of the United States Army twice. The first was Washington, who, after his resignation and subsequent presidency, was prevailed upon by John Adams to take up the sword once more during the war scare with France in 1798–99 and served in that capacity for some six months.[26] The other, who is better remembered for his opportunism rather than highmindedness, treachery rather than devotion, and greed and love of intrigue rather than duty, was one James Wilkinson. Wilkinson had risen to the rank of brevet brigadier-general during the Revolution and became a member of the newly organized board of war. His involvement in the Conway Cabal, however, forced his resignation of both posts.[27]

Wilkinson received a commission as lieutenant-colonel in the regular Army in 1792. Five months later he was promoted to brigadier-general all the time still receiving a pension from Spain, to which he had sworn an oath of allegiance in 1787. Anthony Wayne's death in December 1796 left Wilkinson the Army's senior officer. Subsequent appointments of George Washington and Alexander Hamilton to that post in 1798 and 1799 saw Wilkinson transferred to the southern command (both Washington and Hamilton, when in uniform, out-ranked Wilkinson). In June 1800 Wilkinson was back as the Army's senior officer, a position he held until 1812. As the senior officer, he held no real responsibility for commanding the Army; he merely held his departmental post, which in 1805 included the governorship of the Louisiana Territory. It was during this time that he received a $12,000 bounty from the Spanish, was named in profiteering scandals involving Army contracts and became involved in the celebrated 'Burr conspiracy'.

Secretary of War John C. Calhoun pushed through Army reorganization in 1821, creating eastern and western departments as well as the title of com-manding general. Owing to the retirement of the only other regular major-general in the regular Army, Andrew Jackson, who did so to become governor of Florida, the appointment went to Jacob J. Brown. Appointed a major-general in 1814 he was in overall command at the US's only real bright spots in the land war of 1812, the battles of Chippewa and Lundy's Lane. It was during Brown's tenure that the formal title Commanding General of the Army was first used. But as William Gardner Bell explains, the new title did little to clarify the senior officer's responsibilities and

> [R]aised more questions than were answered ... if the president was commander in chief of the army, what was the role of the commanding general? As his position was not defined constitutionally nor by statute or regulation, what was his relationship to the president, the secretary, the bureau chiefs ...?[28]

General Winfield Scott

It was Winfield Scott who put his personal stamp on the antebellum Army. His 20-year tenure as commanding general combined with his extraordinary military success and attendant prestige, intelligence and diplomatic skills to make him the most influential soldier since Washington. It was at the trial of Aaron Burr in 1807 that Scott would get a sense of the man to whom he would report as a junior artillery officer in 1809 – James Wilkinson.[29]

Swept up by a fit of martial fervor upon hearing the news of the incident between the Chesapeake and the Leopard, Scott eventually received a regular commission as a captain of field ('flying') artillery on 3 May 1808. He quickly recruited his battery from the Richmond and Petersburg area and proceeded, per orders, to New Orleans. Before long his vocal criticism of his commanding general for his involvement with Burr earned him a year's suspension. He was found, under the sixth article of war, to be guilty of behaving with contempt toward his commanding officer. His actions were sanctioned for being 'unofficer-like; but not ungentlemanly', as Scott was rather proud to recall.[30]

Owing to the highly political nature of conferring commissions, Scott describes in his memoirs an officer corps divided into two factions depending on which political party had sponsored their appointments. This caused a great deal of political turmoil and tended to polarize the officer corps, with each faction rallying behind the senior officers of their respective parties. Though very much a political partisan himself, Scott decries this circumstance in his memoirs.[31]

Though he personally pursued and championed military professionalism throughout his career, that quest did not interfere with Scott's political interests. Indeed, for his entire tenure as general-in-chief he was fairly immersed in national politics, the irony being that he was so bad at it. Even before he was placed in command of the Army, Scott was being considered as presidential material. Owing to his enormous prestige as one of the few genuine heroes of the land war in 1812, and his diplomatic success in settling a border dispute in Maine with the British in 1839 (a feat which would be repeated in Oregon in

1852), Scott was an attractive candidate for the Whigs.[32] Whig newspapers lionized him in ink and, though he described himself as a 'quiet Whig', by November 1839 his interest in national office grew even as his actual prospects ebbed. On a trip to Detroit 'he mixed politics with his military duties [and] [t]hough what he saw was not encouraging, he had by then become convinced that he would win'. The nomination, however, went to another prominent Whig military man – William Henry Harrison. Scott was, during the entire political process, commanding the Army's eastern department of the United States. Again, in 1844, Scott was, briefly, considered by some as a viable candidate. This time, though, Democrat James K. Polk was elected.

THE MEXICAN WAR AND ITS AFTERMATH

Perhaps the most remarkable feature of the war with Mexico from our perspective is that it was prosecuted by a commander-in-chief with one political view and a conviction as to how that view should be applied to the war, and pursued by a general-in-chief who held an opposing political view and conducted his campaign accordingly. Polk wanted Mexican territory for American expansion. 'Like the war, Manifest Destiny was mainly a Democratic doctrine.'[33] Indeed, the Whigs in Congress had originally voted against the war. Not completely against expansion and the spread of American republicanism across the continent, Whigs were opposed to the use of force in so doing.

After hostilities with Mexico commenced, Polk conspired to cut off Scott completely from effectively influencing the campaign, because of the latter's political aspirations. Brevet Major-General Zachary Taylor was sent to the disputed Texas–Mexico border and enjoyed immediate and sustained military success. Though Taylor was also a professed Whig, he was deemed less of a political threat by Polk's people, that is until his victory at Resaca de la Palma, after which a delegation of 'leading Whigs' asked Scott to step aside in 1848 in favor of Taylor.[34]

The idea of an amphibious landing at Vera Cruz, first suggested by Senator Thomas Hart Benton, was seized upon by Scott who, in a remarkable display of talent and industry, formulated a plan of campaign based on that of Hernando Cortez.[35] In the planning and execution of the invasion of Mexico, political intrigue and maneuvering by President Polk led to the attempted appointment of General Thomas Benton to command the invasion of Mexico.[36] In Scott's words, 'a grosser abuse of human confidence is nowhere recorded'.[37] Congressional opinion favored Scott's appointment, however, and in a campaign which was heralded by no less an authority than the Duke of Wellington as 'unsurpassed in military annals', Scott entered America's martial pantheon.[38] Being a stalwart Whig and a product of his time, Scott did not ask his commander-in-chief for a political/military mission statement, conducted the crucial campaign of the war and, with the administration's chief negotiator Nicholas Trist, mediated the subsequent treaty as a Whig. He wanted a quick campaign culminating with the capture of the Mexican government and a negotiated peace that would not leave an injured and perpetually hostile neighbor to the south. He reluctantly complied with Polk's demands that the Mexican government pay the bills of the occupying American Army. Together, after much travail, Trist and Scott produced the Treaty of Guadalupe Hidalgo in 1848, which stipulated among other things that the US government assume the 'debt owed by Mexico to American citizens and pay Mexico $15 million for the territory thus transferred'.[39] Polk was incensed, but a Whig-controlled House of Representatives and a war-weary Senate ratified the treaty.

Still in uniform Scott was the Whig candidate for the presidency in 1852. As early as 1850 he had been considered by many highly placed Whigs as the party favorite, despite the fact that the incumbent, Millard Fillmore, was a Whig. Scott's convoluted and inept campaign, however, led to his defeat and the victory of the dark horse Democrat, Franklin Pierce.

THE CIVIL WAR: McCLELLAN AND GRANT

Winfield Scott was two months short of his 76th birthday when the rebel-held shore batteries at Charleston Harbor opened fire on Fort Sumter on 12 April 1861, beginning the Civil War. At the request of Secretary of State William Seward, Scott prepared a missive 'outlining four approaches he thought the new President might take in dealing with the seceded states'.[40] Scott offered four options including political and military initiatives.[41] No one at the time gave the old general's words any credence. However, one piece of advice in Scott's proposals was acted on (besides a naval blockade) and that was to locate an able and young general to command the Army in the field. The command went first to Irvin McDowell, then, after the disaster at Bull Run, to another West Point graduate who had garnered laurels in a campaign in western Virginia: George Brinton McClellan, who had learned warfare from Scott in Mexico.

As noted, the Army's senior officer ranks before the Civil War were 'dominated by non-United States Military Academy Graduates and therefore by men who were not yet fully professional officers'.[42] McClellan's tenure as general-in-chief, though brief, is significant to our examination because it marks the beginning of the ascent of the true professional to that office. McClellan, being the first 'professional', West Point graduate to ascend to the office of general-in-chief, it is with him that 'an examination of the historic details of American civil–military tensions ... must begin'.[43] Whether or not this fact was appreciated at the time, in July 1861 the Union turned to McClellan as its savior. This was a war, however, which was completely removed from national experience.

In December 1861 Congress established the Joint Committee on the Conduct of the War. As Bruce Catton put it, this 'was a flaming portent in the sky for all soldiers who might come to command in the armies of the Union: the civil authority was going to ride herd on the generals, and woe to the man in shoulder straps who failed to please it'.[44]

This was a new wrinkle in the time-worn face of war. Bruce Catton writes, this was a point that

> General McClellan never quite understood. How could he? No general had ever had to understand anything of the kind before. He was not merely the commander of an army in a nation at war; he was the central figure in a risky new experiment which involved nothing less than working out, under fire, the relationships that must exist between a popular government and its soldiers at a time when the popular government is fighting for its existence.[45]

While there is some question regarding the overall impact of the committee on operations during the war, it is generally agreed that it was mainly negative. McClellan was unaware of this shift as was, arguably, every one else in uniform at the time. This sea-change in warfare involved more than the creation of the committee; the very nature of the war was changing. Previous conflicts were of no value as far as this lesson was concerned. But the war in which McClellan found himself at the center

> went all the way to the heart and it could not be left to the regulars. Nobody had yet discovered how a democracy puts all its power and spirit under the discipline of an all-consuming war and at the same time continues to be a democracy ... it was going to be a tough time for soldiers.[46]

Though he was general-in-chief for only 130 days, McClellan's stormy relationship with the Lincoln administration both as general-in-chief and as commander of the Army of the Potomac, had profound effects. Like all the commanding generals before him, McClellan had no code, regulation or tradition of dutifully carrying out the policies of the administration militarily. His commander-in-chief, who was trying to hold together a disparate coalition of moderate and conservative Democrats with moderate and radical Republicans, was not forthcoming with policy guidance. McClellan, therefore, acted as he willed.

A constructive rapport between McClellan and his president was doubtful from the outset. Quite apart from the young general's narcissism, McClellan was a Democrat and his views on how the war must be conducted made it impossible for him to support the commander-in-chief fully. Like Scott before him, he attempted to conduct a war according to his own political ideology. But, unlike his predecessor's, this war was changing. It was becoming a war quite unlike the Mexican War, which was a limited conflict fought essentially over borders. The nature of this war was different. The Civil War was a people's war, a war of causes, culture and beliefs. 'As a conservative, McClellan held war goals that were antithetical to those of the Republican Party.'[47]

McClellan was courted early and openly by the Democrats as a possible presidential contender in the fall of 1861. 'The General was silent about his political ambitions, but he was vocal in his political views. He was a Democrat, he was opposed to wartime emancipation and he did not care who knew it.'[48] Additionally, 'McClellan seemed to think that the government had no right to announce a policy he did not like and that the adoption of such a policy would ... hamper him in his conduct of operations'.[49] He was equally unreceptive to any attempt at civilian meddling in military operations. Manifestations of McClellan's contempt for his commander-in-chief are legendary.

In fact, if we consider Lincoln's proclamation of 15 April 1861 as an expression of his military policy, Lincoln's initial view on the conduct of hostilities was not so distant from McClellan's.[50] Lincoln, though, as the war continued, sensed its change and adapted; McClellan did not.

The Committee on the Conduct of the War started hearings on the inactivity of the Army of the Potomac in December 1861, and it became clear that the more radical wing of the Republican Party was not going to tolerate a general who espoused the political beliefs and, therefore, the military policies of the Democratic Party. The dormancy of the Army of the Potomac 'had brought a storm of criticism upon the government ...'.[51] In all justice, the task which faced McClellan when he took command of the Army of the Potomac, and then of the entire Army was Herculean. The committee, whose understanding of the immense military challenges facing McClellan was abysmal, never understood that. The perception that resulted was not only of an unreliable military leader, but of a dangerous political adversary. A more dutiful and supportive commander would have sensed that the months of inactivity around Washington had caused serious harm to the administration. Lincoln himself cannot, of course, escape censure for this development. It was certainly within his power to get the general to move, and he did try, but he did not choose to force the issue until March.

The Changed Nature of the War

McClellan's lack of accomplishment on the peninsula is the subject of volumes. McClellan's dismal performance and his equally lackluster showing before, during and after Antietam caused Lincoln finally to remove him from command. Just as critical, though, was McClellan's political incapability. In the end he conspired with others to make himself a political figurehead and as such he not only incapacitated himself as an executor of the policy of his civilian master, he made himself a primary target for a political faction growing ever more powerful in Washington. The committee 'strove not only to remove McClellan from his command and to discredit his conservative approach to war but also to strike him down as a political alternative to the Republican administration'.[52] The war was changing, 'from now on it would all be grim. Which meant, finally, that McClellan's part in it was finished.'[53]

President Lincoln, with Secretary of War Edwin Stanton, took over the direction of the war from March 1862 until Major-General Henry Wager Halleck was installed as general-in-chief the following June. Halleck continued in that post until the permanent rank of lieutenant-general was resurrected and bestowed upon Grant in March 1863.

Ulysses S. Grant was the antithesis of McClellan. Serendipitously, he was of a mind with the man whom he would serve as general-in-chief. Grant became aware of the different nature of the Civil War after his close call at Shiloh in April 1862. As James McPherson correctly asserts, total war was inaugurated at Shiloh.[54]

As with his awareness of the changing nature of the war, Grant had a canny sense for the politics of the war's most inflammatory issue: emancipation. Late in 1861 Grant penned a letter taking his father to task on the issue of fighting the war to free slaves. These thoughts are echoed in Lincoln's well-known reply to an emancipation editorial by Horace Greeley in the New York *Tribune*. Responding in August 1863 Lincoln explained:

> My paramount object in this struggle is to save the Union, and is not either to save or destroy slavery. If I could save the Union without freeing any slave I would do it, and if I could save it by freeing all the slaves I would do it; and if I could save it by freeing some and leaving others alone, I would also do that.[55]

While Grant's military abilities were undoubted, Lincoln was concerned about his political aspirations. Though Grant repeatedly denied both publicly and privately any interest in public office, Lincoln needed further assurance. Replying to a letter from Grant's long-time friend, J. Russell Jones, about his political future, Grant asserted, 'Nothing could induce me to think of being a presidential candidate, particularly so long as there is a possibility of having Mr Lincoln re-elected.'[56] Lincoln's relief at reading these candid words at an interview with Jones was evident.

Grant's Objectives

Once in office, Grant's great mission in the spring of 1864 was to defeat the rebel Confederate armies by November. His campaign plan for 1864 was designed to do just that. For the first time during the war, all armies on either side would work in concert toward the same goal – victory. Though his own campaign against Lee languished before Petersburg in the summer of 1864, the campaigns of his best subordinates were turning the tide not only militarily but politically for the Union. Sherman had, by the end of August, taken Atlanta; Sheridan was, at the same time, thrashing Jubal Early in the Valley. Grant in his memoirs speaks of these as political victories, for they would help get Lincoln reelected.

In order to fulfill this political design militarily, 'Grant taught us war is annihilation, and he did so because he brought to the fighting of an American war an indispensable horse sense about American politics ... once a moral nation like America fully committed itself to the war, victory had to be total.'[57] Grant's political as well as military perception saw the Union through to that total victory. The victory was costly: Union casualties from battlefields such as the Wilderness, Spottsylvania, and Cold Harbor totaled more than 45,000.[58] Grant, unlike all the others, remained in command, for 'unlike countless other generals, Grant always remembered to defer to Washington – even in times of exaltation or desperation. Grant sensed that by doing so he could give the politicians victories.'[59]

THE POST-CIVIL WAR ARMY

After the war and Lincoln's death, Grant faced a political challenge that must have made those encountered during the war seem simple and straightforward. President Johnson was desirous of dismissing Stanton as secretary of war. He was unable to do so directly due to the Tenure of Office Act. He therefore decided to dismiss Stanton and appoint Grant to his office *ad interim*. Against Grant's advice, and wishes, Johnson decided to carry out his scheme in August, when Congress was out of session, gambling that when it returned it would approve the move due to Grant's popularity and what Johnson considered to be his own unassailable constitutional position. This was something of a defining moment for Grant: would he remain a simple soldier, or had the presidential 'grub' got to him?[60]

In the end, Grant 'went over' to the Republicans. Fearful that if he defied Congress by replacing Stanton as the president desired, his own political future would be compromised, Grant 'allowed' Stanton to resume his office and thus broke faith with his commander-in-chief. He wanted the presidency himself and was now a 'creature of private ambition rather than public service'.[61] A general-in-chief who had, in time of war, redefined his office for the good of his service and the Republic had, in time of peace, allowed personal ambition to return that office to the ill-defined morass where he had found it.

William Tecumseh Sherman and Modernization

Though he did not have the survival of the Union on his plate, Sherman's tenure as general-in-chief was dogged for most of its life-span by three dangerous and politically volatile challenges: Reconstruction, the Indian wars and constant reductions in numbers. It was in the face of these three external problems, coupled with a consistent restriction of his own power and authority as general-in-chief, that Sherman distanced himself from political engagement.

> Sherman hated Washington politics and bureaucracy. Tactless, uncompromising, impatient, he never came to terms with official life in the capital. His failure to adjust cost the Army badly needed political support during a period of declining fortunes and made his term of office – a constant personal frustration.[62]

Referring to his appointment as general-in-chief in 1868 as 'the dreaded banishment to Washington', Sherman found himself in the midst of the political cesspool he considered that city to be and in proximity to that political faction he loathed: the radical Republicans.[63]

Sherman's well-publicized antipathy toward politics and politicians was directed most fervently at the radical faction of the Republican Party and, therefore, at its creation, Reconstruction. He viewed radical Reconstruction as an anathema and strongly opposed the use of the Army in it. He attacked, in public, government policies such as the Ku Klux Klan Act which authorized the use of federal troops to combat racial intimidation, and 'insisted that if his terms to [Confederate General] Joseph Johnston had been followed Reconstruction would have settled itself'.[64] Sherman's greatest interest, however, lay in the opening of the west. It was here where troops were most needed, not in the south carrying out the radicals' program of persecution. After the passage in 1874 of yet another bill reducing the size of the Army (this time to 25,000), Sherman placed the blame squarely on the Republican Party. That party had, in his opinion, 'passed every law that could be devised to put down and oppress the real soldier'.[65]

The simple fact was that a Congress still highly charged with the radicalism left over from the Civil War was not going to support a commanding general who publicly disdained its policies. Even before Sherman's appointment he and President Grant were in agreement on revising the Army command structure. Grant was determined, it seemed, to strengthen the office of commanding general. Sherman's commission contained a section giving the Army's senior officer more authority over all 'the chiefs of staff corps, departments and bureaus', who would, according to this commission, 'report to and act under the orders of the general commanding the Army'.[66] Six days later, Grant appointed his wartime aide, John Rawlins, Secretary of War. Rawlins demanded that the part of Sherman's commission giving the general his added authority be revoked. Grant acceded to Rawlins. An infuriated Sherman resolved to put this slight behind him and perform his duty.

In 1874 Sherman's resentment of and frustration with official Washington reached its peak. Caught in what he considered an impossible position between the Department of the Interior, with its Indian Bureau blaming every depredation on the Army, and the Secretary of the Army, W. W. Belknap, overruling him at every turn, Sherman moved his headquarters to St Louis, Missouri. (This had been done before: Winfield Scott had moved Army Headquarters to West Point twice during his tenure.) He did not return until Belknap was replaced by Alphonso Taft, a judge from Cincinnati. Whereas McClellan had earlier put himself in an untenable position due to his tenacious and public adherence to a partisan political ideology, Sherman's complete inability (or unwillingness) to participate in any sort of political engagement was, in its own way, just as harmful.

> [T]he grizzled veteran would have to face Congressional committees and explain to them as best he could why the Army needed more men and more money ... His brutal frankness would alienate certain pressure groups ... and in trying to cope with those who could give him the things he needed – men and money – he showed his weakest side. How to fight politicians effectively, he was never able to learn.[67]

This lesson may be summed up simply. No matter how fervently one may wish it or how hard one may try to achieve it, avoidance of political engagement by the senior military in the American republic, even by someone as formidable as Sherman, is impossible.

The Aftermath

Four more men would lead the Army as commanding general: Philip Sheridan, John Schofield, Nelson Miles, and Samuel Young. Sheridan, who thought Sherman 'threw in the sponge' when it came to asserting the commanding general's authority, spent his tenure in an unsuccessful attempt to bring the Army staff under his dominion. John Schofield, demonstrating humility absent in Civil War days, saw 'individual efforts to achieve "higher command, greater power, and more unrestrained authority" as evidence of "ambition inconsistent with due military subordination and good citizenship"'.[68] His tenure was remarkable for the fact that he acted as a chief of staff rather than a commanding general who was constantly seeking greater authority. With the ascendancy of Nelson Miles, however, the quest for greater authority within the Army returned. Like most of his predecessors, Miles's tenure was marked by bitter feuds with bureau chiefs and the secretary of war. The one event that brought much of this to a head was the war with Spain in 1898. Nelson Miles was constantly at odds with his civilian superiors throughout the war and its aftermath as a result of commenting publicly and inappropriately on operations, embroiling himself in naval controversies and devising plans to take Cubans and Puerto Ricans to the Philippines to talk to insurrectionists.

It was Elihu Root, Secretary of War in 1899, along with the last commanding general, Samuel B. M. Young, who brought about the reforms that produced the chief of staff system, with Major-General Young serving as the Army's first chief of staff. The new system helped redefine lines of authority and modernized the service, but the question of political engagement remained unaddressed.

THE MILITARY ACADEMY, WEST POINT

As the single professional institution in the Army during this entire period, the influence of the United States Military Academy at West Point, New York, must be considered. As Professor Russell Weigley has explained, due to the relatively small number of graduates of the Military Academy and the dominance of non-graduates in the antebellum Army (especially before the war of 1812), the influence of the academy and its alumni was negligible. He also asserts that 'the Civil War nurtured the American professional officer corps', and therefore '[t]he professional officer corps that thus emerged from the American Civil War was one whose code of conduct included unprotesting obedience to the civil authorities'.[69] The US Military Academy at West Point nurtured this code and instilled it in the majority of the professional officers in the post-Civil War period.

This institution was not, however, immune to the effects of national politics. The Civil War politicized West Point as well. 'As the war went on, the Army and the Academy, which usually reflected the Army's views, became more and more Republican in their orientation.'[70] The Republican Party advocated a stronger central government and thus a military establishment which relied more on the regular Army than on state militias. Ironically, it was the Republican Party that would generate the 'anti-army' legislation and anti-academy sentiment that plagued Sherman through much of his career. This shift toward the Republicans was open, and was led by the academy's senior officers.

There is little doubt that West Point served during this time as the essential means for professional socialization in the Army. That a cadet would take with him after four years at least a whisper of the predominating political views of those who taught him is only logical. Though the academy constitutes only an undergraduate education, Douglas MacArthur realized that the future leadership of the Army would, most probably, start their education for that task at the academy. He sought to widen education by adding the social sciences, including economics and political science, to the curriculum; this was an effort that was resisted for years by the academy's academic board.

The Army now requires officers to progress through professional educational stages. Just as in the past, there is constant adjustment, especially in the more senior schools such as the Command and General Staff College, of the curriculum in order to address the necessary subjects of history and politics. These attempts at making officers' professional education more academic are constantly under fire by those who insist that the emphasis be on war fighting. The answer lies in the civilian educational system. Promising officers must receive top post-graduate education in those social sciences in order to fill the void in the professional educational system. In the private sector their ideals as well as their intellect will be challenged, providing the services with leaders prepared for the challenges of the new century.

CONCLUSIONS

Political engagement by the military is not, by any means, a modern phenomenon. It has been a fact of life, for better or worse, in the United States' experience since the Republic's beginning. In the nineteenth century, there being no legal, traditional or regulatory prohibitions against it, the amount and tenor of the engagement was pretty much left to those involved. Whether the political engagement was constructive, as in the case of Grant and Lincoln, or destructive, as in the case of McClellan and Lincoln, was a matter of personality, ideology and philosophy. Clearly, however, as Sherman's tenure as commanding general suggests, political engagement is avoided only to the detriment of the services. The American political/military experience indicates that political engagement is inescapable and crucial to the services as well as to the country. Given its inevitable and critical nature the military leader must bend his or her efforts to ensure that the engagement is constructive. In order to ensure constructive political engagement the military officer must be well versed in the history and politics of the Republic and aware of his or her place in the political system. So that promising officers can be adequately prepared for this role they must receive high caliber postgraduate education. This is not possible within the services' educational system, nor is it proper or beneficial that it be conducted there. This sort of preparation must be conducted in the private sector.

Involvement in politics by senior military officers is a part of American history. But most of this political–military intermingling was narrowly focused on the activities in Washington and the national government, with little spillover into American political life in general. It is also the case that during this early period, the United States was concerned primarily with its internal stability and development. Indeed, the United States did not gain stature as a major power until the twentieth century and such power was shared among a number of major powers. It was not until the late twentieth century that the United States emerged as a superpower and, later, as what some call the lone superpower. This changed the role of the military and brought it into a more complex and closer relationship to policy decisions and strategy formulation affecting the military institution. Thus, the involvement of the military in constructive political engagement is now a necessity going beyond the confines of the Washington establishment. However, this earlier period offers insights into examining the role of political engagement in the current period and beyond.

4

Civilian and Military Cultures

The US military must operate within the American cultural framework if it is to maintain the trust and support of the American people. As pointed out in Chapter 2, questions have been raised about the current concept of military professionalism. These spill over into military culture and its interpretation and integration into American culture. Culture refers to a way of living and norms and values that are passed on from one generation to another. This is reflected in language, the arts, the media, and a variety of visible matters such as architecture and entertainment. The roots of culture rest in the norms and values shaping the way of life that underpins the political–social–economic system. However, the changes in American society and its changing demographics have brought with them different interpretations of American culture. This has resulted in much debate about the essence of American culture.

For any number of Americans, the past four decades have been a search for the meaning of American culture. From the 'flower children' and the 'me' generation of the 1960s, the 'baby boomers' and Generation 'X' and the malaise of the 1970s, the so-called 'greed' generation of the 1980s, and, for some in the same generation, the 'noble cause', to the multicultural, diversity, and, for some, the 'so what' generation of the 1990s, it seems that traditional notions of American culture are being challenged from various directions. For older Americans, these newer generations seem a far cry from the 'we' generation of the 1930s and 1940s. That generation suffered through the economic depression and responded with little complaint and gallantly to the country's demands and sacrifices in World War II. This has added to generational differences and interpretations of American culture.

The attempt to come to grips with present-day American culture is reflected in books and popular commentary on the issue.[1] Some argue that a more definitive cultural base may be evolving. Others point to the major divisions in American culture that reflect an increasing fragmentation of the meaning of Americanism.[2]

> On the right, you have the globalized economy people who say we're not citizens of any nation, the nation state is finished, we are a globalized economy, citizens

are consumers, nothing more ... Then on the left, you have the multi-culturalists and the politically correct who really do want to change this country, and are really changing this country. And their vision is a world broken down into group rights, which are essentially ethnic, which are religious, which are gender, which are racial, which are all the things that I wanted to get away from in this country, all the things I thought we were fighting against with civil rights, with freedom for women, et cetera.[3]

In any case, there is still much debate about American culture and its value base. The debate about American values and culture, multiculturalism, diversity, bilingualism, and dual nationalities in the last part of the twentieth century surely will spill over into the twenty-first century. In the process many may be left wondering about the meaning of American culture. However, the roots of military culture remain in a traditional notion of American culture. This makes it particularly difficult for the US military to fix on the meaning of Americanism as it is reflected in society, and in turn shape military culture and military character accordingly.

CULTURE AND SOCIETY

From a traditional perspective, American culture rests on values which are based on what is esteemed and absolutely essential as the philosophical, legal, and moral basis for the continuation of the American system, in other words, those principles from which the American political system and social order derive their innate character and give substance to American culture. Much of this evolves from the classic Greek tradition, the Judeo-Christian heritage, Anglo-Saxon principles, and theoretical dimensions expounded by philosophers such as John Locke, John Stuart Mill, and Jean-Jacques Rousseau.[4] Many of these elements and principles are enshrined in the Declaration of Independence and the Constitution.

Notions of diversity have always been a part of American culture. Today, multiculturalism and diversity have become particularly prominent in the eyes of many Americans. Multiculturalism stresses the importance of the cultures associated with various ethnic and racial groups. Hispanic, African, Irish and Jewish cultures, among many others, have been important in adding to the rich cultural heritage of the United States. At the same time, national unity necessitates that these cultures be placed within the framework of American culture. That is, while retaining the heritage of old world or other world cultures, Americans must give first priority to the meaning of American culture, if there is to be any degree of unity and commitment to the idea of 'America'. Thus, the first question is: what is American culture?

American cultural roots have at least six dimensions particularly relevant to

American national interests and the US role in the international world.[5] It is the view here that these have been, and remain, the traditional basis of American culture and the basis for military culture.

First and foremost, America has its roots in the European culture and the Anglo–Saxon heritage. Discussing America's heritage, a member of the Board of the United States Institute of Peace wrote,

> Though not a European nation geographically ... America is the daughter of Europe. A close look at American society reveals a whole whose parts are assembled from every continent. The union of these parts depends on the heritage of Western civilization – on a belief in the enduring values of the civilized world of Europe contained in its thought and literature, its art and music, and its economic and political legacy.[6]

The recognition that the roots of American culture rest in the legacy from Western civilization was expressed by President John F. Kennedy in his inaugural address. Referring to the 'we' generation of World War II, he said:

> The torch has been passed to a new generation of Americans – born in this century, tempered by war, disciplined by a hard and bitter peace, proud of our ancient heritage – and unwilling to witness or permit the slow undoing of those human rights to which this nation has always been committed.[7]

The reference to 'ancient heritage' seems to be an allusion to the formation of the American Republic and to its roots, which are found in Western civilization with all that that entails, regarding Judeo–Christian heritage, classical Greek civilization, and Western philosophy.

Second, Americanism requires allegiance to the United States and the Constitution. The first allegiance of individual American citizens should be to the principles embodied in the Declaration of Independence and the Constitution, and under these principles to a united America. Traditional views stress that all other cultural factors must be placed within this allegiance. Moreover, this means that 'governors' and those who have been elected to rule, owe their power and accountability to the people and to the principles spelled out in the Constitution. The people are the final authority regarding who should rule. Further, there is a continuing responsibility of the 'governors' as well as those appointed to positions in the system, to rule and function according to the moral and legal principles embodied in the concept of 'power to the people'. The right of the people to change 'governors' is absolute. In this respect, there must not be any one consuming power dominating government or establishing its own rationale for rule. The furthering of individual worth necessitates limited government with no absolute and permanent focal point of power. This notion is embodied in checks and balances and in the separation of powers of the three branches of government. To ensure this, rule and governance must be open. In the main, this means decisions and policies openly arrived at with input from a variety of formal and informal groups. The system of rule must be accessible to the people and their representatives. This is the essence of 'open systems'. In brief, power belongs to the people.

Third, it follows that there is an inherent worth to any one individual in his or her relationship to others, to the political system, and to the social order. In the most simple terms, every person is intrinsically a moral, legal, and political entity to which the system must respond. Each individual has the right to achieve all that he or she can without serious encumbrance, other than those that protect other individuals and those required for the protection and survival of the homeland. Individual worth must, therefore, be reflected in economic, political, and legal systems.

This includes the right of self-determination. It follows that each nation-state has the right to determine its own policy and to govern itself as it sees fit. An important corollary is that the people within that nation-state also have the right of self-determination. From the point of view of the United States, this means that through a mechanism of free and fair elections, people within each nation-state have a right to determine by whom and how they will be ruled, with the option of replacing their rulers as they see fit. All of this is to operate within a system of laws and peaceful change. However, US policy has been inconsistent in applying self-determination with democracy. The break-up of nation-states as a result of the self-determination of groups within nation-states challenges the international status quo but also challenges US policy. Should US policy support self-determination or sovereignty of nation-states? Is the maintenance of existing nation-states more important than supporting the emergence of autonomous entities or new states? According to some, self-determination must be used selectively, depending on the importance for US national interests.

However, the right of self-determination in international terms is complex and troubling. While US policy gives credence to self-determination, its application is often shrouded in contradictory views and policies. This stems from the claims of self-determination conflicting with those of the right of sovereign states.[8] This was (and is) a simmering issue in Bosnia-Herzegovina and the cause of conflict in Kosovo – a province of Serbia, in Yugoslavia – in 1998 and into 1999.

Fourth, from the American perspective, policies and changes in the international environment must be based on the first three dimensions. Thus, the concept of peaceful change brought about by rational discourse between nation-states is fundamental. Resort to war can only be acceptable if it is clearly based on protection and survival of the homeland and the American system, and this only if all other means have failed. In this respect, diplomacy and state-to-state relationships must be based on mutually acceptable rules of the game.

Fifth, for the United States, it is a fundamental proposition that systems professing the values of a liberal democracy such as the United States, and seriously attempting to function according to them, must be protected and nurtured. Further, nation-states whose values are compatible with those of the United States are thought to be best served by an international order based on the same values.

Sixth, there is a moral underpinning to American values that owes its inception to the Judeo-Christian heritage. For many Americans, therefore, this instills a sense of humanity, a sensitivity to the plight and status of individuals, and a search for divine guidance. All of this adds a dimension to what is seen to be proper and just in the minds of many Americans, and is considered by many to be beyond the legal definition of government.

In a broader context, American culture has roots in the notion of Western civilization – the West. This does not mean that there was a smooth transition from the classical Greek systems to American-style democracy. Indeed, according to David Gress, the notion of the West 'grew by paradox and contradiction out of jungle of desires, ambition, and greed that is human nature, always and everywhere'. He concludes that

> Universalism – the idea that everyone wants democracy and free markets, and will get them – is wrong because the world is not the West. On the other hand if Western elites forget their roots and launch themselves into the illusions of a conflict-free multiculturalism, they will risk bringing down the West and with it an essential building block of tomorrow's multipolar world order. The West owes it to the world not to disappear.[9]

It is not suggested that the values from Western civilization are perfectly embodied in the American system, nor is it suggested that all of the important dimensions of American culture are included. It is further acknowledged that not every American agrees as to how the cultural principles spelled out here are defined and applied. It is also the case that some will disagree as to what is presented here as basic elements of American culture. It is recognized that these principles may not reflect the realities of the internal debates and strife over such issues as racism. Also, there are many historical examples of value distortions and their use to disguise other purposes. The American Civil War, for example, was a watershed in the shaping of American culture in notions of human rights, equal rights, and slavery. The results of the Civil War reaffirmed the cultural principles embodied in the Constitution and the Declaration of Independence. Yet today there is still debate about the meaning of the Civil War.

The fact is that in the American system, no matter how imperfect, these values stem from the founding of the nation and formation of the American Republic. Now they are embodied in the Constitution and the American political–social system. Further, the system of rule and the character of the political system have institutionalized and operationalized these values, no matter how imperfectly. The expectations of many Americans and their assessment of other states are, in no small measure, an application of these values. For these Americans, there is a sense of absolutism in what is embodied in these principles. It is the view here that what is identified as the roots of traditional American culture is seen by many US military professionals as the basis of Americanism.

AMERICAN VALUES: INTERNATIONAL DIMENSIONS

The collapse of the old order in Europe following World War I set the stage for the further evolution of democratic systems in Europe, on the one hand, and oppressive fascist or Marxist-Leninist systems, on the other. Until that time, the *Pax Britannica* had provided a sense of stability and order to European affairs as well as to the United States and its relationships with Europe. But for any number of Americans, involvement in World War I to save Europe seemed a mistake. The US withdrew into a splendid isolationism which only ended after the start of World War II.

Even in the aftermath of World War I, Americans had been accustomed to a world dominated by the European order compatible, more-or-less, with the general nature of American values and national interests. While this was an imperfect order, it was not threatening to what Americans felt was the proper order of things and their own value system. At the beginning of the twentieth century, American values seemed to be best expressed by the progressive period of Theodore Roosevelt's presidency, by Woodrow Wilson's 14 points in the aftermath of World War I, and in the 1930s by Franklin Roosevelt's New Deal, focusing both on individual Americans and on the government's responsibility to them.

In earlier years, there seemed to be little need to translate these values for use in the external world. America's interest only rarely extended beyond its own shores. Yet it was also at the beginning of the twentieth century that the United States became a world power with the acquisition of territory resulting from the Spanish–American War. A decade later, involvement in World War I was seen as a way of making the world safe for democracy and subduing a tyrannical old world power. In the aftermath, however, most Americans were glad to see their government distance itself from the old world again and focus on internal domestic matters. 'It's their problem, not ours', was a common American attitude with respect to Europe and the outside world. Isolationism during the 1920s and 1930s, in the main, was characteristic of American foreign policy.

In between the two world wars, Americans presumed that American interests were also world interests, that American values were morally unassailable and therefore were those to be sought by the rest of the world. In this context national security was primarily a narrow view focused on the protection of the American homeland, which required only minimum armed forces and limited strategies. Further, there was little need to struggle with issues of American values and how to protect them in the external world, except occasionally in terms of international economics.

World War II changed all of that, even though most Americans wanted no part of the European War up to the bombing of Pearl Harbor in 1941. Although America's desire was to return to splendid isolationism in the aftermath of World War II, the United States was in the world to stay. It became clear that American responsibilities now extended beyond the nation's borders. It was also becoming clear that democracy and American values could not be nurtured and expanded by simply 'staying at home'. Democracy made political and moral demands that required its nurturing in all parts of the world. Beyond protection of the American homeland, what did the United States stand for? And how did it intend to achieve these goals, whatever they were?

These questions were less difficult to answer in the negative – that is, America was against Marxist–Leninist systems and the 'Evil Empire', as well as other authoritarian systems. Containment became the major US policy to prevent the expansion of the Soviet Union. Positive responses to such questions were seen in the US role in rebuilding Europe – the Marshall Plan and the North Atlantic Treaty Organization (NATO). All of this placed the United States in a leadership role of the West, a reflection of the earlier Puritan view of the 'chosen people'.[10] This probably provided the moral basis for involvement in the Korean and Vietnam wars.

But the end of the Cold War and the emergence of a new security landscape made many Americans feel that it was time to focus on domestic issues. There was a turning inward, reinforced by the conviction that the danger of major wars had diminished considerably and that the United States had won the Cold War. But this new landscape was muddled and lost in the 'fog of peace'. Indeed, some even argued that America would miss the Cold War.[11] But as the twentieth century came to a close and America prepared for the next century, it seemed clear that it was deeply involved in many parts of the world, economically, politically, and militarily. Moreover, many Americans felt that globalization and the lone superpower responsibility made America a virtual world hegemon. This further prompted many Americans to presume that American values, such as human rights, self-determination, and liberal democracy, were essential parts of foreign policy and national interests.

AMERICAN VALUES: THE DOMESTIC SETTING

The characteristics of the American domestic environment complicate the difficulties of coming to grips with American culture. As stated earlier, during the 1990s Americans became concerned with the meaning of American culture, particularly in relation to the emergence of issues of multiculturalism and diversity. Some critics argued that while the United States may never have been a melting pot, it did benefit from the waves of immigrants who brought with them a rich cultural heritage. But this heritage, according to critics, is being promoted at the expense of Americanism. That is, the notion of American cultural heritage and Western tradition in which the roots of democracy lie, are being eroded by increasing prominence of other cultures and loyalties. The greatest charge is that such a development can lead to the 'balkanization' of the United States. Regardless of the pros and cons, it is clear that demographics and cultural issues can have an impact on the national security policy, strategy and the US military. American involvement in Africa, for example, must surely be sensitive to the views of Americans of African descent. The same is true with respect to Latin America and American Hispanics.

Efforts have been made (and are being made) to promote the notion of multiculturalism and diversity. Unfortunately, some of this is being done at the expense of the unifying notion of Americanism. This is particularly the case in many institutions of higher education. To be sure, other cultures and demographic diversity lends uniqueness, richness, and strengths to the notion of Americanism. But, for many Americans, the fear is that multiculturalism and diversity can be taken to such lengths that the concept of Americanism becomes eroded and lost in the maze of cultural distinctions and loyalties. There is also the fear that multiculturalism will bring with it cultural confrontations and the continuation of age-old animosities spilling over from foreign lands. For some, this is aggravated by raising the notion of diversity to such a priority that it erodes individual quality and capability: that is, diversity subordinates individual character.

All of this is made more difficult by political correctness and moral–ethical traits reflected in segments of American society. As General Colin Powell writes,

> And Lord help anyone who strays from accepted ideas of political correctness. The slightest suggestion of offense toward any group … will be met with cries that the offender be fired or forced to undergo sensitivity training, or threats of legal action. Ironically for all the present sensitivity over correctness, we seem to have lost our shame as a society. Nothing seems to embarrass us; nothing shocks us anymore.[12]

There are also some historical revisionists who are critical of the Founding Fathers because of what they see as hypocritical posturing on issues such as slavery. But these revisionists have in turn, been challenged for their 'Johnny-come-lately' efforts to discredit the long-term accomplishments of the Founding Fathers in shaping the American democratic system.

Part of American culture also rests in the notion of the messianic spirit. Religion has been an important component in shaping American culture. This is seen in the view held by many that the United States as the leader of the West must be a moral as well as a political–military leader, and that moral principles must guide the behavior of governmental officials and the military. Although a number of Americans feel that religion has no place in a democratic and secular system, history seems to prove otherwise. The messianic spirit reinforced by the historical role of religion is an important factor in the evolution of American culture. As one authority writes, 'Religion was present at the creation of the American political system, and was one of several elements contributing to the design of governmental institutions and to the core beliefs that grew into national political culture.'[13]

An important part of how the United States responds and perceives the international security setting is the view of its own historical experience, including ideology, culture and character of the political system. A great deal has changed since the end of the Cold War. This was also the case at the end of World War II. Each generation has witnessed enormous changes in relations between nation-states, the nature of conflicts, and the nature and character of adversaries. Indeed, change has become so commonplace that it is a truism that the only permanent thing in the world is change. The uncertainty of the strategic environment, combined with increasing questions about the United States as the lone superpower and world hegemon have created an unsettled, if not fearful, mood about the ability of the United States to promote its values in the world environment.

Yet debate and disagreement over American culture reflects differences in defining American values and, in turn, has an impact on notions of national security and national interest. This makes it difficult to design and adapt strategy and policy that is intended to foster American values and reinforce American culture. If Americans disagree on such fundamental matters, how can they become the focus of clear strategy and policy?

MILITARY CULTURE

The complexity of the American domestic landscape, combined with the debates over the meaning of American culture, make it extremely difficult for the military to maintain a 'fixed' and compatible cultural identity with the civilian culture. This is based on the view that military culture evolves out of the broader American culture (in the traditional sense) and basic American values. Making it even more difficult for the military is that the military raison d'être makes certain demands that differ from those of society in general. These rest on the notion that mission success requires absolute attention to authority, training and skills that focus on killing the adversary, and on a physical and psychological preparedness to engage in stressful and highly demanding operations to perform the primary mission of the military. But these differences must still be within the orbit of American democracy. That is, military culture must be nurtured by principles accepted and supported by the American people.

In the context of American culture, the military has defined basic concepts that underpin military culture. The US Army culture rests on the concept of duty, honor, country. The Navy stresses honor, courage, and commitment, while the Air Force focuses on integrity, service before self, 'excellence in all we do'. The Marine Corps focuses on honor, courage, and commitment. The totality of these concepts shape military culture. In more simple terms, military culture stresses honor and devotion to duty, unqualified service to the nation, and subordinating self to the greater good. This translates into a complex set of values encompassing morals, trust, and integrity. In turn, standards of behavior are expected to conform to these in absolute terms – a clear distinction between right and wrong. The challenge for the military is the translation of these values into individuals' behavior while maintaining and reinforcing them within the military system.

A particularly compelling view of the differences between military and civilian culture is Thomas Ricks's *Making the Corps*.[14] Although focusing specifically on the Marine Corps, Ricks provides insights that are generally applicable for all of the military services. Following a Marine platoon composed of individuals from all walks of life through basic training, Ricks shows the impact of rough absolute standards of right and wrong as well as success and failure.

> In a society that seems to have trouble transmitting values, the Marines stand out as a successful and healthy institution that unabashedly teaches values to the Beavises and Buttheads of America. It does an especially good job of dealing with the bottom half of American society, the side that isn't surfing into the twenty-first century on the breaking wave of Microsoft products. The Corps takes kids with weak high school educations and nurtures them so that many can assume positions of honor and respect.[15]

Reviewing the book, John Hillen notes that the book is 'a powerful indictment of many other institutions in American society'.[16] The Marines instill a sense of discipline and moral and ethical standards, and a view of the world quite different from the general notions of American society. It is interesting to note that basic training in the Marine Corps is not gender integrated.

Regardless of the efforts at trying to harmonize attitudes over race, gender, and homosexuality, the military system is an authoritarian system driven by the need for combat cohesion and unit effectiveness.[17] This leads to the need for the absolute authority of those in command, subordination of individual rights to the rights of the group and the unit's purpose, and the focus on the unity of effort based on values of Americanism. While due respect must be given to multiculturalism and diversity, the first commitment must be to the United States and the Constitution. This is a critical element in Americanism. Military training, indoctrination, and commitment are aimed at these cultural roots. All other cultures are secondary. Moreover, diversity can not be so defined as to erode the unity and 'oneness' in service to the state. This is the essence of the military culture and must be placed within the framework of the American democratic system.

At the same time, within these parameters, individual dignity must be maintained. This is no easy proposition. It never was. However, no amount of effort can change this 'democratic authoritarianism' without first changing the military's relationship to society and the professional military ethos. This is at the core of the internal travails of the military and the concern of those about the so-called gap between military and society (see Chapter 6).

However, there are some who criticize the military for not stoutly defending the military culture. According to Hillen, 'the military (with the once again conspicuous exception of the Marine Corps) is failing to defend its own culture and its own hierarchy of values'.[18]

Military culture also shapes military lifestyle and the family environment. In the military profession as perhaps in no other, lifestyle and responsibility extend to an individual's family. The military professional lives in a world in which there is virtually no place to hide. Almost all activities are conducted within the official organizational structure. The military profession becomes a total way of life, not only for the professional, but also for his or her family. It is assumed officially as well as unofficially by superiors and peers, as well as by subordinates, that the quality of family life is a direct reflection of the professional capability and stature of the military professional.[19]

The closeness between the family and the military profession is basic to military culture. This closeness is well-expressed in a passage written a generation ago and still relevant to the military family and military community.

> The officer and his family are members upon arrival at a station of the social and cultural life of the military community. The feeling of 'oneness' or 'belonging' is a natural outcome of the singleness of purpose of the military mission on which all are engaged. It is enhanced by the fact that the problems, the hopes and expectations, and even the fears, within one military home are similar to those in other military homes.[20]

The same is true of non-commissioned officers and petty officers.

To be sure, in the current period any number of military families live off-post and are more involved in the civilian community. Also, contrary to past practices, many military wives work off-post and do not become deeply involved in military social life. But the fact is that the military mission and the linkage with the total military community affects military family life in a way not generally characteristic of the civilian community. It is also the case that any number of families in the Navy and Marine Corps, for example, must deal with constant deployment, often six months every year. The stress on family life is particularly troubling for those in such units.

In the process of reinforcing the military culture – as noted earlier, a culture that is rooted in the physical and psychological notions of killing others – and yet ensuring that the military operates within the principles of American democracy, the military profession must have its voice heard regarding military needs in order to serve the nation effectively. And its voice should clarify the meaning and principles underpinning the military's raison d'être.

What makes all of this difficult for the military is the fact that the debates about the meaning of American culture and efforts by some to subordinate traditional views to those of group rights and various versions of American culture, have created a mixed and unclear cultural bag. The military focuses on a specific cultural focal point – the willingness to serve, to offer one's life for the country. This translates into an Americanism that remains rooted in the elements identified in the first part of this chapter. Regardless of other legacies and heritage, the driving force for the military remains the notion of Americanism. This places the military in a complicated and challenging relationship to society in general and to other cultures.

CONCLUSIONS

There will always be some distinctions between American civilian and military cultures, and these evolve from the very purpose of the military. Yet, as noted earlier, such distinctions must be within the orbit of the American democratic system. The military cannot act or be seen as a business corporation, a social group or any other type of group characteristic of society in general. It is a profession with a unique and demanding purpose with a set of values and principles that are essential to its purpose. To demand something other than this is to destroy the very purpose of the military.

A majority of Americans have little or no military experience, nor does it seem that they have much contact with military life. The same holds true for many elected leaders and for most in the so-called 'American elite' group and members of the media. At the same time, the relatively good economic times in the mid-1990s and beyond have made it more difficult for the military to retain the requisite number of well-qualified and motivated individuals, many of whom are attracted by well-paid, less strenuous positions in the civilian economy. All of this has added to the perception of a gap between civilian and military cultures.

To demand that the military replicate the characteristics of society in general is to demand that the military change its primary purpose and fashion itself as another socio-economic institution in the American system. If this is the case, then the military will be placed in a position that relies on social affinity and the good graces of society for its existence. Yet it is also clear that military professionals and their families are first and foremost citizens of the United States. They are involved in the political realm and have political choices. The domestic cultural environment and the strategic cultural landscape force the US military to be sensitive to the debates and disagreements about the meaning of American culture and relationships with various world cultures. This is no easy proposition. The military must not only remain within the orbit of the American system and its cultural base, it must be prepared to engage in contingencies in different cultures – many of which may be contentious in terms of traditional American culture.

It is not clear that those in public life and many in the populace have a clear understanding of the distinctions between military and civilian cultures. For some these distinctions appear to be incongruous to American democracy. And for others, the military is viewed as another government institution whose culture and values must reflect society. Surely, it is incumbent upon those in the National Command Authority and military professionals to convey to the American people and its elected representatives the meaning of military life and the essence of military culture.

> The task before us should be obvious. It is to reinforce, not undermine the military culture – a culture that remains rooted in the psychological and physical notions of killing the enemy – while maintaining its loyalty to the principles of democracy and civilian supremacy. At the present time, that task is not advanced by silence. On the contrary, the voice of the military profession must be heard regarding the military's need if it is to serve the nation effectively. It is particularly important for the military profession to respond to those who dogmatically and erroneously associate the US armed forces with a particular political preference, bureaucratic interest group, or subversive conspiracy.[21]

5

The National Security System

In the immediate aftermath of World War II and the onset of the Cold War, the United States established a national security system that, in the main, remains in place today. However, the unclear international landscape in the post-Cold War period and into the twenty-first century has complicated the meaning of American national security. This has raised questions about the appropriateness of the existing national security system as the world moves into the next millennium.

In contrast to the Cold War era, the translation of national interests into a clear national security policy has become a vast gray area. This has been compounded by the closer linkage between national security and domestic policy. Now many national security issues are difficult to isolate from domestic policy. All of this calls into question the meaning of national security.

For any number of Americans, national security now not only encompasses national interests, but American values. Still others link US security with world security. Thus, the notion of national interests and national security has been broadened to include a variety of matters that go beyond military considerations. This has led to a lack of clarity about the dimensions of national security and, at the same time, a lack of clear vision about US national (grand) strategy. It also makes it difficult for the US military to focus clearly on its role in national security and on the kinds of threat and contingency for which it must be prepared. Complicating this is the question about the relevancy of a Cold War system into the twenty-first century.

These uncertainties have led to debates and disagreements about the meaning and concept of national security. According to one account, 'The debate is about what kind of policy and what kinds of military capability the United States will have in the future. One aspect is the changed world environment ...'[1] These matters are examined in subsequent chapters. But, at this juncture, the focus is on the national security system and its organizational structure, and the military role in the national security decision-making process.

THE NATIONAL SECURITY STRUCTURE

While the president is the focal point of the national security system, there are any number of structures and relationships within that system that have an impact on the decision-making process and implementation of national security. The National Security Establishment, created by law and designed to provide the president with an advisory and operational instrument, is a formal policy-making instrument and an instrument for implementing national security policy.

Figure 5.1: Organization for National Security

National Security Council	*National Security Council Advisors*
[National Command Authorities]	Chairman, Joint Chiefs
President Vice-President	Director, Central Intelligence
Secretary of Defense Secretary of State	

Figure 5.1 shows the organization for national security.[2] It is presented here only as a reminder of the formal structure and a way of distinguishing this from the realities of the decision-making process. Often, however, the character and personality of the president has led to the creation of informal and parallel structures and processes for developing national security policy. This sets up a series of policy power clusters that form a national security network driving the National Security Establishment and the formal policy-making process. The relationship between and within these power clusters and their power are dependent upon the way the president exercises his leadership and his views on how the National Security Establishment should function.

There are three major power clusters affecting national security: (1) the policy triad, consisting of the Secretary of State, Secretary of Defense, and the National Security Advisor to the president; (2) the Director of the CIA and the Chairman of the Joint Chiefs of Staff; and (3) the White House chief of staff and counselor to the president. While the policy triad is the most important, all of the power clusters have a role in shaping national security policy. They represent critical parts of the National Security Establishment and operate in ways that reflect presidential leadership style and mind-sets of those within the three power clusters. As such, these may or may not be compatible with the formal National Security Establishment. In other words, the national security decision-making process is much more fluid and dynamic than is suggested by the formal structure. Similarly, the policy-making process is not as rational and systematic as may be suggested by the formal policy process.

The working of the national security system may be more realistically shown in Figure 5.2. This policy triad is an informal system and the internal dynamics can differ considerably from the formal structure.

Figure 5.2: The Policy Triad

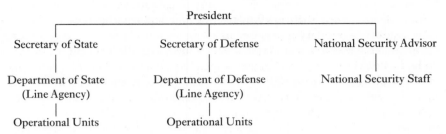

Note: The Secretaries of State and Defense each wear two hats: staff advisor to the president and operational department head. Their perspectives on national security are usually conditioned by the capability of their departments to implement policy and strategy. The National Security Advisor, however, has no operational units. His national security staff is just that – a staff agency. The National Security Advisor and his staff attempt to provide a presidential perspective and to stand above departmental issues. Perceptions, mind-sets, and responsibilities differ between the two secretaries, and particularly between the two secretaries and the National Security Advisor.

The relationship of individuals within the power clusters to the president, perceptions of their relative power, and their leadership skills affect the exercise of power and have an impact on the decision-making process. The relationship between the Secretary of State, the Secretary of Defense, and the National Security Advisor (the triad) are important in shaping the decision-making process. That is, the personality of each and how each views the national interest, the use of military force, and the international environment, determine the interplay within the triad and the impact on presidential perspectives and policies. In addition, how each personally relates to the president is critical. Also, the leadership skills of the Chairman of the Joint Chiefs of Staff – the chief military advisor to the president – and the CIA Director, and the relationship of each member of the triad to the others affect the totality of the national security system. In brief, the interpersonal skills and individual qualities all play an important role in determining the focus of power within the National Security Establishment.

From this, it is clear that the decision-making process in the national security system is replete with power-plays and personal relationships. This becomes even more complicated when the relationships and power structure within the various staffs – military officers and civilian staff – involved in the national security system are injected into the decision-making process. This is also the case within the Department of Defense and between the Department of Defense and the Department of State.

The structure of the Department of Defense includes both a military and a civilian dimension. The nature of the military profession and the education and socialization of many civilian officials and employees shape the institutional posture – at least in terms of the Washington establishment. This is supposed to provide a military perspective in response to national security issues, as one would expect. In turn, there is a fundamental orientation within the department to seek adequate military manpower levels and resources to develop the most sophisticated weaponry, and to provide for a satisfactory level of compensation and social services for its service personnel. This goes hand-in-hand with the effort to develop a skilled military which can perform effectively in war. As discussed earlier, these efforts have been expanded to include a variety of situations short of war – operations other than war – and a number of political–military situations that, in the past, were primarily matters for the Department of State.

This institutional orientation often places the Department of Defense in opposition to the efforts of the Department of State. This is not to suggest that there is not a mutually acceptable goal to solve problems as peacefully as possible. But the fact is that the 'stick' component in the 'carrot and stick' relationships between states is usually in the hands of the Department of Defense. Yet, given the nature of operations other than war, the Department of Defense is often seen as an arm of the Department of State by critics and as an operational element of the Department of State by the military. This raises a number of questions not only in terms of institutional relationships and power-plays, but of those between individual civilian and military staff officers.

THE MILITARY AND THE POLICY PROCESS

The traditional military professional posture rests partly on the premise that the military does not become involved in the political dimension of the policy process. Hence, because the policy process is invariably a political one, military professionals are supposed to distance themselves from it, at least formally. Moreover, because formulation of national strategy is in turn closely linked to the political process, military professionals are not usually considered to be directly involved in that process.

In addition, the joint military perspective necessary in the national security policy process is often difficult for military professionals to maintain – career success comes through their respective services. Even the members of the Joint Chiefs of Staff (JCS) with their dual roles, usually tend first to their service responsibilities. The same is true of joint staff officers. Although how they perform on the joint staff and their relative efficiency is determined by the JCS, for officers on the joint staff, service perspectives and career considerations often override a joint perspective. Service parochialism and professional socialization instilled over a long career are difficult to overcome by a three-year assignment to the joint staff.

Another basic problem is that the role of the military in the policy process and formulation of strategy is affected by role conflict. The technology drive in the military, sophisticated battlefield weaponry, electronic warfare, and the evolution of an intricate organizational defense structure have shaped the military establishment along lines of civilian corporate and managerial systems. Interestingly enough, the Marine Corps is making an effort to incorporate the capability and knowledge of industry and academia into its command and control system. In order to be well prepared to conduct military operations,

> US military leaders will need to tap into detailed expertise outside the military – companies doing business in a particular region, academics with years of study in an area or subject, or another segment of the government that does not primarily deal with military issues.[3]

A great deal of effort in senior service schools has been aimed at developing officers capable of dealing with the complexities of the technological age. As a consequence, military managership has become an important factor in career success and military efficiency. But not everyone agrees with that perspective. Many military professionals and critics argue that the real need within the military services is leadership. According to this view, emphasis on managership and associated skills must be secondary to the ability to lead and command units in war. Reliance on technology shifts the focus away from the psychological–social dimensions of human behavior, reducing competency in the art of leadership. (See Chapter 2, 'The Military Profession'.)

Notwithstanding its presumed distance from politics, the military is involved on many fronts: weapons-acquisition process, budgetary matters, and relationship with Congress, among other things. Further, contemporary conflicts, whether they involve strategic nuclear weaponry, are unconventional in character, or evolve out of operations other than war, include important political factors. Indeed, most US military operations in the 1990s have been (and are) characterized by inextricable political and military factors. Cases in point include US involvement in the Gulf and in Bosnia-Herzegovina. For military professionals to be effective, therefore, they must acquire political as well as military skills. At a minimum, military professionals must be able to deal with political dimensions of conflict. No longer are such considerations clearly distinct from the operational environment, if they ever were. One aspect of this is the linkage between military professionals on staffs in the National Security Establishment and their formal and informal impact on policy decisions.

NATIONAL SECURITY AS A CONCEPT

National security in the post-Cold War period and beyond has expanded to incorporate any number of non-military matters. That is, the use of the military is now only one factor in designing and executing national security policy. Indeed, it can be argued that for many Americans the economy and issues of the global village may now have a higher priority in national security than military considerations. Thus, military factors have become but one dimension of national security policy. This makes it particularly difficult to design military strategy in the context of a variety of non-military dimensions.

Traditionally, there have been three overriding priorities in national security interests. First, protection of the American homeland and the survival of its political system. Second, maintenance, nurturing, and expansion of open systems – this generally means democratic systems. The concept of open systems is used here with the idea that there are various forms of democracy and, indeed, there may be socialist systems that have established the basis of openness and are non-threatening to neighbors and to world peace. Third, protection against those states developing military capacity to threaten seriously the US system.

These observations are the basis for defining national security policy. National security policy is that part of government policy primarily concerned with formulating and implementing national strategy to create a favorable military environment for US national interests. An integral part of this is to prevent the effective use of military force by the nation's adversaries or potential adversaries in obstructing or denying US ability to pursue its national interests as defined in the broader strategic landscape. But as noted earlier, the new international landscape encompasses a variety of issues that many now see as security issues. In addition to economic and environmental issues, the effort to develop international stability, respond to refugees, and counter terrorism and international drug cartels, among other matters, have become part of national security. This is further broadened by the expansion and support of American values such as democracy and human rights.

There is also a great deal of overlap and intermix between foreign policy and national security policy. Traditionally, national security differed from foreign policy in at least two respects: (1) national security purposes are more narrow and focused on the security and safety of the nation; (2) national security is primarily concerned with actual and potential adversaries and their use of force. This meant a military emphasis that is not usually the case in matters of foreign policy. However, in the new international security landscape many see national security policy overlapping with foreign policy; indeed, sometimes they are almost indistinguishable.

It is also the case that for many policy-makers and nationally elected leaders, national security has become more than the capacity to conduct wars in the international arena. Some scholars argue that,

> The concept of 'security' must include protection against all major threats to human survival and well-being, not just military threats ... Given the multiplicity of pressing world hazards, the concept of 'national security' must be integrated with that of 'world security' ... In today's interdependent world ... the quest for

security is rapidly becoming a *positive sum* process, whereby national well-being is achieved jointly by all countries – or not at all.[4]

How to incorporate American national security into world security in a realistic fashion is difficult to determine. Moreover, the tendency in such perspectives is to view virtually every external matter as a national security issue.

INTERESTS, SECURITY, AND THE USE OF FORCE

It is the view here that national interests and national security policy must be carefully crafted and applied according to priorities delineating survival (vital) interests from others. Too often national security is used synonymously with *any* interest and value, raising the specter that all interests and values are survival priorities. If national security policy and strategy followed such a pattern, the United States would be placed in a position of having to defend virtually everything, with the end result of being unable to defend anything, a repeat of Sun Tzu's admonition. If almost everything is a matter of national security, then the concept of national security becomes virtually meaningless.[5] Resources and forces would be scattered throughout the world and rarely would be in a position to bring sufficient force to bear on a particular issue that may well be a survival matter.

> The United States cannot and should not do everything. For the most part, it should attend to larger security problems worldwide while it supports its allies and like-minded countries who have responded first to global security needs in their own regions.[6]

From such a perspective, national security should rest primarily on the notion of a high propensity for the use of military force in a combat environment. To do so requires some distinctions between domestic policy and national security as well as between foreign policy and national security policy. The primary distinction rests in the propensity for the use of military force and the acceptance that the military is the primary instrument in the implementation of national security policy. While many other matters are important in the overall concept of national interests, they may best be incorporated into foreign policy and implemented by non-military organizations and institutions. This is not to suggest that the military has no role in foreign policy – armed diplomacy.[7]

The use of the military, or the threat of its use, in the conduct of diplomacy was well illustrated in the US/UN–Iraq confrontations in 1998, and NATO operations in Kosovo in 1999. The build-up of NATO forces in the Balkan area was an important factor in maintaining pressure on Yugoslav President Slobodan Milosevic to accept NATO diplomatic resolution of the Kosovo crisis. Similar measures have been in place against Iraq and Saddam Hussein. Into the middle of 1999, there was no resolution to either crisis; although NATO had taken control of Kosovo, Milosevic remained in power. US policy-makers seem to have accepted that no resolution to either crisis is possible while both leaders remain in power.

Yet, as Craig and George note,

> The use of force or the threat of its use in diplomacy raises a central, difficult question in the theory and practice of foreign policy: under what conditions and how can military force and threats of force be used effectively to accomplish different types of foreign policy objectives at an acceptable level of cost and risk? This has sharply divided American strategic thinkers; it has been a focal point in many controversies over foreign policy since the early days of the Cold War.[8]

Short of clear threats to the territory of the United States, Americans may disagree, and do, over priorities. Even when there is agreement on priorities, there is disagreement about resource commitment and strategy. Nonetheless, a system of priorities provides a way of identifying levels of threats and helps in designing strategies. But all of this must be guided by the meaning of national security and its conceptual dimensions. That said, some concept of national interests is important in sharpening the concept of national security.

NATIONAL INTERESTS

US national interests are expressions of major US policy objectives projected into the international arena.

> We must recognize that America does indeed have national interests in the world, including an extremely important interest in the sturdy legitimacy of the international system as it changes over time ... This does not imply that American global hegemony is needed now or in the future – as it was needed to deal with the global Soviet military threat throughout the Cold War. Instead, we need to be both precise and clear about our national interests as the twin military and geopolitical transformations remake the international order.[9]

The purpose of these interests include the creation and perpetuation of an international environment that is not inimical (antagonist) to the peaceful pursuit of American values. It follows that such interests are those that nurture and expand democracy and open systems. Conversely, these interests are those that prevent the expansion of closed systems using force or indirect aggressive means. But all national interests do not automatically translate into vital interests and therefore into a national security concern; that is a priority necessitating or contemplating military involvement.

As stated earlier, at the core of US national interests is the survival of the homeland and the American political order.[10] However, survival cannot be limited to the final defense of the homeland. In the light of today's weapons technology and ideological imperatives, among other things, the concept of survival of the homeland means more than retreating to the borders of the United States and threatening the total destruction of any who attack.

If national interest is invoked only in those cases where the homeland is directly threatened and its survival is at stake, then the concept is of little use. Indeed, it may be too late if Americans wait until survival is at stake. If the concept of national security is to have any meaning in terms of policy and strategy, then it must mean something more than survival of the American homeland. It is the interpretation and application of this broader view that sparks a great deal of debate and disagreement between the executive and legislative branches of government and between a variety of groups in the American political arena, including the media.

A useful way to try to distinguish various priorities in the concept of national interests is to view these from the perspective of priorities: core (first order), contiguous (second order), and outer (third order):

Range of Options

CORE	**CONTIGUOUS**	**OUTER**
(First Order)	(Second Order)	(Third Order)

First order: vital interests.

Protection of the homeland, and areas and issues directly affecting this interest, require a total military mobilization and resource commitment of the nation's total effort.

Second order: critical interests.

These are areas and interests that do not directly affect the country's survival or homeland, but in the long run have a high propensity for becoming first-order priorities. In the immediate period, these have a direct influence on first-order priorities. Such interests are measured primarily by the degree to which they maintain, nurture, and expand open systems. Military force may be the instrument of choice, but not necessarily the only instrument.

Third order: serious interests.

These are areas and issues that do not seriously affect first- and second-order interests, but do cast some shadow over such interests. US efforts are focused on creating favorable conditions to prevent such interests from developing into higher order ones. Unfavorable third-order interests serve as a warning to second-order interests. A variety of non-military instruments probably are the most appropriate.

All other interests are peripheral in that they are placed on a watch list. This means that there is no immediate impact on any order of interests, but these matters should be watched in case events change them to a higher order of interests. In the meantime, these peripheral interests require few if any US resources.

However, the National Security Establishment, policy-makers, and the US military rarely have the luxury of endless debate. Nor do they have unlimited time or all of the necessary facts in any given situation. Yet policy must be made and strategy options examined and implemented regardless of these conditions, even while debates and disagreements remain intense. The fact is that at some point in time policy must be decided upon and implemented. Before that is done, US national interest for that particular situation must be identified and articulated. At the same time, national interests over the long range must be considered.

Although Congress has an important role in these matters, custom, usage, and constitutional powers have usually given the president the basis for articulating the meaning of American national interests. Initiatives in foreign and national security policy usually rest with the president.

In summary, five points need to be restated. First, American values as they apply to the external world are at the core of national interests. But values cannot be so construed as to reshape national interests into commitment of military forces in every instance in which American values may be challenged. Second, national interests do not mean that US strategy is limited to the immediate homeland of the United States. These may require power projection into various parts of the world. National interests and national security are closely linked. But these interests must be differentiated in terms of vital (core) and other interests. This should be the critical aspect of national security. Third, the president is the focal point in defining and articulating American national interest. To do this effectively, the president must demonstrate leadership and understanding of the domestic and international setting. Fourth, there must be a degree of consensus of the American public and national leaders regarding the translation of national interests into the use of military force. Fifth, the US military must function within the context of the first four points.

NATIONAL POWER

The ability successfully to carry out national security policy is a direct result of the power the nation possesses and its ability to use that power effectively. But here again, we are faced with problems of definition. National power can be seen from two dimensions. It can be defined in universal terms and also with respect to power in any given situation. In the first instance, national power can be measured by a variety of indicators, ranging from the total number in the armed forces, to the ability of a nation to mobilize for war, to the nation's economic capacity. In such cases, only relatively large states favored by large populations and resources can become powerful.

But, in any given situation, large states may not have usable and effective power. In such cases, smaller states may have power based on other considerations. For example, in the case of Vietnam, many argued that the United States did not have usable power to bring the Vietnam War to a successful conclusion. Yet the minor state of North Vietnam had more effective power in that particular case and was eventually able to prevail. It may very well be that the Soviet Union/Russia faced a similar power relationship with respect to the Afghanistan War, 1979–88 and to Chechnya in 1994–96.

In brief, national power is a complex and often ambiguous concept. Nonetheless, there are a number of important elements of national power that a nation must possess if it is to pursue its national interests on a global scale.

According to one authority,

> National power ... is a mix of strategic, military, economic, and political strengths and weaknesses. It is determined in part by the military forces and the military establishment of a country but even more by the size and location of territory, the nature of frontiers, the population, the raw material resources, the economic structure, the technological development, the financial strength, the ethnic mix, the social cohesiveness, the stability of political processes and decisionmaking, and, finally, the intangible quantity usually described as national spirit.[11]

It is from this concept of national power that we design a more abbreviated view that may be a useful road map of the national security landscape. National power is based on four major elements: military power, geostrategic importance, national character, and psychological sustenance.

Military power is a measure of the total (aggregate) physical attributes of the armed forces of a country. This includes such indicators as the quality and quantity of equipment, mobility, and combat effectiveness (skills, leadership, and will to fight).

Geostrategic importance refers to the location of the country in terms of international economy, international security, and the national security of other states. For example, the Strait of Hormuz in the Persian Gulf area is of geostrategic importance, given its international character as a waterway to oil resources, among other things. Further, geostrategic importance includes the availability of important resources within the country, its climate and terrain. All of these provide a measure of geostrategic importance.

National character is measured by such things as the homogeneity of the population, its size and growth, population education and skills, economic system and capability, the degree of commitment to the political system, and the legitimacy and efficiency of the governing structures. Because of its highly subjective nature, some discount its relevance to national power. Nonetheless, it is important in providing insights into the nation's political processes and cohesiveness.

Finally, *psychological sustenance* is an intangible part of national power. This is an obvious subjective dimension and, as expected, the most difficult to measure. The fact is that all of the elements of national power may be useless if the people of a nation are unwilling to use these in the pursuit of national interest. Moreover, if other states perceive that the nation with power is hesitant to use it and its people are divided over the proper courses of military action, then such states will ultimately perceive it as a 'paper tiger' whose power is based solely on rhetoric. Similarly, even when a nation has all of the other elements of power, its own people may perceive such power as useless, and for all practical purposes, diminish the nation's real power.

Thus, military power as well as the other elements of power are real only if buttressed by national will, political resolve, and staying power, and an effective strategy to pursue national interests. At the same time, there must be a commitment to persist over the long run – staying-power to see the matter through, once the nation is committed.

Measuring national power is even more complex than each of these elements individually suggest. The problem becomes acute in trying to link these elements, determine their relationships, and identify their total impact on other states. Yet attention to national power does provide a sense of the relative power of the country. It also focuses attention on the need to translate national power into usable power and link it through the National Security Establishment and the policy process to the pursuit of national interests.

THE INTERNATIONAL LANDSCAPE

The international security setting affects the US national security policy process in a number of ways. The international landscape is characterized by contradictory forces creating complexities and difficulties that are often intractable (unmanageable) in terms of US national security (see Chapter 7). Thus, there are limits to what the United States can do in any given national security issue (except in clear cases of survival – vital interests). This has become even more difficult in the security landscape of the late 1990s, where real threats to American vital security interests have diminished. The difficulty now is to determine what and who are threats to US national interests.

In addition, the international security setting is not a neat and clearly delineated order, nor is it necessarily driven by a set of rational forces. On the one hand, there are a number of commonalities with each security issue. On the other hand, there are distinct characteristics associated with each security issue and challenge. Thus, each US national security issue may require a unique set of responses. This may require a broad policy being implemented by a variety of strategies, at times appearing to be contradictory. Further, the traditional concepts of military force may have limited utility in such a setting.

US national security policy also may require secrecy or covert operations. Given the nature of the US system, trying to undertake effective covert operations promises to be difficult at best and ineffective at worst. This makes it difficult for the United States to develop a coherent policy and strategy to respond to the most likely conflicts – unconventional ones, which may require indirect approaches and secrecy. Further, the resurgence of Congress in the national security policy area (some call it congressional micromanagement) and the continuing debate and disagreement over the defense budget add to the problem. This is particularly true when such policies and strategies stray from mainstream American views and ways of war.

Finally, the problem of strategic cultures poses a relatively new issue for US national security. Strategic cultures evolving out of non-Western traditions govern the political and security orientation of many states in the southern hemisphere as well as of China and India. The character of conflicts and the meaning of victory or defeat may differ in foreign strategic cultures in contrast to US strategic principles.[12] Yet the United States cannot compromise its strategic culture without eroding its legitimacy and capacity as a major world power. Maintaining and nurturing its culture in both domestic and international arenas is an essential part of its identity.

The major conclusion is that there are a set of boundaries, constraints, and limitations that cannot be separated from the operations of the US national security establishment. Neither can the policy process be viewed in isolation from these considerations. As a result (and always aside from real threats to the homeland), there is likely to be a great deal of disagreement and debate within the United States regarding national security. Disagreements are likely to occur within the National Security Establishment, between the Establishment and other branches and agencies of government, and between all of these and the public in general; the intensity of the disagreement increases in direct proportion to the size of the gap between policies and strategies on the one hand, and well-established American perspectives and political–military posture on the other.

When we add to this the differing views of allies and adversaries and their national security efforts – particularly in the post-Cold War era – it is not difficult to conclude that simply examining the National Security Establishment or the policy process does not do justice to the complexities and complications inherent in US national security.

All of this is exacerbated by the diffusion and decentralization of power within the US political system, not only within and between the various branches of government, but also within the general population. Participatory politics and single-issue politics, the erosion of political party cohesion, the policy role of the media, and internal power problems within the government have made it almost impossible for the president to undertake any foreign policy or national security initiatives that are perceived as outside the mainstream or that appear to challenge American constitutional principles. To induce changes successfully and to place his own stamp on national security policy, the president and his allies must build a political base within the government and the general public, as well as convince the media of the appropriateness of new policies and strategies.

The American fear of concentration of power ingrained in the constitutional principles of separation of powers and checks and balances has provided clear limitations to the exercise of power of any one branch of government. Yet these restraints can also prevent effective response to challenges that require a concentration of power. The legalities of constitutional practice may have little influence in the international security setting, where power and politics are often inextricable. And it is in this context that the US National Security Establishment and the process by which security policy is formulated and implemented meet their greatest test.

CONCLUSIONS

The national security system remains wedded to a Cold War syndrome. Yet the issues facing the United States in the last part of the twentieth and into the twenty-first century go beyond the vestiges of the past. To be sure, past experience is important in designing the security system for the future. But such a design also requires some sense or vision of the strategic landscape. For the US military, the problem is not only its proper role in the national security system now and its role in new systems, but also its impact on strategic visions with due regard to the realistic capability of the military. This is complicated by the fact that 'The role of force in diplomacy will continue to pose a difficult dilemma for American foreign policy.'[13] The underlying problem is the reconciliation of political and military considerations, while trying to achieve diplomatic solutions.

Military strategy, operational doctrine, and force structures are key elements affecting military capability and the military professional ethos. And these matters must be placed into the decision-making process of the national security system. Equally important, such matters must be incorporated into the political dimensions of any national security policy. All of these considerations affect the scope and substance of national interests, national power, and the willingness to support the use of military force in a variety of contingencies. And, surely, elected leaders and the American public need to know the military professional perspective on such matters.

As Hoffman concludes:

> The risks and costs incurred when the sword is employed are high. The costs of intervention must be measured against the values of the interests being advanced

or defended. Civilian officials need to spend a greater amount of time studying the military, understanding its challenges as a profession, and wrestling with the intricacies of its employment ... Without such an understanding it is very doubtful that the 'ultimate decision', the decision to send America's sons and daughters into armed conflict, will be wisely made.[14]

An important step in developing 'such an understanding' rests with the military profession. This requires reaching out into the public realm and presenting the military perspective. This means that the military perspective must be an integral part of the national security policy process and incorporated at all levels of the national security system. Politics is an integral part of this system.

6

Civil–Military Relations

As pointed out earlier, the military's relationship with American society is going through a difficult period of adjustment brought about by the changes in the international and domestic environments. Much of this evolved from the differences between civilian and military cultures and disagreements about military and politics. In the long term, the substance of military professionalism and the qualitative nature of civil–military relations will have a major impact on the US military's capability to respond to the new security landscape. This chapter examines US civil–military relations in the new security era and draws conclusions on what all of this may mean for military professionalism and US national security policy.

There is a great deal of literature on civil–military relations, particularly in a historical context. In the current period, there are different views about the civil–military relations, evolving from different interpretations of history, varying analytical frameworks, and different views about the role of military professionals and civilian leaders. Too often, however, the scope of relationships as seen in the current period is driven by perspectives that overlook the substance of military professionalism. In reality, the relationship between society and the military is complex and multidimensional:

> Military professionalism and civil–military relations are closely connected. The values and beliefs that form the substance of military professionalism determine in no small measure the role of the military in society, establish the boundaries and criteria for military behavior, provide norms for the military subsystem, and establish the professional posture vis-à-vis civilian elite ... the character of military professionalism places the military subsystem in its 'orbit' within the political system and, in so doing, establishes the reference point from which civil–military relations evolve.[1]

Combining theoretical concepts with the realities of international life necessitates placing the study of civil–military relations and military professionalism in the context of the security landscape and conflict characteristics that are part of that landscape. This adds to the complexity of the analysis. Yet it is clear that there are historical patterns and principles that shape civil–military relations and military professionalism.

During most of its history, the United States considered the US military, particularly the Army, as a distinctly secondary adjunct to the political system. The historical aversion to standing armies evolving from the revolutionary period and the cautions expressed by the Founding Fathers about the dangers of large standing armies are deeply rooted in the American psyche. When faced with major conflicts, the US military, composed of a small number of regulars, was expanded by the influx of citizen-soldiers. These episodic surges of the US military were quickly followed by demobilization and reduction of the military.

Although written over two decades ago, James Alden Barber's view seems relevant today. He wrote,

> American attitudes toward the military services and the role played by the military in the social and political systems of the United States have deep roots in the American heritage ... From England the colonists inherited a distaste for a professional military and a distrust of a standing army. These attitudes have permeated American civil–military relations ever since.[2]

It is also the case that during the nineteenth and into the twentieth century senior military men openly engaged in politics. This was an expected phenomenon. At the senior level there was no 'wall' between the military and external politics. Further, internal military politics over 'turf' building was characteristic of the same period – that is, it consisted of arguments and power plays over roles and missions.[3] Between the two world wars, however, visible military professional involvement in the political realm seemed to happen rarely, if at all. Politics and the military seemed to be clearly separate, except under a specific civilian-ordered mandate.

World War II marked a new period in civil–military relations. Following the victory over Germany and Japan, the United States attempted to return to its historical posture of demobilization and back to normalcy. However, the rise of the Soviet Union to superpower status and the onset of the Cold War forced a change. The US could not base its security on a small military. It also could not revert to its historical isolationist security posture. One consequence was the emergence of a more visible and prominent national security establishment and military system as integral parts of the American political scene. This development was not without its civil–military consequences. The so-called 'Battle of the Potomac' and 'The Revolt of the Admirals' were triggered by efforts to design a new national security system, unifying the armed forces and establishing various roles and missions for the military services (see Chapter 2).

TheVietnam War marked a watershed in civil–military relations. The involvement of the United States in Vietnam not only triggered anti-war protests, but eventually caused some military professionals to question the conduct of the war as well as the conduct of some in the military. The character of the war and some aspects of its conduct by the military had a negative impact on civil–military relations. The 1980s and President Reagan's labeling of the military involvement in Vietnam as a 'noble cause' led to the easing of the Vietnam trauma. This moved civil–military relations into a more comfortable pattern.

As pointed out in earlier chapters, with the collapse of the superpower system, the prospect of major wars between major powers has considerably diminished. At the same time, a new world order has emerged; but its shape remains obscure and the world is characterized by ill-defined threats and uncertain challenges. Complicating this new environment, the US domestic political–economic system is in a period of transition. Demographic and economic changes combined with lowered expectations of involvement in major wars has turned the attention of many Americans to the domestic political–economic environment and global economics. But US military contingencies remained focused on preparing for wars and on the international environment, with increasing pressure for it to become involved in socially relevant contingencies, many having to do with support of indigenous governments and humanitarian missions. However, in 1998 and into 1999 the majority of Americans seemed to be satisfied with the economy and supported the status quo. According to Thomas Dye, 'President Clinton has enjoyed continuing economic growth, throughout his years in office, which helps to explain his reelection victory in 1996 and his favourable job ratings in public opinion polls …'.[4] This was the case even through the impeachment of President Clinton in 1999, but its aftermath may bring distrust of the president's political motivations, even though the president was acquitted by the Senate.

How all of this can be translated into civil–military relations is a difficult proposition, and has led to varying views about civil–military relations. These perspectives need to be examined before conclusions are drawn about current implications and what these may mean into the twenty-first century.

SCHOLARLY PERSPECTIVES

As pointed out in Chapter 2, the study of civil–military relations in the United States gained some impetus in the 1950s. The works of political scientist Samuel P. Huntington and sociologist Morris Janowitz incorporated the study of military professionalism into the study of civil–military relations.[5] This is not to suggest that scholars ignored the subject earlier.[6] But Huntington and Janowitz seemed to crystallize matters by expanding the analysis of military professionalism and civil–military relations at a time when Cold War issues prevailed.

In one of the more recent studies on civil–military relations, Don M. Snider and Miranda A. Carlton-Carew identified four trends as,

> potentially responsible for strains in civil–military relations: (a) changes in the international system ... (b) the rapid drawdown of the military; (c) domestic demands on the military and society's cultural imperatives; and (d) the increased role of nontraditional missions for the military.[7]

The authors discuss the substance of these trends and conclude that US civil–military relations are not in 'crisis'. But they argue that there is a need to develop a healthier relationship between the military and society. In the book, a number of authors offer their own interpretations of civil–military relations; most do not agree with the crisis school.

In reporting on a civil–military symposium James Burk writes,

> At the moment, we cannot conclude with any confidence that the current fractiousness in civil–military relations is a cause for concern, much less evidence of a crisis. Fractiousness, after all, is only disagreement over policy: it is the expected state of affairs in an open society, and its lack may be a surer symptom than its presence that a democracy has fallen on hard times.[8]

Other scholars note that the military is a political instrument. Accordingly, military professionals need to develop a sophisticated understanding of and sensitivity to the American political system and the political–social environment.[9] Some further argue that involvement in political decision-making is an integral part of military professionalism. However, such involvement would be driven by military purpose and not political partisanship. Clearly, these notions have an impact on civil–military relations.

In the light of the differing views about proper civil–military relations, it is important to examine the forces shaping such relations and identify what is acceptable in a democratic system. In the broader scheme, civilian expectations coupled with the need for military effectiveness and the dimensions of military culture create countervailing forces. In turn, this shapes the character of civil–military relations, suggesting that there is something more than one particular formula.

DIMENSIONS OF CIVIL–MILITARY RELATIONS

Earlier studies identify a number of key components of civil–military relations which include political leaders and elected officials and their aggregate view of the role and function of the military, the state of the political–social system, the degree of penetration of society by the military – and the military by society.

Civil–military relations must also include military professionalism, as this affects the military's views of society and society's views of the military. At the same time, it is important to consider military professionalism as a matter in its own right and as an institutional factor. The dynamics and relationships between these components shape the composite notion of civil–military relations. And it is clear that there is no simple view of civil–military relations.

Political Leaders and Politics

There is little question that civilian control and supremacy are established institutional and constitutional facts within both political and military systems. One reflection of this is that most military professionals have generally refrained from direct public statements against elected officials and politicians. But in the current era, it is also clear that military involvement in political decisions on foreign policy and national security policy is a necessary, if not publicly proclaimed, role. Even so, military professionals operate in a complex environment, often faced with a political dilemma.

According to Joseph Ellis and Robert Moore,

> Perhaps more than any other group, the military is victimized by a divided allegiance; on the one hand, they are charged with carrying out dictates of the elected or appointed civilian leaders; on the other hand, as the Americans most intimately acquainted with the implementation of our military policies, they are most likely to have personal qualms about the effectiveness of their policies.[10]

This was clearly seen during the Vietnam War. Disagreements about the control and conduct of the war developed into confrontations between political leaders and military professionals. A number of military professionals believed that the military operations in Vietnam were unduly affected by political interference from civilian sources in Washington. As the war became increasingly difficult to prosecute, domestic political support eroded and ultimately led to US withdrawal. While this did not necessarily generate a 'stab in the back' mentality, it did create some bitterness within the military profession and disenchantment with political leaders.

> The country that sent us off to war was not there to welcome us home. It no longer existed ... Many of our countrymen came to hate the war we fought. Those who hated it the most – the professionally sensitive – were not, in the end, sensitive enough to differentiate between the war and the soldiers who had been ordered to fight it. They hated us as well ...[11]

In the broader scheme of things, not only did the role of military professionals affect civil–military relations during this period, civilian images and perceptions also had some impact on these relations. In the main, civilian and military perspectives were not only contradictory, they created 'friction' in civil–military relations.

In the new world order and into the next century, the scope and dimensions of military commitments invariably involve an inextricable political–military linkage. This is not only true internationally but also domestically.

This was one of the themes in the work by Michael Handel.[12] In examining the focus of the US military on classical works on strategy and war, the author states, 'The faculties of the US war colleges and students who graduated in the late 1970s and early 1980s, gradually (and for some reluctantly) understood that war and politics could not be separated as was often assumed.'[13] In the aftermath of World War I and into the 1930s, however, it was assumed that involvement in politics was unprofessional.

In contrasting the role of Prussian/German military in the Franco–Prussian War of 1870 and World War I and after, Handel notes that

> the German generals were involved in politics in order to shape the nation's military and political strategies. In contrast, the US military in Vietnam experienced the opposite problem – that of considering any involvement in politics as unprofessional or even 'dirty'. That produced a Jominian type of separation between the political leadership and military strategy, which were viewed as independent fields of activity.

The fundamental issue is under what circumstances, or if at all, the military should become involved in politics. In an endnote Handel writes,

> it appears that either too much or too little involvement in politics can create serious problems. No military organization on the highest levels can avoid becoming involved, or trying to influence, political affairs as they pertain to the conduct of war.[14]

The problem is to develop a relationship that is appropriate and acceptable to both civilians and the military, while insuring that the military has an appropriate and realistic role in the political decision-making process.

THE MILITARY AND THE MEDIA

Disenchantment with the civilian leadership during the Vietnam War was more than matched by professional disenchantment with the American media. As part of the political landscape, the media has been viewed suspiciously (and remains generally so) by many military professionals. The media's interpretation and reporting of the Tet Offensive in Vietnam in 1968 was a clear example of media bias in the eyes of many military professionals and confirmed their view of the media.

For example, in studying the impact of the media on American politics during the Tet Offensive, Peter Braestrup, a member of the media, concluded,

> The generalized effect of the news media's contemporary coverage of Tet in February–March 1968 was a distortion of reality – through sins of omission and commission – on a scale that helped spur major repercussions in US domestic politics, if not foreign policy ... The media's penchant for self-protection and instant analysis carried the day, and the resulting reporting turned out to be grossly misleading.[15]

The role of the media in the Gulf War (1991) also raised questions about the relationship between the media and the military in general. After eight months of discussion, in May 1992, representatives from the Department of Defense and the news media issued nine principles for war reporting. The tenth principle proposed by the media stated, 'News material – words and pictures – will not be subject to security review.' The Pentagon countered with its own principle: 'Military operational security may require review of news material for conformance to reporting ground rules. This fundamental disagreement could not be bridged, so no principle has been adopted governing control of information.'[16]

The adversarial (friendly?) relationship between the media and the military is an important element in the dynamics between the military and the political system. Many consider the media to be the fourth branch of government because of its ability to shape the political agenda by focusing public attention on what the media considers to be important political issues. In addition, how the military is portrayed and the tendency for the media to seek the dramatic and controversial are often seen by military professionals to be at odds with realities of military life.

The friction between the military and the media was again highlighted in 1998. A report on CNN about the alleged use of nerve gas by US forces in Operation Tailwind during the Vietnam War triggered sharp criticism by the Department of Defense as well as other journalists.[17] The lack of evidence and the uproar caused by the apparent false report led to a retraction and apology by CNN and the dismissal of two producers and a reprimand of the reporter. Although this was reported by only one media source, many probably saw this as another example of the 'friction' and adversarial posture of the media with respect to the military.

Although the media–military relationship is not a replica of civil–military relations, it does reflect military professional suspicion of an institution that links the public to national politics and national institutions. This is exacerbated by the view that many in the media have no real understanding of military culture. This, in turn, affects the media's interpretation and portrayal of military issues and military professionals. (There are, to be sure, individual exceptions to this.) The fear is that misinterpretations and misunderstanding can shape the media's reporting which in turn affects public attitudes and understanding of the military system.

THE CURRENT PERIOD

In the last decade of the twentieth century, civil–military relations have undergone (and continue to undergo) changes. These have laid the groundwork for civil–military relations in the current period and into the next century. Some of this was seen in the early years of the Clinton administration.

In the presidential election campaign in 1992, a potentially disturbing development surfaced. A number of retired US military officers including former Chairman of the Joint Chiefs of Staff, Admiral William Crowe, publicly endorsed the Democratic Party candidate, Governor Bill Clinton. While retired military men and women have supported one or the other candidate in the past, this was usually done unseen, without media fanfare. In 1992, it appeared that not only was Admiral Crowe's endorsement of Bill Clinton made in the public realm, it was given wide television coverage as Bill Clinton and Admiral Crowe appeared together a short time before the elections. In addition, the grouping together of a number of retired officers supporting Bill Clinton seemed to signal an organized effort. For some, this appeared to cross the line, injecting a partisan posture that bodes ill for the notion of military professionalism.[18] By contrast, retired General Norman Schwarzkopf, whose views on Bill Clinton's avoidance of military service and President George Bush's leadership in the Gulf War are well known, declined to endorse anyone publicly in the 1992 presidential elections or become involved in public displays of partisanship.

Another event also seemed to detract from appropriate civil–military relations. The *New York Times* reported that Representative Dave McCurdy 'had approached senior officers at the Pentagon and asked that they exert influence on his behalf ... the officers went to members of President-elect Bill Clinton's transition team and told them they preferred Mr McCurdy to Mr Aspin as Secretary of Defense'.[19] If such activity becomes the established pattern, with future presidential candidates seeking public endorsements from one or another group of retired military officers or active officers lobbying for one or the another candidate for cabinet office, the line between politics and the military profession becomes dangerously partisan and contrary to the principles of military professionalism.

The Military and Society: Changing Dimensions

During most of the Cold War era, the US military enjoyed a relatively comfortable relationship with society. The military purpose was generally accepted by society as legitimate and necessary. It was seen primarily as a 'warrior' profession whose purpose was to win wars. This was reinforced by the existence of a real enemy – the Soviet Union – and the possibility of conflicts with the Soviet Union or its surrogates. Vietnam was an exception. But even during that period, the majority of Americans remained supportive of the US military and prosecution of the war until 1969, following the Tet Offensive and the view that the war had become a stalemate. The post-Vietnam era of the 1980s and the Gulf War seemed to restore much of what was lost in Vietnam.

In the aftermath of the Vietnam War, the creation of the volunteer military system resulted in initially distancing the military from society. Only later did the volunteer system broaden its social representation, increase its quality, and restore its linkage with society. But now, the changed domestic political environment and the prominence of a number of social issues have spilled over into the ranks of the military. This drive for democratization of the military, that is, the drive to reshape the military into a closer reflection of the social shape of society, is not a new issue, but it has emerged as a serious problem for the military in the 1990s. This matter was discussed in more detail in Chapter 4. Here, we touch on these matters as they affect civil–military relations.

Democratization covers a range of issues from women in the military to demographic changes in society and its increasing heterogeneity. Women have carved out an important role in the military. But how that role is to be incorporated into a combat role remains a matter of serious debate, particularly in terms of women in the ground combat arms. At the same time, visible homosexuality remains outlawed in the military, with its 'don't tell, don't ask, don't pursue' policy. Even though the Clinton administration was committed to lifting the ban on homosexuals in the military, arguments pro and con have not yet defined a clear path regarding homosexuals in military service.[20] Further, liberal and radical feminist groups are particularly outspoken against the military over sexual harassment cases such as the Tailhook affair involving US Navy fighter pilots and over sexual harassment of female naval officers.[21] The Lieutenant Kelly Flynn affair in the Air Force and the sexual harassment cases in Aberdeen Proving Grounds as well as the charges brought against the Army's Command Sergeant Major McKinney (all except one later dismissed) highlighted the problems in the military services.[22] The same holds true for lesbian and gay activist groups who charge the military with discrimination. Combined with demographic changes and the increasing heterogeneity of the American populace, the military finds itself struggling with social issues that affect force composition and its professional value system. (Chapter 10 examines these matters as they relate to force structure.)

In contrast to many earlier periods, the US military is now becoming more aware of and sensitive to political–social issues emanating from society. For example, in an issue of *Military Review* the lead articles were on 'The Army in American Society'. The editor in chief wrote that in 1991, the *Military Review* sponsored a writing contest to examine 'relationships between Army, government and people ... Every entrant underscored the idea that Army problems reflect society's problems and that the Army's virtues echo those of America.'[23]

All of these matters are compounded by the changed military force structure and stationing of many military units in the United States. Among other things, there are questions on what impact this will have on standards of enlistment, reenlistment, and retention on minorities and women, and on the relationship between military and local civilian communities. The range of issues cover important parts of civil–military relations and the quality of military life.

> It is generally recognized ... that there has been a significant penetration of the military by society in Western industrial democracies. Similarly, there has been a degree of penetration of society by the military. In other words, the military has increasingly been influenced by values, attitudes, skills, and expectations of civilian life.[24]

Although written more than a decade ago, this view remains relevant today, even though there is much debate about the degree of military congruence with society.

Finally, as is the case with political leaders, the successor military generation is a new breed. Those with Vietnam experience have passed from the scene, to be replaced by the Gulf War generation. The experience in the Gulf War may become the reference point for strategic perspectives and operational guidelines. At the same time, operations other than war such as those in Bosnia-Herzegovina in 1998 and beyond, may serve as a reference points at the other end of the spectrum. While such missions are not likely to be the basis for general doctrine, they have affected (and will affect) readiness and the quality of military life in a negative way.

In this respect, recent research has pointed to an increasing sensitivity on the part of many military professionals to domestic attitudes and the domestic political–social environment.[25] From the evidence, it seems clear that domestic political and social matters have become an increasingly important factor shaping the military professional ethos. While all of this must be included in the military professional/civil–military equation, it is reasonable to ask to what end.

International Dimensions

Civil–military relations are affected by the nature of military involvement and the characteristics of the conflict. When the military is committed to what many call operations other than war or lesser conflicts, questions are raised about political objectives and proper use of the military. Military professionals are drawn into such issues, raising questions about proper relations between the military and civilian authorities and the American public. This is particularly the case when there is no clear evidence of challenges to national security/ national interests (see Chapter 5).

In the broader international context, the drawdown and deployment of most of the Army to the continental United States, for example, necessitates a rethinking of the traditional professional world view that looked primarily to external threats as the driving force of the military system. While such a view will remain an integral part of professional mind-sets, an increasing concern with domestic issues, domestic contingencies, and non-combat missions have become part of the professional world, although most military professionals are likely to place them on the periphery.

All of this is complicated by the fact that many elected officials see few contingencies in the external world that will require the use of US military forces, particularly ground forces, in *combat*. Yet since the end of the Gulf War in 1991, the US military has been involved in any number of operations short of war – operations other than war with the potential for combat. But there remains some reluctance on the part of many Americans and members of Congress to commit ground forces outside the United States or within the auspices of the United Nations when clear political objectives are lacking and US national interests are unclear.

The political environment in the United States is not likely to lead to a broad consensus on the commitment of US ground forces into foreign areas except under clear strategies and objectives. The US involvement in Bosnia-Herzegovina is a case in point.[26] However, once the military is committed, the decision will probably be supported by a majority of the American people and elected national leaders. But committing the military in circumstances short of actual war, or commitments that lack clear US national interests and are strategically obscure will probably be questioned and debated by the American people and their representatives. 'None of this means that US military force cannot have a decisive impact in some ethnic conflicts. But it does suggest that the odds will never be good and that the United States must approach the use of force with extreme circumspection.'[27]

In this respect, the Weinberger doctrine (named after former Secretary of Defense Caspar Weinberger) may rise from the dustbins of history and become the criterion for the use of military force.[28] The strict application of this doctrine precludes the use of military force except in clearly defined circumstances and according to very specific criteria. In sum, in the hands of civilian leaders, applying the Weinberger doctrine can serve as an important means for exercising strict civilian control over the commitment of the military.

The so-called Powell doctrine seemed to reaffirm the major elements of the Weinberger doctrine. Following the US involvement in Panama, General Colin

Powell stated his own convictions regarding the use of military force. 'Have a clear political objective and stick to it. Use all the force necessary, and do not apologize for going in big if that is what it takes. Decisive force ends wars quickly and in the long run saves lives.'[29]

NEW DIRECTIONS?

Civil–military relations in the remainder of the twentieth century and into the twenty-first are likely to follow one of several paths. In the late 1970s, Huntington argued, 'Recent trends in the US military establishment have been in the direction of lower levels of congruence and, to a lesser degree, lower levels of interaction in relation to civilian society.'[30] He concluded that 'the dilemma of military institutions in a liberal society can only be resolved satisfactorily by a military establishment that is *different but not distant from* the society it serves'.[31] Written two decades ago in the aftermath of Vietnam, the Huntington view may well be accurate for the contemporary period.

Another scenario is offered by Herbert Garfinkel: 'To despise the military is to open the way for an oppressive form of civilian supremacy that would ultimately endanger our democratic values by leaving the nation effectively defenseless.'[32] In light of the changing role of the military and the American successor generation, such a scenario may not be far-fetched.

Still another recent perspective argues that,

> Most Army professionals perceive the world through orthodox lenses and from traditional value systems ... Army professionals saw little change in their own professional status ... This is true, even though a body of professional views surfaced which were more concerned about the nature of the political system and the policy process than mainstream professional views. This concern was expressed primarily by Army professionals who had recently completed full time civilian graduate education or who were in such a program.[33]

The most realistic assessment may be that all three perspectives may be partially correct and parts incorporated into the various perspectives in the National Security Establishment, Congress, and the American public. For most military professionals, the last scenario may be the most appropriate, with attention to the political realm and the national security decision-making process.

Education and Enlightened Advocacy

To respond successfully to these challenges, the military profession must resist a return to an isolationist posture separating it from society in the belief that this will inoculate it from the ills of society and allow the military to get on with its business. Yet it cannot allow itself to be placed in a relationship with society and its political leaders that is determined solely by those who may have little realistic understanding of or sensitivity to military life or the problems faced by the military profession. To guard against this, the military profession needs to reshape its professional ethos and incorporate 'enlightened advocacy' and education – a broader intellectual perspective on politics and conflicts.

More than two decades ago, similar views were expressed by a retired US Navy officer.[34] Focusing on the notion of military professionalism in the future, he wrote,

> the military role will be more sophisticated than in the past. The Korean and Vietnam wars demonstrated that merely being 'firstest with the mostest' and possessing ability to crush the opponent no longer leads necessarily to a satisfactory military solution ... Members of the military profession must be more sophisticated and better educated in order to appreciate the complementary role of the military in the conduct of diplomatic affairs. Conversely diplomatic and political leaders must develop a better understanding of the military profession.[35]

This means that the education of military professionals must go beyond battlefield skills and include knowledge and understanding of the political, social, and economic factors shaping American society and the international order. As suggested earlier, part of this has to do with understanding strategic cultures that evolve from non-Western ideologies and political systems. Civilian graduate education for a number of military professionals is important in bringing into the system an intellectual thrust to deal with these new landscapes.

Civilian education is an important element of enlightened advocacy. In brief, the military profession must offer an intellectually sound view of the capability of the military and those policies and strategies that offer the best path to achieving success. This means that the military profession cannot remain distant from the American political system – one that precludes its role in politics. It must become involved in that part of the political process that focuses on national security and defense policies. This is not to suggest partisan politics. If the military profession falls into that trap, its legitimacy will surely be eroded. Yet it is also the case that to remain passive and allow misjudgments and misguided policies and strategies to emerge from the political arena without a thorough debate on the military's perspective is also a step in eroding the military's legitimacy. Equally important, to allow this to become an institutionalized procedure will reduce the military's ability to respond to security challenges.

Multimilitary Systems?

From a broad perspective, a subtle shift in the military system may be taking place. As a result new notions of military professionalism may be evolving (see Chapter 2). Given the increasing technological character of conventional warfare and the prominence of technical, administrative, and logistical dimensions of military capability, it is likely that there will be a clearer distinction between ground combat forces and other services and arms. And there may even be a sharper distinction between special operations forces and the rest of the military. The relationship between ground combat arms and the role of the Federal Reserves and National Guard reflects this distinction. There is a growing effort to remove much of the combat arms focus in the total reserve force to combat service support or combat support. Thus, such responsibilities as military police, civil affairs, and logistical missions are increasingly passed on to the Federal Reserves and National Guard. Indeed, the National Guard has been tasked for domestic counter-terror responsibilities. But it is important to note that Reserves and National Guard personnel are involved in Bosnia and the Sinai under the same rules and regulations as regular US forces; US forces operate under the auspices of the UN. (See Chapter 10 for a more detailed discussion of the role of active and reserve forces.)

Ground combat forces continue to stress leadership and command of combat units as the key to success, both for the institution and for individual careers. While other services and arms recognize this, they are just as likely to stress that success in war is contingent upon success in the support and service arms. It is in the support and service arms that one finds the concept of multi-professionalism well established.

The existence of a multimilitary system and the importance of one or the other type of military professionalism has been a characteristic of the military for a number of years, albeit one that remains within the confines of the military profession. The notion of dual professions and multiple professions has become increasingly important in the technological age. This need not be a divisive factor within the military as long as it is recognized that regardless of such notions, the primary purpose of the military remains unchanged. While the notion of more than 'one' type of military is unlikely to gain official endorsement, its roots are in place. Nonetheless, this raises questions about the meaning of civil–military relations. Can there be but one type of civil–military relations at all levels of the military and civilian system? The more realistic view may be that there are various dimensions of civil–military relations ranging from the highest levels within the Beltway to the civil–military community interactions at the local military base/post. This surely contradicts the notion of an all-encompassing civil–military monism.

Civil–military relations and military professionalism in the new security era are faced with reconciling a profession that in the past was driven by a primary focus on the battlefield and skills specifically related to success in war, with a number of new forces that may only be incidental to the traditional ethos. In this respect, the military profession is faced with trying to reconcile the need for military effectiveness with democratization and increasing technological advances. Although the military has eagerly accepted and incorporated a variety of civilian-type managerial and technological dimensions, it has serious difficulty in responding to democratization. The question now is how the military can respond to the new forces while insuring that it establishes an acceptable relationship with society and still maintains effectiveness in performing its primary mission – success in battle.

One answer is provided by Johnson and Metz. They argue that throughout changing relationships between the military and society, there has been a distinct pattern. Some are evolutionary, others are more dramatic.

> Throughout the process, there is an attempt to sustain equilibrium and balance between the military and its civilian overseers ... the array of tools held by civilians more than counterbalances the military's more coherent method for cultivating individual skills ... The lifeblood of the equilibrium is constant adjustment shaped by open, informed debate from all segments of the National Security Community.[36]

We would add that this debate also should be open to all segments of the American public.

CONCLUSIONS

In the current period, there is much disagreement about civil–military relations.[37] Part of this disagreement stems from assessments of the meaning of military professionalism another from interpretations of the historical relationship between elected leaders and the military; still another part stems from convictions that civilian supremacy is jeopardized when military professionals become involved in any way in the political process. And finally, another part of the debate revolves around disagreements over time periods, frameworks, and data. These issues and various approaches will not be repeated here. In the most simple terms, the issue is the political role, if any, of the military profession, and how such a political role may impinge upon civilian supremacy. Our theme remains that military professionals have a legitimate political role of constructive political engagement. Without such a role, it is difficult to see how civilian supremacy can be sustained, or military concerns expressed, and military challenges met.

In responding to the issues raised here, the military must not be a passive actor in shaping the character of civil–military relations. Yet it must be recognized that the military is not the only actor in determining the character of military professionalism. The perceptions and attitudes of political leaders, the state of domestic politics, and social conditions constitute the context within which the military system must operate. This is made more complex by the international order and the security challenges emanating from it.

American political leaders and the public, in general, must understand that the military is part of the political system and, as such, is both a military and a political instrument. This has not been the historical view and, for some, may deviate from the notion of civilian control and supremacy. But the fact is that in the new world order and in maintaining its links with society, the military cannot simply dwell on a battlefield orientation. The nature of conflicts and proper civil–military relations require that the military professional develop a sensitivity to the political–social character of the American system and understand strategic cultures; cultures that may perceive conflicts in terms that are different from Judeo-Christian notions. Such sensitivity must be institutionalized within the military system and become a part of the professional ethos. At the same time, these new dimensions must replace the latent civilian views that often rest on anti-military attitudes and fears of the 'man on horseback'.

In terms of civil–military relations, this means that while retaining and reinforcing the notion of civil control and supremacy, the military cannot remain a silent partner. It must move closer to the political system and yet retain enough distance to ensure that it does not become another civilian institution, losing its capability to win wars. There is no fixed formula for determining the proper balance. At the least, however, the role of the military must be constantly examined to ensure that there is a degree of homeostatic equilibrium. This begins with efforts by civilians, in general, and political leaders, in particular, to develop a realistic understanding of military professionalism. It also means that the military must go beyond battlefield skills and develop a sophistication and realistic understanding of politics, the American political system, and the military's proper role in democracy.

As pointed out earlier, complicating the political–military equation is that in the not too distant future, a new generation of elected officials at every level of government will take over the reins of government. Few, if any, will have had military experience. While this may not necessarily lead to inappropriate political–military policies, it may create an environment in which strategies, political–military policies, and decision-making lack sensitivity to the realities of military life. If this is the case, military professional views of politics and elected leaders are likely to reflect the disdain and disenchantment of the Vietnam years. In the final analysis, military profession engagement with the political–social system should be the course of action. But this must be balanced by the raison d'être of the military. Social and political accommodation is not a substitute for combat effectiveness. But the profession must make a serious effort to provide national leaders and the general public with some sense of the realities of military life. Moreover, both civilian and military have yet to come to grips with the new world order and what this means in terms of civil–military relations and military professionalism. Without some success in such efforts in both civilian and military worlds, it may well be that the 'soul' of the military will be a thing of the past.[38] If this be the case, than it is questionable whether the US military will be able to respond effectively to the challenges emerging in the new security era, and much less retain the trust and support of the American people.

PART III

THE NEW WORLD ORDER AND
THE UTILITY OF MILITARY FORCE

7

The New World Order

The superpower world has been replaced by what is being called the 'new world order' by some and the 'new world disorder' by others. Trying to come to grips with these changes and trying to determine the direction of world politics is virtually a speculative adventure. This makes it difficult to design a framework to study world politics. 'Because world politics is complex and our images of it often discordant, it is not surprising that scholars differ in their approaches to understanding the contemporary world.'[1]

It seems that the end of the Cold War opened the door towards 'ordered chaos' in the international world. Indeed, for some the new world order reflects the disorder of the 1930s. What seems clear in the new world order is that there is a degree of disorder, shifting and evolving forces and ideologies that make it extremely difficult to come to grips with an international system. Indeed, the notion of ordered chaos may be an optimistic view of the new world order. In brief, the relative predictability of the superpower era differs considerably from the new world order.[2] 'The end of the Cold War has not only eliminated the armed-to-the-teeth standoff between the US and the Soviet Union, it has eroded the discipline the two superpowers had previously imposed on their client states.'[3]

Although the international landscape has yet to evolve into some predictable pattern, there appear to be at least three major reference points shaping the characteristics of the new world order.[4] First, the system has changed from one driven by superpower relations to one driven by the concept of lone superpower and regional multipower relations. Second, economic interdependence and notions of the global village provide an integrative thrust to the international landscape. Third, while there are centers of stability, the periphery is unstable. This has led to a variety of conflicts, and issues have surfaced creating global centrifugal forces.

In sum, in one dimension, the world has become safer and more interdependent. In another, the world has become more dangerous and fragmented. This schizophrenic political order poses problems in translating US national interests into meaningful policy objectives and strategic guidelines.

CHARACTERISTICS

While the final shape of the new world order remains elusive, the three reference points given above offer a basis for identifying a number of characteristics of the new world order which have an important bearing on US foreign policy, strategy, and the utility of military force.

First, the dissolution of the Soviet Union led to the disappearance of the 'Evil Empire'. Combined with the resulting collapse of the superpower era, this has led to a new strategic landscape characterized by a number of ethnic, religious, ideological, and nationalistic conflicts – or a combination of some or all of these, many of them emerging from the old Soviet Union. At the same time these conflicts have been compounded by the reshaping of some state systems, for example, in former Yugoslavia, and the potential for breakdown in some existing states. In all of this Russia remains a major player on the world scene, particularly with its existing strategic nuclear stockpiles, its resources and population, and its influence with the independent republics. Its potential as a major power remains, even though in 1999 Russia was struggling to reform its economic system and trying to resolve its internal political problems.

Second, regional hegemons and power clusters have evolved and are evolving. Local major states are attempting to dominate their regions. For example, Iran and Syria may be embroiled in an implicit struggle over control of events in the Arab Middle East. One or the other may well be attempting to be the leader of the Islamic world. The Islamic movement plays a major role in such matters, as do the evolving Israeli–Palestinian peace efforts. China and India are developing the wherewithal and military capacity to confront each other and to dominate East and South Asia. Also, Brazil occupies a major place in the Latin American system, as revealed by the difficult economic problems faced by the country in late 1998 and their impact on the Latin American system. The difficult economic problems faced by the country in late 1998 and extending well into 1999 and the flotation of the real had a major impact on the region as well as the world economy. In west Africa, Nigeria has developed into a regional hegemon.

Third, there are a number of troubled states. These are facing internal struggles and trying to respond to destabilizing forces. Particularly important to the US and Europe was that in late 1998 and into 1999, Russia was a troubled state, owing to its economic and political turmoil. The category of 'troubled state' had become an acceptable international term several years earlier. In 1994, Bosnia-Herzegovina, Somalia, Rwanda, and Haiti were cases in point. In 1998 and into 1999 the Democratic Republic of the Congo (formerly Zaire) was embroiled in internal conflict. Similar problems existed in Europe, where in 1998 and into 1999, Kosovo and continuing unresolved issues in Bosnia-Herzegovina dominated the Balkan area. Economic and political problems also characterized Asia. Indonesia's internal strife and violence in 1998 and 1999 was partly a result of the collapse of some Asian economies, including its own, as well as of its repressive political policies. Further, a number of former Soviet republics were in the process of trying to create effective political and economic systems, establishing law and order, and defining their relationships with other states. An example of such problems is the conflict between Christian Armenia and Muslim Azerbaijan over Nagorno-Karabakh. An Armenian Christian enclave in Azerbaijan, Nagorno-Karabakh engaged in a war of independence with the help of Armenia. After the Armenian part of Nagorno-Karabakh gained its freedom from Azerbaijan, a cease-fire was established. But the issue remains unsettled with divergent US, European, Russian, and Turkish policies at play in the Caucasus, supporting one or the other indigenous groups. In late 1999, the issue of Nagorno-Karabakh remains unresolved.

Fourth, there are a number of rogue regimes in the world. These support terrorist groups and are involved in trying to undermine the ability of other governments to respond to international as well as domestic issues. Such states are seen as undermining international norms. The United States has accused Libya and Syria, among others, of such policies. Other states such as Iran and Iraq have been developing nuclear capability in defiance of the United Nations. As discussed earlier, into 1999 the continuing problems between US/UN and Iraq over UN arms inspections, humanitarian issues, and weapons of mass destruction confirmed Iraq as a rogue regime. The testing of missiles by North Korea in 1998 confirmed its role as a rogue state.

Fifth, international economics have created what some call a global village. At the same time regional economic groups have emerged. The European Union (EU), the North American Free Trade Agreement (NAFTA), the evolving Association of South East Asian Nations (ASEAN), and the Asia Pacific Economic Cooperation forum (APEC) bind regions together in trade pacts. The 1994 General Agreement on Tariffs and Trade (GATT), paving the way for the World Trade Organization, reflected a global economic vision. In 1999, 11 of the 15 EU members began using a common currency, the Euro, established by the 1992 Maastricht Treaty to strengthen the regional economic group. All of this underpins the increasing globalization of economic matters. At the same time, economic ills of one country affect the global economic system. In the late 1990s, this was the case in Japan and Russia, as well as other states such as Brazil, South Korea, and Thailand.

Sixth, many old alliances and treaties have become irrelevant, NATO being the exception. But some question the future relevance of NATO in a world so radically changed from the Cold War period. At the same time, former enemies may become friends, and former friends may become adversaries in the economic realm, challenging the economic power of the United States, for example. Also, new adversaries are evolving, perhaps not constituting a threat of the same magnitude as the former Soviet Union, but regional threats, nevertheless that may challenge US national interests.

Seventh, there is a widening economic and military gap between developed and developing industrial democracies and most of the Third World. The concept of the Third World is simply intended to denote a distinction in types of political systems and strategic cultures that are different from Western systems and cultures. This is not intended to denote a monolithic world in the southern hemisphere nor one that is characterized by a common set of economic and political systems. This gap is the basis for continuing conflicts within the Third World and between certain Third World systems and the United States and the remainder of the West.

Eighth, the United Nations has become increasingly important in the international arena. In 1998 the Secretary-General of the UN, Kofi Annan, appeared to have resolved the confrontation between US/UN and Iraq's Saddam Hussein. But in 1998, Operation Desert Fox made it clear that there was no such resolution. In 1999, the continuing clashes between Iraqi air defenses and US/British aircraft seemed to indicate that there was no end in sight to the dispute short of the overthrow of Saddam Hussein. The UN is also involved in a variety of peacekeeping and peacemaking operations such as in Bosnia-Herzegovina. This is also to be taken into account when regarding the UN's activities as supporting the notion of globalism, challenging the notion of state sovereignty.

Throughout most of the Third World, there are other phenomena that affect the international system. For example, increasing urbanization leads to the growth of shacks and shanty-towns housing large numbers of unemployed and underemployed people, who suffer from severe economic deprivation.

Indigenization also characterizes many parts of the Third World. This refers to serious efforts by a country's elite to strengthen the position of indigenous culture to ward off foreign intrusion as well as to reinforce their own standing with the indigenous population. Needless to say, such trends not only affect the immediate region, but also places these issues in the international arena, and on the agenda of the United Nations.

Further, the distinction between issues of national and transnational significance is becoming increasingly obscure. This not only adds to the diminution of the importance of state boundaries, but it increases the possibility of intrusion into individual states by international associations and organizations as well as by international drug cartels and terrorist groups. Moreover, loyalties of individuals may be offered to other than state systems, to religious and ideological movements, leading to alternative concepts to state-centric views of international politics and order.

THE CLASH OF CIVILIZATIONS

One of the most challenging efforts to explain changes in the international environment was presented by Samuel Huntington.[5] He argued that future conflicts would be a clash of civilizations:

Groups or states belonging to one civilization that become involved in war with people from a different civilization naturally try to rally support from other members of their own civilization. As the post–Cold War world evolves, civilization commonality ... is replacing political ideology and traditional balance of power considerations as the principal basis for cooperation and coalitions.[6]

With specific reference to Western values and system of government, Huntington noted,

Western ideas of individualism, liberalism, constitutionalism, human rights, equality, liberty, the rule of law, democracy, free markets, the separation of Church and state, often have little resonance in Islamic, Confucian, Japanese, Hindu, Buddhist, or Orthodox cultures.[7]

There are, however, critics of Huntington's view. For example, Shireen Hunter argues that

Huntington elevates the role of civilization as a factor shaping behavior of states far above that accorded to earlier universalist determinants of state behavior ... Huntington therefore does not address the interaction between civilizational factors and other factors and the role of determinants in mitigating or enhancing the impact of civilization.[8]

Then, focusing on the issue of civilizations and relationships between Islam and the West, Hunter criticizes the generalizations and 'sweeping statements' that are used to describe relations between the West and Islam. 'On the basis of both historical experience and current conditions, relations between Islam and the West cannot and should not be discussed in overly general terms.'[9]

Other critics of Huntington's view have made any number of valid points. However, it is also true that religious loyalties and foreign strategic cultures may be developing transnational groupings, superimposing them over traditional state structures.

From another perspective Nye states that 'international politics is a realm of self-help where states face security dilemmas and force plays a considerable role. There are mitigating devices like the balance of power and international organizations, but they have not prevented all wars.'[10] Nye notes that there are futurists who believe that there will be a decline of the territorial state with the development of new structures to create world stability. He places them in four categories: world federalism, functionalism, regionalism, and ecologism. Nye concludes that 'Contrary to these four models, the nation–state has not yet become obsolete ... the territorial state and its problems remain central to world politics.'

However, others argue that the era of states is ending. For example, van Creveld writes,

The State, which since the Treaty of Westphalia (1648) has been the most important and most characteristic of all modern institutions, is dying. Wherever we look, existing states are either combining into larger communities or falling apart; wherever we look, organizations that are not states are taking their place.[11]

The characteristics of the new world order and Huntington's view and his critics raise a number of questions for the United States. What role should (can) the US play in shaping the international environment? What remains of the old alliances? Who are friends and adversaries? What is the place in the new world order of the concept of national power? How can such power be utilized to achieve national security objectives? Perhaps the most complex and difficult issue is what do US national interests and national security mean in this new world order? In 1999, answers to these questions remain elusive and troubling.

Ronald Steel argues that

> There is much the United States can and should do in the world, particularly in the economic and humanitarian realm. But this cannot be done while we try to maintain a pretense of global primacy that rests on a diminishing leverage in the military and diplomatic realm ... The American people want the nation to be strong and to stick by its ideals. But they are not interested in grandiose plans of global management.[12]

According to some analysts, however, it is possible that the power and prestige of the US may be declining, affecting its ability to shape world events. This issue was raised by Paul Kennedy in 1987.[13] In a particularly compelling view, two English authors argue that there is a distinct possibility of internal American instability that will affect its ability to maintain the American empire. This is based on the view that in the United States there will be

> Increased regionalism and separatism, enhanced cultural differences and an erosion of US national identity ... In the US ... this is combined with fundamental demographic changes leading to major cultural upheavals, at a time of increasing social deprivation and alienation among the very groups most affected.[14]

While some states resent what they see as the effort by the United States to be a world hegemon, it appears that the United States remains the only power that can affect most parts of the world. This is likely to remain the case into the first decade of the twenty-first century. After that time, there is a potential for other states such as China, India, and perhaps a revitalized Russia to compete with the United States. In any case, there will remain any number of troubled states and rogue states, and others competing for regional hegemony. Changes in the characteristics of the international landscape are being driven by increasing global interdependence, communications technology, and the shape of the conflict environment.

GLOBAL INTERDEPENDENCE

The new world order has focused attention on a variety of issues that cross national boundaries. These include environmental considerations, humanitarian impulses, the drug trade, and, perhaps most important, economic power as instruments of national policy. Many of these issues have been placed in the context of national security (see Chapter 5). Environmental issues, for example, are seen as threats to the survival of the state and to the wellbeing of people. Accordingly, such issues are best resolved by placing them in the category of national interests requiring major financial commitments, humanitarian missions, and even commitment of military force. All of this is to try to ensure compliance with strict environmental safeguards. Similarly, it is argued that unless all peoples have some level of quality of life and are not hounded by hunger and poverty, a serious security environment is created, threatening the security and wellbeing of states and people who are relatively well off. But the most visible dimension of interdependence is economic. Historically, economic strength has been part of national security, but it was overshadowed by the focus on military power. However, in the new era, when many accept the notion of the decreasing utility of military power, economic power has gained a particular prominence as a major component of national security. For some, the use of the economic instrument can now achieve national security objectives unattainable by the use of military power.

Economic power rests primarily on domestic economic strength, that is, on productivity and competitive capability in the external world. This forges a close link between national security and domestic economic and political issues. It is also argued that the ability to bring to bear economic power against other states, both explicitly and implicitly, shapes security and foreign policies. But it is also true that small states with important resources such as oil can have a major impact on larger states whose need for oil is critical. Thus, smaller states in the Middle East, for example, are important players in the national security field by virtue of their oil resources.

The economic dimension is also part of the notion of global village and interdependence. The clear implication is that no state can exist in an economic vacuum; domestic economics are closely linked to the international economic arena. This linkage forges close ties between the domestic economic issues of major states with international economic issues. This is reinforced by the increasing gap – in economic power – between developed industrial states and a number of underdeveloped states in the southern hemisphere. This became particularly troubling to a number of global economic determinants as fears of an economic meltdown spread, triggered by the difficult economic problems of important states such as Japan and Brazil.

From another perspective, economic development is crucial to the wellbeing of any state. The continuation of those in power is in no small measure contingent upon the ability to implement specific policies to further the economic wellbeing of its people. Indeed, the 1992 presidential elections in the United States turned on such an issue. Yet it is also the case that increasing globalization and the rising importance of non-governmental organizations and international business corporations have, in the eyes of many, diminished the role of the state in international economic matters.

In the final analysis, the economic power of an interdependent international community or global village will have an impact on US national interests. The most prominent of these is economic power. This needs to be incorporated into the national security equation to an extent beyond that envisioned in the past. The more difficult problem for the United States is the design of appropriate strategies for responding to interdependent issues and the use of economic power to achieve national security objectives. Complicating the matter is that economic power cannot be viewed in isolation. It must be systematically incorporated with other national security instruments and into strategic planning. In brief, for many US policymakers strategic thinking must go beyond the use of military power, incorporate a variety of instruments, consider a variety of options including economic strategies, and may even demand the creation of new instruments.

COMMUNICATIONS TECHNOLOGY

A revolution in communications technology has not only added to the notions of global interdependence, it has dramatically exposed the workings of government and the political instability characterizing much of the international environment.[15] Moreover, it has made information available almost instantaneously throughout the globe. This has been called the information age. The technological revolution in communications promises to continue unabated. What does this mean in terms of the new world order and national security?

Not only does the ability of government to communicate across national boundaries almost at will reinforce the notions of interdependence, but it reshapes diplomacy and can provide a wealth of information on any particular state or groups of people. Equally important, the ability to use satellite communications makes it increasingly difficult to control the media and to censor news reports.

Further, such technology has had an impact on the ability to conduct wars. The highly sophisticated communications networks established by the coalition against Iraq in the 1991 Gulf War was an extremely important factor in controlling forces and in conducting a successful military operation in Kuwait. This was particularly true in the use of air power, air-to-ground missiles, and surface missiles. Also, the ability of news personnel to use satellite communications provided instantaneous reports on battlefield operations throughout the globe. Further, through the use of the communications network, command centers in Washington had a better grasp of military operations even than commanders in the field in Saudi Arabia. These developments have driven the notion of a revolution in military affairs.[16]

At another level, the dramatic increase in the number of personal computers, fax machines, and camcorders, among other things, in the possession of individuals throughout the world increases 'people power' and offers direct person-to-person communications across national boundaries. Total government control over such communications is difficult if not impossible to achieve.

The implications seem clear. The access to information and the ability to transmit information quickly and relatively cheaply not only links states more closely, but also people. Moreover, authoritarian systems which had a monopoly on communications now find it harder to maintain such a monopoly. Also, the ability of governments to shape the news and give it a particular spin is more difficult, given direct access to a variety of news sources made available by the communications explosion. Some argue that this development has reshaped the notion of state sovereignty.

Those in the US National Security Establishment need to take account of communications technology not only in designing national security strategy, but also in implementing security policies, collecting and evaluating intelligence information, and in the political–psychological dimension of national security issues. It is also the case that in the use of military force, care must be taken regarding the role of the media and access to information that ultimately comes with military operations. National security has become, on the one hand, a more complex arena with the communications technology. On the other hand, it has become a more visible arena as access to information by more governments and individuals increases. It is becoming increasingly difficult to find a place to hide.

THE CONFLICT ENVIRONMENT

The changes in the international environment and the security landscape have changed the conflict environment. There is a popular view in the United States that the possibility of major wars has considerably diminished. Nonetheless, there remains underlying concern about nuclear proliferation and the proliferation of missile technology. For example, in 1998, India's detonation of underground nuclear devices followed by those of Pakistan heightened international concern over possible confrontations between India and Pakistan, and India and China. Subsequently, the firing of a missile by Iran that can reach Israel and other equally distant targets in the Middle East, and North Korea's missile firings in 1998 sharpened the concern about missile proliferation, particularly by states enmeshed in territorial as well as cultural disputes.

Yet it is the case that the more immediate challenge stems from the fact that there are any number of lesser conflicts and unconventional conflicts in the world ranging from the former Yugoslavia, the Caucasus, areas in southeast and southwest Asia, sub-Saharan Africa, and parts of Latin America. Further, the potential for conflicts remain high in the Middle East and on the Korean peninsula. The most likely conflicts in the remainder of the 1990s and into the next century may not necessarily follow the patterns of conventional conflict such as those in the 1991 Gulf War. Many are likely to be unconventional conflicts encompassing everything from revolution and counterrevolution to terrorism and counter-terror operations. This was highlighted dramatically in August 1998 with the terror bombings of the US embassies in Nairobi, Kenya, and Dar es Salaam, Tanzania, with the loss of many lives and injuries to thousands, including a number of Americans.

Even though the US/UN involvement in Bosnia-Herzegovina seemed, on the surface, to follow conventional lines, the fear was that these not only could expand, but eventually include unconventional conflict. The same holds true for the Kosovo conflict which began in 1998 and continued into 1999. Moreover, the United Nations command and control system for such conflicts came under criticism, not only for the hesitancy with which decisions were made, but also because of the very limited response to overt Serbian military efforts. This also was the charge of critics of US policy regarding the Serb–ethnic Albanian clashes in Kosovo in 1998 and 1999.

The threat of terrorism came to the fore with the attacks on the US embassies in Nairobi and Tanzania. The US struck suspected terrorist bases in Afghanistan, and a factory in the Sudan allegedly producing a component for nerve gas. Although the US publicly proclaimed this to be a new phase of its security concerns, the fact is that the issue of terrorism has been a long-standing one in the United States. In any case, the international terrorist threat transcends state boundaries and adds to the complexities of the new international order.

The attacks on suspected bases for terrorist activities in Afghanistan and Sudan by the United States may also add to the concern among some nations that the United States has become arrogant, imposing its version of politics and international tranquility upon the rest of the world. With states such as China, India, and Russia having the potential to develop into powers capable of challenging it, can the United States continue to view itself as a world hegemon or as having international responsibilities beyond the scope of other states? If so, what type of US military system and force structures are applicable and what does one make of national strategy and military strategy?

CONCLUSIONS

The continuities from the Cold War era and the major characteristics of the post-Cold War period shape the new world order. And more specifically, these fashion the security landscape that is emerging in the new world order. Thus, legacies of the nuclear age and the Vietnam War combine with the changing conflict environment, interdependence, and communications technology to underpin the shape of the new world order. All of these developments create dilemmas for the United States because they contain contradictory forces and pose difficult and serious challenges. For our purpose, how these developments are perceived and interpreted, and how US policy and strategy are designed to respond, are part of the broad patterns of the politics of policymaking and affect the shape and mind-sets of those in the National Security Establishment. In turn, this shapes the role and capabilities of the US military.

In sum, the new world order that emerged (and is emerging) in the 1990s and beyond remains unclear and ill defined. On the one hand, the shape of the old order and its end seem relatively clear. On the other hand, the shape of the new order and its political-military ramifications remain unclear and shrouded in a fog of peace. But certain developments are beginning to outline the future landscape. In one dimension, the world has become safer and more inter-dependent. In another dimension, the world has become more dangerous and fragmented.

These uncertainties, combined with short-term and long-term interests, not only challenge the effectiveness of US foreign and national security policy, but create challenges for the US military. The fundamental question is how the military prepares for the strategic landscape. How long can the United States sustain its role as the lone superpower-world hegemon? In that context, how should the US military shape its military strategy and doctrine? Finally, should not the military profession convey to the American people and its elected repre-sentatives the challenges and difficulties these pose for the military?

8

US Strategy and Conflict Characteristics

The new world order has created a great deal of confusion and debate about the meaning of US policy and national (grand) strategy. This confusion is reflected in various views about the concept of strategy. While some use the term as an all-encompassing framework designed to impose American interests and values on the world, others use the term as a specific outline for US policy. Still others conceive of strategy as a visionary vehicle for confirming the United States as the lone superpower.

In any case, we need to heed Clausewitz's caution. Writing in the eighteenth century, Carl von Clausewitz concluded: 'Strategy borders on politics and statesmanship or rather it becomes both itself ... in strategy everything is simple, but not on that account very easy.'[1] Recently, Palmer noted:

> The term 'strategy', derived from the ancient Greek, originally pertained to the art of generalship or high command. In modern times, 'grand strategy' has come into use to describe the overall defense plans of a nation or coalition of nations. Since the mid-twentieth century, 'national strategy' has attained wide usage, meaning the coordinated employment of the total resources of a nation to achieve its national objectives.[2]

The term 'strategy' as used in this chapter refers primarily to national strategy (grand strategy). From time to time references will be made to what some call national military strategy, focusing on 'the generation of military power and its employment in state to state relationships'.[3]

At the highest level, grand strategy is the usual label given to the way in which a state intends to pursue its national security goals. From this a number of other strategies are designed that are focused on specific regions or issues. Thus, there is military strategy, economic strategy, political strategy, psychological strategy. Also, for example, there is a US strategy for the Middle East and other parts of the world. No wonder there is confusion in using terms such as strategy, policy, and doctrine.

In examining the concept of grand strategy, two authorities write that 'Four grand strategies, relatively discrete and coherent arguments about the US role in the world, now compete in our public discourses. They may be termed neo-isolationism; selective engagement; cooperative security; and primacy.'[4] The authors examine each of these in detail. They conclude, in part, that an ad hoc approach is the best that can be expected. When a crisis develops, a more focused choice may be required.[5]

There is, of course, more to these terms than this brief explanation. But the differences seem clear: policy refers to goals, national strategy is the means to reach these goals. It follows that strategy or strategies cannot be realistically designed and implemented if policy is unclear or vacillating. In our view of US strategy, the terms policy and strategy are used as indicated here.

Complicating the study of strategy and its application is the confusion within segments of the American public about the nature and characteristics of conflicts in the new world order. In this respect, it is not clear that the American public, in general, and elected officials, in particular, fully understand the range of conflicts, their characteristics, and impact on American domestic politics. As noted earlier, views about the US role shape the notion of grand strategies. These in turn, reflect the views about US intervention in responding to conflicts. While some see virtually all conflicts as opening the door to world conflagration, others view most as local and limited, requiring little or no American response. As suggested by one analyst, the propensity for the new interventionism seems to focus on wars of conscience and missionary zeal.[6] Following such perspectives, it is conceivable that involvement in military operations can easily lead to open-ended embroilment in an unconventional conflict environment, with all that portends regarding domestic political reaction and political–military complications.

US national strategy into the twenty-first century remains clouded in uncertainty. While there are broad elements such as mobilizing resources to ensure protection of the American way of life and supporting democracy, the more specific elements of strategy seem absent. This is probably to be expected, given the uncertainties of what the next century will bring. The broad strategic elements seem relatively clear, but strategy also requires some sense of how resources will be mobilized and used to achieve policy goals. This also requires some sense of the costs incurred. An important part of strategy is response to unconventional conflicts – conflicts short of war, and not presenting a serious threat to national interests. That is, how to mobilize resources and forces to succeed in a variety of conflicts at the lower end of the conflict spectrum. This part of the strategic picture is a particularly gray area with the Vietnam syndrome lurking in the background, buttressed by the debacle in Mogadishu, Somalia, in 1993.

VIETNAM

The concept of unconventional conflicts in military doctrine remains wedded to the experience of the Vietnam War. This left a legacy that still permeates military thinking since it not only placed the military in a position in opposition to the American way of war, it created contentious civil–military relations (see Chapter 6, 'Civil–Military Relations').

Reflecting on his Vietnam experience, General Norman Schwarzkopf concluded that the war had 'demoralized our soldiers and wrecked our credibility with the American public ... I *hated* what Vietnam was doing to the United States and I *hated* what it was doing to the Army. It was a nightmare that the American public had withdrawn its support.'[7]

It is also the case that any number of military professionals are bitter about the role of the military in the conduct of the Vietnam War.[8] For example, the My Lai incident was particularly troubling for most military professionals as well as for the American public. In brief, in March 1968 in the village of My Lai in South Vietnam, Lieutenant William Calley and other members of Charlie Company, Task Force Baker of the Americal Division, were involved in the slaughter of hundreds of Vietnamese civilians – old men, women, and children. Compounding this incident, there appeared to be a lack of aggressive response, with self-protection and institutional loyalty preventing a clear investigation of the incident.[9] American antiwar activists focused on the My Lai incident as one reason why US involvement in the war was immoral.

More than 25 years after the war, the disagreements and debates about the US role in Vietnam remain. This is not unexpected, given the experience and aftermath of the war. Indeed, recent publications raise additional concerns about the so-called lessons of Vietnam and the impact on the US military. Three publications provide particularly excellent insights into the Vietnam War. The authors and short titles are as follows: Timothy J. Lomperis, *From People's War to People's Rule*, H. R. McMaster, *Dereliction of Duty* (cited in earlier chapters), and Jeffrey Record, *The Wrong War*. While the book by Lomperis questions the notion of a particular lesson of the Vietnam War, the books by McMaster and Record focus on US military–civilian inadequacies.[10]

For example, Record writes,

> I contend that, whereas the primary responsibility for the US share of the war's outcome clearly rests with civilian decision-making authorities ... the military's accountability was significant and cannot and should not be overlooked ... US military leadership not only warmly supported the Johnson administration's decision to enter the very kind of open-ended land war on the Asian mainland whose avoidance had been a traditional – and strategically wise – staple of American military planning ... It also submitted, without effective protest, to civilian-imposed restrictions on military operations that it regarded as crippling to reasonable prospects for a decisive resolution of the conflict in Vietnam.[11]

Although for many Americans the reality of Vietnam may recede into the background, it will color the way wars are perceived. In the long term, because of its divisive nature and the withdrawal of the United States from Vietnam leaving its ally to face the enemy with little material backing from the United States, the Vietnam War is likely to remain an enduring memory in the US military system. This legacy underpins the problems faced by the US military when engaged in operations other than war (OOTW), unconventional conflicts, and the post-Cold War conflict environment.

EVOLUTION OF POST-COLD WAR STRATEGIES

The groundwork for national security and military posture into the twenty-first century was established by the Bush administration during the Gulf War in 1991 and the drawdown of military forces in the aftermath of that conflict. This was followed by the Clinton administration's deeper reductions in the military and the efforts to broaden the notion of national security. In all of this, what appeared to be lacking was a clear strategic vision and a clear basis for national security. Needless to say, this made it difficult to design military strategy and doctrine, and force structure.

The Bush Administration

George Bush acceded to the presidency with a great deal of credibility, particularly from the viewpoint of many in the military. Having served as a combat pilot in World War II and with experience in government as vice president, President Bush had the credentials to establish himself as an experienced and knowledgeable commander-in-chief. He understood the military culture and relied on military operational skills once a decision was made to commit the military force. This was well demonstrated in the Gulf War in 1991.

In a speech at Aspen, Colorado, in August 1990, President Bush outlined a broad strategy for 'reshaping our forces' for the new security landscape. The president stated in part,

> The size of our forces will increasingly be shaped by the needs of regional contingencies and peacetime presence ... A policy of peacetime engagement every bit as constant and committed to the defense of our interests and ideals in today's world as in the time of conflict and Cold War.[12]

Elaborating on the president's statement, Secretary of Defense Dick Cheney proposed four major elements of a new US defense strategy.[13] *Strategic defense and deterrence* necessitates a 'diverse mix of survivable and highly capable offensive nuclear forces'. In addition, this required worldwide protection against limited ballistic missile strikes. *Forward presence* requires that some US forces remain overseas as a visible sign of US commitment and serve as a credible deterrence. Further, such forces would be the base for engaging in other contingencies. *Crisis response* means that US conventional forces 'must be able to respond rapidly to short-notice regional crises and contingencies that threaten US interests'. And finally, *force reconstitution* is based on the need to 'maintain the ability to reconstitute a larger force structure if a resurgent threat of massive conflict returns'. Thus, in addition to retaining high-quality personnel and a capable industrial and technological base, total force policy has an important role in force reconstitution as well as in all other elements of strategy.

In a further elaboration of strategy as it applies to the Army, the then Secretary of the Army Michael P. W. Stone stated that the Army must be prepared to fight two concurrent regional conflicts. This was based on what was labeled MRC (Major Regional Conflict) East and MRC West.[14]

Also, from the US perspective, the various alliances and treaties established during the Cold War period appeared obsolete, at least in their original intent and substance. Further, a new set of relationships emerged with former adversaries including Vietnam. Others pointed to the need for a new policy with respect to Cuba. Equally important, the Pacific Basin area emerged as a potential for power projection and conflict as China and Japan vied for advantage in the area.[15]

The high point in the Bush administration was the Gulf War in 1991 (operations Desert Shield and Desert Storm). This was the first major use of US military forces in the post-Cold War period, in a conventional, but limited, war. And this was done under the auspices of the United Nations. The major causes and conduct of the war are well known and need little elaboration here. Suffice it to say that President Bush created a coalition of forces that included Western and Mid-East nations. The coalition forces were successful in defeating Iraq and liberating Kuwait, although Saddam Hussein remained in power in Iraq.

General Norman Schwarzkopf provided a graphic view of how President Bush viewed the military role:

> President Bush called shortly before eight p.m. – the first time we'd spoken since Christmas eve … I was struck by what the President had chosen *not* to say: he'd given me no order and hadn't second-guessed the decisions I'd made, and the detailed questions he'd asked had been purely for clarification. His confidence in the military's ability to do its job was so unlike what we'd seen in Vietnam that the conversation meant the world to me.[16]

In the aftermath of the Gulf War, the Bush administration implemented plans for the drawdown/downsizing of military forces and reduction of the defense budget. Moreover, during the last part of the Bush administration questions were raised regarding the use of military in operations short of war – operations other than war. The utility of military force in the post-Cold War era became a major issue that spilled over into the Clinton administration. In any case, the conduct of the Gulf War became a reference point for designing military forces and strategy in the future.

The Clinton Administration

In 1997 President Bill Clinton's view of US national security was spelled out in *A National Security Strategy for A New Century*.[17] In concluding, President Clinton stated:

> Today, closer to the start of the twenty-first century than to the end of the Cold War, we are embarking on a period of construction to build new frameworks, partnerships and institutions – and adapt existing ones – that strengthen America's security and prosperity. We are working to construct new cooperative security arrangements, rid the world of weapons that target whole populations, build a truly global economy, and promote democratic values and economic reform … Our engagement requires the active, sustained support of the American people and the bipartisan support of the US Congress.[18]

President Clinton's calls for support of the American people and a bipartisan Congress were also made in earlier national security statements. These were made in the context of uncertain efforts in Bosnia and Somalia, and the commitment of US forces to Haiti to protect President Aristide. These earlier statements by President Clinton brought a sharp rejoinder from Harry Summers. 'There is a credibility chasm between what Clinton says and what he does.'[19]

Further, one authoritative group concluded,

> One of the most striking features of the current period is the mismatch between our rhetoric and our resources. The administration's announced strategy of enlarging the community of democratic market-economy nations implies a growing demand on resources. The end of the Cold War, however, has resulted in a steady and substantial decline in defense spending and other resources for intervention.[20]

US strategy was subject to more questions in the aftermath of the India–Pakistan nuclear confrontation in 1998. The India–Pakistan stand-off raised increasing fears of regional nuclear war. The nuclear issue is a reflection of the continuing struggle over control of Kashmir. The Kashmir issue evolved over India's (a Hindu nation predominantly) control of Kashmir, a state in which Muslims are a majority, and the evolution of the Muslim separatist movement challenging Indian rule. Most observers felt, however, that the ongoing issue of Kashmir would not lead to armed conflict, other than border skirmishes. Coming on the heels of the issue of the transfer of nuclear-associated technology to China by the Clinton administration, many were left wondering about the principles of US strategy. While the Clinton administration argued about the need to develop and maintain acceptable relations with China, critics argued that the Chinese were able to develop missile technology because of American technology exports to China authorized by President Clinton. This raised questions about the need for strategic missile defense and led to a renewed call for the development of such defenses, reminiscent of the 'Star Wars' debates during the Reagan administration.

The increased concern about nuclear confrontation resulting from the India–Pakistan stand-off raised more questions about the nature of conflict in the post-Cold War period and into the twenty-first century. This was compounded by the surge in terrorist activity reflected in the terrorist bombings of the US embassies in Kenya and Tanzania. And with regard to such questions the US military was placed in a position of needing to demand a re-examination of its nuclear war posture, its defense against missiles, as well as its role in countering terrorism. In the broader scheme, the US military profession was faced with restructuring military forces to face challenges in the twenty-first century.

RESTRUCTURING OF THE US MILITARY

Budgetary Issues

As noted earlier, in response to the end of the superpower era, the Bush administration planned a reduction in the US military over a five-year period. This included the trimming of the defense budget by billions of dollars and the reduction of military manpower.[21] Moreover, for the first time in decades, most of the Army was to be stationed in the continental United States. In 1993, the then Secretary of Defense Les Aspin announced that the Clinton administration was planning even deeper reductions in the US military.[22] For the military, not only was the additional cut in defense dollars difficult to absorb, but the reduction in total strength raised fears about the military capability to respond to a variety of contingencies. The new budget revised the earlier Base Force concept and evolved from a 1992 study on ground-force structure by then Congressman Les Aspin.[23] In that study, a number of options were presented. These options evolved from four conceptual structures using the forces employed in Desert Storm as the reference point. Also included were views on the use of Federal Reserves and National Guard – the Total Force concept. This was the basis for the Bottom Up Review and the drawdown of the US military and reduction in defense spending.

Defense spending and military force structure are shown in Figure 8.1 and Table 8.1.[24]

According to Congressman Floyd Spence, chairman of the House National Security Committee, although the proposed 1999 Defense Budget was slightly over US$270 billion in budget authority, it was 'a 1.1 percent real decline from

Figure 8.1: Defense Budgets, 1986–98/99
(constant FY 1998 $US Billions)

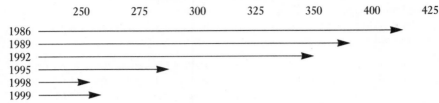

Source: adapted from Floyd Spence, Chairman, House National Security Committee, *National Security Report*, Vol. 1, Issue 2 (Washington, DC), April 1997, p. 1; and Spence, *National Security Report*, Vol. 2, Issue 3, May 1998, p. 1 in which he reports that 'Between fiscal year 1999 and fiscal year 2003, the President's defense budget falls $54.4 billion short of keeping pace with inflation.' See also Baker Spring and John S. Barry, *Current Budget Priorities May Have Serious Defense Consequences*, A Report of the Heritage Center for Data Analysis (the Heritage Foundation, Washington, DC: June 4, 1998), pp. 4–5. On p. 6, the authors write 'Defense outlays were $300.1 billion in 1990. In 1997, they were $271.6 billion. This 9.5 percent reduction in current dollars terms represents a 26 percent reduction in real terms between 1990 and 1997.'

Table 8.1: Military Force Structure, 1990–98

	1990	*1998*
Army divisions	18	10
Reserve component brigades	57	42
Navy battle force ships	546	346
Aircraft carriers (active and reserve)	16	12
Air Force fighter wings (active and reserve)	36	20
MEFs (Marine expeditionary force)	3	3
Strategic nuclear forces (by 2003)	About	18 ballistic missile submarines 94 B-52 H bombers 20 B-2 bombers 500 Minuteman III ICBMs (single Warhead)
Active duty manpower	2,069,000	1,395,778
Reserve manpower	1,128,000	About 885,322

Source: adapted from Floyd D. Spence, Chairman, House National Security Committee, *National Security Report* (Washington, DC, 1997) and from Floyd D. Spence, Chairman, House National Security Committee, *Summary of Major Provisions, HR 3616: National Defense Authorization Act for Fiscal year 1999 (Conference Report)* (Washington, DC, 1998), pp. 9–10. See also Congress of the United States, *A CBO Study: Enhancing US Security Through Foreign Aid* (Washington, DC: Congressional Budget Office, 1994), p. 20. See also Floyd Spence, Chairman, House National Security Committee, *National Security Report*, Vol. 1, Issue 2 (Washington, DC, 1997), p. 2, and Les Aspin, Secretary of Defense, *The Bottom Up Review: Forces for a New Era* (Washington, DC: Department of Defense, 1993), p. 17.

current defense spending levels ... [and] is more than $54 billion short of keeping pace with inflation over the next five years, and is 39 percent lower from mid-1990s defense-spending levels'.[25] Moreover, critics pointed out that the plans for reduction of forces had little to do with strategic planning, but rather with the shifting of resources to domestic programs.[26]

> Largely self-inflicted *economic* weaknesses now indirectly threaten our national security ... Despite the euphoria over America's success in the war in Iraq, the 1990s will be a decade of new and increasing tensions for the United States between international needs and economic constraints. As the full implications of being the world's largest debtor dawn on us *and* on the rest of the world, the gap between our interests and our capacities will become larger, more obvious, and more painful.[27]

However, in late 1998, after prodding by the Joint Chiefs of Staff, President Clinton recommended a $1 billion increase in military spending. But many in Congress 'expressed doubts about Clinton's commitment to improving military spending given his suggestion that there might be budgetary limits to how much of an increase might be feasible'.[28] According to the same source, the 1999 defense authorization is considered a 'band-aid'. '"This is not a long-term answer to the military's growing personnel problems," said a House aide who worked on the compromise.' A case in point is the 1999 NATO intervention in Kosovo.

In subsequent sessions over the budget, all parties agreed to add $9 billion to the defense budget. However, only slightly over $1 billion was allocated to combat readiness resources. 'Amazingly, at the beginning of the year, the Pentagon brass and President Clinton were pronouncing the all-volunteer military in robust health – as the joint chiefs have been regularly asserting since the end of the 1991 Persian Gulf war.'[29]

Department of Defense and Service Issues

During the first years of the Clinton administration changes in the various structures of the Department of Defense were made. Secretary of Defense Les Aspin began restructuring the Defense Department in early 1993. Among others, an Assistant Secretary of Defense for Democracy and Human Rights and an Assistant Secretary of Defense for Arms Proliferation were established.[30] These changes seemed to move in a political–diplomatic direction, prompting some to see a mini-Department of State emerging in the Department of Defense. It also appeared that the Assistant Secretary of Defense for Special Operations and Low Intensity Conflict (SO/LIC) was de-emphasized, based on Secretary Aspin's view that it was a leftover from the Cold War. Some argued, however, that the Assistant Secretary of Defense for SO/LIC was an innovative structure intended to go well beyond the Cold War. Secretary of Defense William Perry, who succeeded Les Aspin, returned to the more traditional structure of the Department of Defense. In 1999, William Cohen, who replaced William Perry as Secretary of Defense, appears to be continuing the traditional Department structure.

Another potentially serious problem has emerged. This is the renewing of inter-service rivalries.[31] While such rivalries historically have been part of the military system, with the reduction in defense budgets and planned reductions in military manpower, these disputes take on special significance. Battles over missions, turfs, and defense budget allocations, are emerging in full array. These were signaled by the publication of various manuscripts designed to rationalize the importance of each service in future conflicts. For example, the monograph by Sullivan and Dubik, *Land Warfare in the 21st Century*, emphasized the technical revolution occurring in ground forces and the impact this would have on land warfare, underpinning the importance of ground forces in any future conflict.[32] The Air Force monograph, *Global Reach – Global Power* and the Navy's ... *From the Sea* are similar efforts on the part of each of those services.[33]

More specifically, the Air Force developed a 'halt phase strategy/doctrine'. This was apparently in response to the Quadrennial Defense Review, which air power advocates saw as undermining Air Force capabilities by reducing personnel and resources. The halt phase strategy/doctrine is analyzed and critiqued in a recent monograph by Earl Tilford, Jr, published by the US Army War College.[34] The author introduces the study by noting the 'heated debate over alternative strategies. The outcome of this debate may well shape the kind of forces with which the United States will maintain its security well beyond the first quarter of the twenty-first century.'[35] He goes on to write, 'The Halt Phase Strategy/Doctrine ... focuses on using air power as the primary force early in the conflict.' While Tilford acknowledges that this air power approach may indeed be useful for the twenty-first century, he argues that this is 'an approach to a form of future warfare that is becoming less likely as time goes on.' Among other criticisms he writes that such a strategy or doctrine is a 'rearward-looking strategy', concluding that 'it is land forces that exercise direct control over people and resources'.

It is no wonder that in the Foreword to Tilford's work, the Director of the Strategic Studies Institute writes, 'Many will disagree with Dr Tilford's conclusions and air power enthusiasts are sure to take exception with him.'[36] This may well reflect the ongoing debate within Air Force circles about the focus of the Air Force mission into the twenty-first century.

The Navy's view on strategy was well presented by Rear Admiral James B. Hinkle writing in the *Armed Forces Journal International*.[37] He praises the Quadrennial Defense Review as 'an extraordinary opportunity to take stock and engage in important security dialogue while also telling the remarkable Navy–Marine Corps story'.[38] The author briefly discusses Navy–Marine Corps involvement in recent global commitments, operations short of war, and diplomacy. 'In its documents "From the Sea" and "Forward ... From the Sea", the Navy displayed the foresight and organizational vitality to move from the familiar and traditional "blue water" Navy to increased emphasis on naval expeditionary capabilities.' He stressed the Navy's ability in power projection. The author concluded, 'That's why US Naval forces will continue to be persuasive in peace, compelling in crisis, and capable in every aspect of war.'

The responses by the various services not only indicate a particular view of the strategic landscape, but also an effort to identify their military turfs. But in the broader scheme of things, the strategic landscape remains uncertain, making it difficult for any military service or military strategy to set their strategic sights in concrete. Yet it is also the case that the military services tend to place great weight on conflicts that encompass advanced technology and cyber-space visions. But others see future conflicts to be in the unconventional category with minimum relevancy to hi-tech weaponry and strategy.

The varying strategic perspectives of the various military services reflect disagreements over the definition of 'jointness'. According to one account, 'Our belief is that the rhetoric of jointness has surpassed its reality.' [39] Accordingly, there is a need for joint operations. But, 'which and how forces are used in specific circumstances ought to depend on their comparative advantages. There will be times when only the Navy and/or the Marine Corps are relevant; other times when neither are relevant; and times when they complement the other services.'

The debate over jointness is also one involving Congress and disagreement over strategy. In responding to the efforts of a member of Congress over joint experimentation, Owens examines the concept and concludes that 'The problem with such a conception of jointness is that it threatens to replace the traditional American approach to defense planning – strategic pluralism – with an approach called strategic monism.' [40] His definition of jointness focuses on integration, which the author believes will stifle service initiatives and offer a strategic perspective removed from reality.

Owens also argues that 'Strategic pluralists maintain that the US has separate services for a reason: no one service can be expected to effectively address the complete spectrum of military operations in every medium.' He tags joint experimentation and strategic monism as a 'dangerous myopia', noting that it leads to a centralized bureaucratic view of strategy.

In a rejoinder, Senator Coats writes, in part,

> The complexity and variety of missions anticipated in the 21st century compels jointness. While single-service command structures and organizations may have been adequate in the Cold War and before, they must now be transformed to address the rapidly changing strategic environment and to take full advantage of the revolution in technology. Jointness in war fighting is no longer an option; it is an imperative. [41]

The debate goes on.

THE STRATEGIC LANDSCAPE AND CONFLICT ENVIRONMENT

The diminishing prospect of major wars between major powers has shifted attention to a variety of lesser wars and unconventional conflicts. Increasing attention is on a variety of ethnic, religious, and nationalistic conflicts such as in the former Yugoslavia and on peacekeeping operations as in Somalia. At the higher end of the conflict spectrum, the 1991 Gulf War represented a form of European scenario providing for some American guidelines for the future.[42]

> Resurgent forms of ethnic and religious violence and new forms of transnational conflict differ from traditional aggression across frontiers – but they may be equally destructive to global security. Low-intensity conflict and secret warfare – including the use of terrorism by states, private groups, and revolutionary movements – threaten the international order in new ways that transform the manner in which policymakers, diplomats, and the public must approach questions of peace and security.[43]

Complicating the conflict landscape are conflicts associated with coalitions between drug cartels and revolutionary groups, particularly those operating out of Latin American states.

The conflict environment makes it difficult clearly to identify adversaries and even more difficult to spell out political–military objectives. Indeed, even in the aftermath of the 1991 Gulf War, some criticized the operation because it did not finish the job by deposing Saddam Hussein as president of Iraq, although this was clearly not the assigned mission. In any case, the likely conflict characteristics make it difficult to garner the necessary support of the American people to engage in military operations.[44] This is particularly true with respect to sustained, long-term operations. Low-visibility military operations may succeed for a time, but many see the use of military force as a blunt instrument not particularly relevant to the political–military problems likely to face the United States in the immediate future.

In the final analysis, conflicts in the new strategic landscape are likely to be less than major, less threatening to US national interests (at least in the short run), and are likely to fall within the full range of unconventional conflicts and a variety of peacekeeping missions – that is peacekeeping, peace making, and peace enforcement. More often than not the peacekeeping environment lays the groundwork for unconventional conflicts. Humanitarian missions have also become part of expected military contingencies, for example, Hurricane Andrew in Florida and the initial effort in Somalia. Historically, the military has effectively performed humanitarian missions and a variety of other missions under the current label of 'peacetime engagements'.[45]

In the period before World War I, concerns were raised about the deployment of the military and its wartime missions. 'Despite the fact that reformers argued that the Army, Navy, and Marine Corps should concentrate upon their wartime missions, all the armed forces found themselves busy with constabulary duties beyond the border of the United States.'[46]

Similar concerns have been raised in the current period. Moreover, the notion that the US military can engage in humanitarian and peacekeeping missions on a consistent basis raises serious questions about the impact of the US military presence in various parts of the world. Also, the capability of the military and its effectiveness in responding to a range of unconventional conflicts, including response to the drug cartel–revolutionary coalition and international terrorism, remain questionable.

While the US military must maintain its capability to deter nuclear conflict, respond to weapons of mass destruction, succeed in conventional conflict (including the emerging third-wave warfare – warfare in the post-industrial era; the first wave being the agricultural revolution, the second being the industrial revolution), it must be particularly concerned about operations other than war and unconventional conflicts. And it is the latter conflicts and missions that are the most likely contingencies and the conflicts of the future. And these conflicts are not likely to follow conventional scenarios. As Callahan writes, with respect to ethnic conflicts, 'Despite all the uncertainty that now characterizes international affairs, there can be no doubt that the United States will inevitably face horrible new dilemmas abroad that arise from ethnic violence.'[47] Yet, if history is any guide, the US military will remain fixed on wars of a conventional nature and technological developments that affect weaponry and communications – much of this has a minimum impact on effective response to operations other than war and unconventional conflicts.

Conventional Wars and Beyond

In the post-Cold War period, the uncertain and dangerous world still requires that the United States maintain some level of effective strategic deterrence and develop defenses against nuclear as well as chemical weapons. The move by both Russia and the United States to reduce stockpiles of strategic weapons and the unlikely conflict between the United States and states evolving from the former Soviet Union have reduced the need for maintaining strategic forces on the scale of the past 50 years. More pressing for the US military, however, is the need to maintain the ability to engage effectively in conventional war at relatively short notice. Many point to Desert Shield, the offensive against Iraq in 1991, as a model for the future. In that operation, according to many analysts, active forces were able quickly to challenge and 'stand off' the adversary until the arrival of reconstituted forces in the form of reserves and National Guard units. Equally important, in the Gulf War the United States was able to develop and maintain a coalition strategy which brought to bear not only United Nations pressure on Iraq, but also a variety of forces from other countries including some from the Middle East.

The Air Force takes particular pride in its performance in the Gulf War and more recently over Kosovo/Serbia. Indeed, this seems to have laid the groundwork for Air Force plans into the twenty-first century.

> Whatever its purposes and genesis, *Global Reach – Global Power* gave voice to exactly the rapid, lethal air power which the Air Force employed in the Gulf War. The precision, decisive air power employed in the Gulf positioned the Air Force out in front of the other services for the force cutback debate following Desert Storm. It was developing a clear vision of its future, and it demonstrated that it was ready to carry out that vision.[48]

This view stressed 'secondary and rapid force projection'. It also envisioned that space and information technology would be likely characteristics of future conflicts.

However, Desert Storm must be taken as a model only with a great degree of caution. While the United States can draw important lessons from the Gulf War, it may also be likely that future adversaries have also drawn a number of important lessons, the most important being not to challenge the United States overtly, visibly, or conventionally. Indeed, adversaries may have learned that the most effective way – and least threatening to them – to achieve their objectives may be by covert operations and unconventional warfare using surrogates and/ or third parties. These may be what some label as 'asymmetrical conflicts'.[49] In the long run, conventional wars such as the Gulf War may be the least likely contingencies for the United States. This does not mean that regional conflicts will necessarily diminish, but it does suggest that US involvement may be the least optimum strategy. Indeed, such involvement may exacerbate the situation.

Operations Other Than War

Non-combat contingencies are under the label 'operations other than war' (OOTW), labeled by some as 'military operations other than war' (MOOTW) and also as 'stability operations'. According to US Army doctrine, in operations other than war, 'Army forces and soldiers operate around the world in an environment that may not involve combat.'[50] These contingencies range from arms control, support to domestic civil authorities, humanitarian assistance and disaster relief to peacekeeping operations, peace enforcement, and support for insurgencies and counterinsurgencies.[51] There are other contingencies based on the ability to provide administrative and logistical support to political and diplomatic efforts aimed at drug control/abatement. It is usually the case that activities in operations other than war stem from civilian-initiated and implemented policies, strategies, and efforts. The key is that the role of the military, and this is especially true of ground forces, is in direct support of civilian efforts – military initiatives are minimal, if undertaken at all. In brief, the military role remains secondary to the political–diplomatic effort, whether initiated by the United Nations or the United States.

In the current period, the US military is struggling with reconciling commitments to operations other than war and maintaining effectiveness in its primary mission. 'The Army's primary focus is to fight and win the nation's wars.'[52] Yet it is also clear that support for insurgencies, counterinsurgencies, and counterterrorism poses the most serious problems for the mainstream military. It is difficult for mainstream military forces to engage successfully in such operations (termed here as unconventional conflicts) beyond limited administrative and logistical support without becoming engulfed in indigenous struggles and raising the specter of another Vietnam. In our view, it is also true that virtually every activity conducted in foreign lands under the rubric of operations other than war can lead to unconventional conflicts or, according to the official label, support for insurgencies or counterinsurgencies. In this respect, unconventional conflicts are critical reference points in coming to grips with most activities labeled as operations other than war.

Unconventional Conflicts

Conflicts following the Gulf War scenario are not likely to characterize the new millennium. It is more likely that conflicts will have their roots in ethnic, nationalistic, and religious differences. And these are more likely to be unconventional conflicts, challenging all of the notions about 'just war' and 'just conduct'. Indeed, unconventional conflicts challenge almost all of the precepts about war in the traditional sense. However, it appears that American perceptions about war and security remain fixed in the traditional-war syndrome, such as the Gulf War and the Cold War. In addition, there may be threats requiring simultaneous military responses.

According to former Secretary of Defense Dick Cheney,

> To help deter low-intensity conflicts and promote stability in the Third World, we must have innovative strategies that support representative government, integrate security assistance and promote economic development. Our approach for doing this is 'peacetime engagement' – a coordinated combination of political, economic, and military actions, aimed primarily at counteracting local violence and promoting nation-building.[53]

The official literature uses the labels 'special operations' and 'low-intensity conflict' (SO/LIC) as well as 'insurgencies' and 'counterinsurgencies'. Over the past years however, various labels have been used to identify basically the same characteristics. These include such terms as 'limited wars', 'internal defense', 'guerrilla war', 'counterguerrilla war', 'insurgency', 'counterinsurgency', 'small wars', 'peacetime engagements', 'operations short of war', and now 'operations other than war' or 'stability operations' encompassing special operations and low-intensity conflict. Moreover, efforts have been made to identify the nature of conflict by degree of intensity: low-, mid-, and high-intensity. The term 'unconventional conflicts' is used here because it focuses primarily on the *differences* between the characteristics of conflict – unconventional and conventional.

Unconventional conflict is defined as revolution, counterrevolution, and terrorism associated with each, encompassing strategies aimed at overthrowing the state or achieving a lesser political goal using unorthodox military operations. This is primarily a political–military struggle over control of the state and involves a broad range of political, economic, psychological, social and military means. It can also encompass ethnic and religious as well as inter-state conflicts. The tactics used are intended to achieve political objectives, often using terrorism and covert operations. The driving strategic principles emanate from Sun Tzu rather than Clausewitz.

Characteristics: Unconventional conflicts have characteristics that are unique and differ considerably from conventional conflicts. These are discussed in detail in a number of publications.[54] Some of the most important characteristics are the following:

1. *Asymmetrical*: For the United States these are limited wars, but for the indigenous adversaries these are wars of survival – total wars. The differences between the US involvement and those of the indigenous adversaries shape mind-sets, resources, and commitments. As an officer in the Chilean Army noted,

> From the US perspective, and based on its strategic reality, the situation in certain countries of the area requires only part of the potential US aid available which, in turn, leads to classification as low-, mid-, or high-intensity conflict. In other words the magnitude of US effort expended determines the classification of any given conflict. The countries involved have a very different viewpoint; for them it is painful bloody war, not conflict.[55]

2. *Ambiguous*: In unconventional conflicts it is difficult to determine at any one time who is winning and who is losing. In the main, conventional criteria for determining success are irrelevant. As the United States learned in Vietnam, conventional yardsticks such as body count, prisoners, and weapons captured may be meaningless. Also, it is difficult, often impossible, clearly to distinguish the adversary's armed elements and personnel from the civilian system.

3. *Unconventional*: Such conflicts are not only unconventional in a strategic sense but also in a tactical sense: terrorism, hit-and-run raids, ambushes, and assassinations are the common operational tactics. 'Revolution is endowed with a dynamic quality and a dimension in depth that orthodox wars, whatever their

scale, lack. This is particularly true of revolutionary guerrilla war, which is not susceptible to the type of superficial military treatment frequently advocated by antediluvian doctrinaires.'[56]

4. *Protracted*: The long-drawn-out nature of unconventional conflicts not only challenges US military doctrine but tends to erode US national will, political resolve, and staying power. Cases in point include conflicts that occurred (or are in progress) in Angola, Bosnia-Herzegovina, Cambodia/Laos, Central Africa, Chechnya, Colombia, Kosovo, Malaya, Peru, and Vietnam. Americans are inclined to see as the proper use of strategy that which seeks the overwhelming use of military force to end the conflict quickly. The Gulf War was seen as the 'model'.

5. *Differing strategic cultures*: Unconventional conflicts are likely to take place where cultures differ from the Western tradition. The Judeo-Christian heritage and the Anglo-Saxon legacy may not be compatible with or relevant in other cultures where unconventional conflicts are most likely to occur. Among other things, the concepts of winners and losers and conduct of conflicts may differ in other cultures. Samuel Huntington's 'The Clash of Civilizations' is particularly appropriate in studying this issue.[57]

6. *Clausewitz and Sun Tzu*: The center of gravity in Clausewitzian terms lies in the adversary's military. Once the military is defeated, the winning power can impose its will on the adversary. This generally means that overwhelming force at the point of decision is the key to success. According to Sun Tzu's precepts, the most successful general is one who wins without fighting. The center of gravity is found in the political–social social milieu. Thus, secret, covert, and psychological operations are critical to success. Further, the key is to penetrate the adversary's political system and erode the will to resist. It is Sun Tzu's principles that characterize successful efforts in unconventional conflicts.[58]

7. *The American way of war*: The American way of war is rooted in such concepts as the moral high ground, clear objectives, a clear beginning and end to any conflict, short duration, and focusing on clearly defined adversaries. Also, the purpose and objectives of the conflict need to be understood by the American people.

> Limited wars, while not preferred, are a frequent occurrence. ... Our cultural orientation is towards large-scale, production-line, conventional warfare. Some find this bias reduces the utility of the US military in lesser contingencies where force or the threat of force could be used as a preventive option or low-cost problem solver.[59]

There also is a military institutional mind-set that US military forces are capable across the conflict spectrum. This is based on the view that preparation for war also prepares the military for operations other than war and unconventional conflicts. This may be a mistaken notion.

US forces are well structured and prepared for high-intensity operations, but less so for peace operations and lower-intensity intervention ... While US forces are sufficient for large-scale intervention, they are not optimized for peacekeeping and other peace operations, or for other types of low-level conflict. These operations demand specialized training and preparation.[60]

While conventional contingencies and major power security relationships remain major concerns, the concept of operations other than war gained prominence in the early 1990s as the United States became involved in Somalia and Bosnia-Herzegovina.[61] For some, many missions in operations other than war are driven by moral indignation, what are considered to be wars of conscience, and video images. If these are taken to their logical conclusions, the US military may become engaged in a variety of operations that may have little to do with national interests. In the strategic landscape of the 1990s and into the next century, operations other than war seem to be becoming the rule rather than the exception. Further, the operational doctrine and the mind-set appropriate for operations other than war differ from the primary purpose of the US military – success in combat. This places considerable pressure on the military to balance the skills, operational techniques, and mind-sets required for success in combat with those required for peacekeeping and humanitarian missions including unconventional conflicts.

> While no one can predict the kinds of conflicts the United States may face in the coming decade, it is reasonably clear that instability and internal conflicts in the Third World are likely ... The most difficult challenges ... are those posed by unconventional conflicts ... [These] pose complex and difficult policy questions for the United States, involving Third-World cultures, different levels of growth, and different types of political systems. The United States has yet to learn how to deal with the driving forces in these non-Western cultures.[62]

CONCLUSIONS

The military services are giving a great deal of attention to information-age warfare/third-wave warfare and trying to develop doctrine to respond to the emerging landscape in the next millennium. This is described as the revolution in military affairs.[63] *Joint Vision 2010* established the guidelines for all military services in preparing for warfare in the twenty-first century.[64] What seems to be lost in the political–military maze is the challenges posed by unconventional conflicts as well as other activities associated with operations other than war as well as international terrorism. In any case, to develop and maintain flexibility to respond to these potential conflicts and challenges necessitates a number of basic military capabilities. Such capabilities include an effective response to conventional wars and beyond, unconventional conflicts, and non-combat contingencies.

The strategic landscape of the twenty-first century lacks the relative certainty of the last part of the twentieth century. As a consequence, the US National Security Establishment faces a serious challenge to design policy and strategy that offers some degree of clarity to the American people as well as to its allies and adversaries. The mixed signals on US and NATO involvement in Kosovo in 1999 is a case in point. Well into the NATO air campaign against Serbia, President Clinton and his national security advisors as well as NATO failed to provide a clear strategy and justification for its intrusion into the relatively weak state of Serbia, the actions of Slobodan Milosevic against the Kosovar Albanians notwithstanding. The US military was faced with a dual dilemma: how to respond to the military action against Serbia (the air campaign) and prepare for the continuing military efforts against Serbia (mission creep?), and how to design military forces for a strategic landscape that the national leadership has yet to define in terms of American national interests.

As emphasized earlier, the US military is in a difficult transition period. From the professional perspective, it is important that military professionals grasp the importance of this period and the critical issues associated with it. And as has been pointed out, these issues go beyond reduction of manpower, redeployment to the United States, and budgetary considerations. The more important issues are at the heart of the military's raison d'être and *esprit de corps*. These rest on strategic coherence, appropriate force structure, and perhaps most important, on cohesiveness and spirit within the military, with OOTW and unconventional conflict challenging all of these.

It is acknowledged that to develop a comprehensive strategy is not an easy task. It seems clear, however, that the military profession must adjust to the new realities of the transition period, one in which major wars may be a thing of the past. Even with an uncertain strategic landscape and questions regarding US national security goals, military strategies and force structures must be reshaped and redesigned. The US military does not have the luxury of standing pat, waiting for a clarification of the security landscape and the certainty of a new world order. At the minimum, strategies and force structures must be attuned to the fluidity of the emerging landscape and must develop some congruence between military posture, new definitions of power, and the utility of military force and this must go beyond preparing for the twenty-first century information-age warfare.

It is the military profession that should, and must, know best what these needs are in order to serve the nation properly. And it should be the military profession that, even under the most critical oversight and control from the nation it serves, ensures that its views and advice are placed in the political arena, regardless of consequences. In the process, society must try to understand that the prime purpose of the military is to kill and break things. But, there is a deeper psychological issue. The military profession is committed to *society-sanctioned* killing that links the American people directly to the *collective killing* of adversaries.

When involvement becomes necessary because of US national interests, those in the political and military realms of authority need to understand the characteristics of unconventional conflicts and what 'operations other than war' mean in terms of such conflicts. In addition, if such involvement is a matter of national necessity, then it may require the Americanization of the involvement with all that this may mean in terms of the American way of war.

Even if the United States did everything right, there is no assurance of success. There are limits to what it can reasonably accomplish without resorting to major war – particularly in delving into foreign strategic cultures. This may well be the primary factor shaping the view of many Americans, both civilian and military – the view that involvement in the Third World and in operations other than war and unconventional conflicts at more than a minimal level will lead to another Vietnam. According to this view, the United States should not be involved unless the issues are clear, the political and military objectives well defined, and there is a certainty that the United States will win. Given the nature of the new strategic landscape, and the characteristics of operations other than war and unconventional conflicts, adopting such a view may leave the field open to adversaries and adversely affect long-term national interests. However, involvement in operations other than war and unconventional conflicts requires a serious rethinking of the meaning of national interests and national objectives combined with a cautious and prudent use of Special Forces and, as a last resort, of the mainstream military – if national interests dictate it. This is not an easy task. As shown in this study, it is one that the United States has difficulty doing effectively.

9

Military Force and Operational Parameters

The previous chapter pointed out the problems facing the US military in trying to come to grips with various dimensions of war and conflict. This raises an even more fundamental question: how should the military be used, that is, what is the most appropriate and effective use of the military in implementing American policy? To be sure, there is less debate when the issue is a clear case of American national interest. This is also the case when there is a clear case of aggression leading to war in the conventional sense. But near the lower end of the conflict spectrum, questions become increasingly troubling regarding the proper use of the military. It is the accepted notion that the US military is to be prepared to act decisively across the conflict spectrum, from operations other than war to nuclear war and war into the twenty-first century and what is labeled 'asymmetrical conflicts'. Yet it is clear that how and if the military is deployed in contingencies and missions short of war raises serious questions. Questions that have to do with, for example, appropriate force, objectives, withdrawal criteria, and combat/non-combat structures.

A road map for the military services in preparing for the twenty-first century strategic landscape is spelled out in *Joint Vision 2010*.

> Focused on achieving dominance across the range of military operations through application of new operational concepts ... JV 2010 begins by addressing the expected continuities and changes in the strategic environment, including technology trends and their implications for our Armed Forces ... This vision of future warfighting embodies the improved intelligence and command and control available in the information age and goes on to develop four operational concepts: dominant maneuver, precision engagement, full dimensional protection, and focused logistics.[1]

This still leaves the question of the utility of military force in less than major conflicts. Such issues have been raised regarding the Quadrennial Defense Review (QDR).[2] The Review apparently seems to maintain the status quo with respect to major regional contingencies, manpower cuts, infrastructure, modernization, and forward deployment. While it has received favorable reviews from many in Congress, critics decry the Cold War mentality that underpins the

QDR while it ignores many contingencies that are encompassed by operations other than war.[3] Similar questions have been raised about the National Defense Panel's report, *Transforming Defense: National Security in the 21st Century*. Although focusing on the twenty-first century, it did have implications for the immediately preceding period.[4]

> Defense choices invariably entail risk; the only question is where we take the risk. A significant share of today's Defense Department's resources is focused on the unlikely contingency that two major wars will occur at almost the same time ... We are concerned that, for some, this has become a means of justifying current forces. This approach focuses significant resources on a low-probability scenario, which consumes funds that could be used to reduce risk to our long-term security ... The Panel believes priority must go to the future. Current force structures and information architectures extrapolated to the future may not suffice to meet successfully the conditions of future battle.[5]

Yet challenges facing the US military evolve from the view that the United States is involved globally and is the lone superpower, if not the world hegemon (see Chapter 7, 'The New World Order'). This means that the military is to be prepared for any variety of conventional and unconventional wars and operations other than war, as well as nuclear war and international terrorism. The challenges of future warfare combined with near-term contingencies place tremendous stress on the US military, stress that a number of military professionals fear will erode combat readiness.

As stated previously, the prime purpose of the military is to win the nation's wars. In the prevailing strategic landscape, however, military missions and operational tempo seem to be driven by operations other than war. Such operations require US armed forces to act primarily as policemen rather than soldiers, challenging the main purpose of the military. This concern was expressed by General Colin Powell: 'We have this mission: to fight and win the nation's wars. That's what we do.'[6]

In an article published in *Foreign Affairs*, General Powell wrote,

> When the political objective is important, clearly defined and understood, when the risks are acceptable, and when the use of force can be effectively combined with diplomatic and economic policies, then clear and unambiguous objectives must be given to the armed forces. These objectives must be firmly linked with the political objectives ... We must not for example, send military forces into a crisis with an unclear mission they cannot accomplish ...[7]

Testifying before Congress in 1993, General Carl Vuono, the former Chief of Staff of the US Army, stated, 'Will today or tomorrow's peacetime commitments leave enough [soldiers] for properly tailoring a robust, major contingency power-projection package? As far as I'm concerned, they will not.'[8] At the same hearing, the late General Maxwell R. Thurman, former commander of the US Southern

Command, stated, 'After a peacekeeping mission ... soldiers have to go through an extensive training regime to regain the level of operational proficiency which they held at the outset of that duty.'[9]

These concerns were confirmed in a recent study by the House National Security Committee. It concluded that involvement in operations other than war is one major reason that 'the readiness of our armed forces is suffering'.[10]

All of this is complicated by the fears of what some call 'mission creep'. That is, the US military is deployed under the rubric of operations other than war with an initially spelled out end-game and withdrawal elements. But as time goes on, slowly but surely the mission becomes expanded and the military finds itself engaged in various operations that may have little to do with the original purpose. A case in point was US military involvement in Somalia in 1992–93. For many, the fear is that mission creep not only requires more resources and personnel, but further obscures political–military objectives.

THE PREVALENT CONFLICT SCENARIO

As earlier chapters have emphasized, the conflict environment into the twenty-first century is likely to be characterized by unconventional conflicts including operations other than war. This is not to deny that conventional conflicts and technological age warfare are serious concerns. But it is the case that the US military may well be much better prepared and culturally oriented towards the higher end of the conflict spectrum. It is also true that weapons proliferation and international terrorism remain serious challenges. But American defensive measures and responses to these challenges are usually seen as responsibilities of agencies and institutions other than the military. This is not to suggest that the military does not have a role in such matters.

Again, the prevailing conflict environment stems from the lower end of the conflict spectrum. For example, a pressing problem for the United States are the drug cartel–revolutionary group coalitions such as in Colombia, Peru, and Mexico. Not only do such coalitions pose a serious threat to the indigenous systems involved, they are a threat to American domestic tranquility and drug-abatement efforts. Further, response to international and domestic terrorism has become a high priority, particularly for the Central Intelligence Agency.[11] This intermix of domestic and international dimensions makes effective US response extremely difficult. In the main, the visible use of mainstream military forces in support of domestic issues is limited to the external environment and normally in support of other agencies. Moreover, effective response to drug cartel–revolutionary group coalitions does not necessarily rest with conventional forces and conventional military doctrine.

In 1992 (and into 1999), another dimension surfaced in the United States, labeled 'wars of conscience'; many of these were triggered by video images – the

CNN factor. The constant media showing of suffering in Somalia and Rwanda, particularly of children, for example, seemed to play on the American conscience and created the environment for committing the United States. These activities are seen as mostly humanitarian responses to the plight of refugees and the turmoil of limited civil war spilling over into the population at large such as was witnessed in Somalia in 1993 and later in Rwanda and Kosovo. Such turmoil does not necessarily challenge or threaten US national interests, but the country is moved by humanitarian concerns. To be sure there are other bases for US involvement, including support of UN efforts. But the experience in Somalia may be a lesson that when the US military is involved in humanitarian efforts, mission creep can result in failure.

What began as a UN-sponsored humanitarian effort in Somalia in 1993 turned into a debacle when the US military was ordered to capture the warlord General Farah Aideed. Not only were 18 Army Rangers killed in the effort, Aideed was not captured. In its aftermath, the failed effort led to the withdrawal of US forces from Somalia, along with other UN contingents.

But it is the use of the military in conventional wars at the higher end of the conflict spectrum that provides the basis for the military to operate according to its primary purpose. The Gulf War showed the capability and effectiveness of the US military. Its use of advanced technology combined with outstanding performance of ground units seemed to suggest that the US was prepared for any contingency. The Gulf War also seemed to show that wars can be concluded quickly with minimum casualties. Yet the character of conflicts in this decade may not follow European-type or Gulf War scenarios.

FUTURE CONFLICTS?

The uncertain strategic landscape with the probability that conflicts will be at the lower end of the conflict spectrum, has led to much debate within military circles and among national security specialists about the characteristics of future conflicts and the need to prepare for the next century. As David Shukman concludes,

> The problem is that revolutions in military thinking do not come easily … Senior officers tend to favour the familiar in hardware and procedures; there is so much else that can go wrong. And the older the forces and the better-established the traditions the harder it will be to recognize the value of change. Yet that is what is required now. The accustomed global patterns of military power and of advances in weaponry are undergoing a transformation. We are only at the start of this process but the first signs of its implications and dangers are there for those who wish to see them.[12]

While many stress the importance of the revolution in military affairs, others argue, however, that the characteristics of warfare remain rooted in the populace and urban areas, and in all manners of unconventional conflicts. These demand the kind of skills and war-fighting capabilities that may have little to do with high-tech weaponry and electronic warfare.

For example, Ralph Peters argues,

> The future of warfare lies in the streets, sewers, high-rise buildings, industrial parks, and the sprawl of houses, shacks, and shelters that form the broken cities of our world ... The US military, otherwise magnificently capable, is an extremely inefficient tool for combat in urban environments.[13]

This raises questions about the utility of military force, military operational doctrines, and long-term support of the American people. But an equally critical issue is how well prepared the US military is to engage in operations other than war (OOTW), including unconventional conflicts shaped by foreign strategic cultures. Will the American people support such involvement, if so, for how long? Can the United States design an effective strategy or strategies that take into account foreign strategic cultures and a variety of non-conventional considerations?

Additionally, asymmetrical wars are a particularly difficult challenge for the US military.[14] This presumes that US adversaries will use their strength against American weakness. That is why adversaries will not necessarily challenge the United States in conventional terms, using conventional ground forces to face US conventional forces. This was well demonstrated in the Vietnam War. Unconventional conflicts are, in the main, asymmetrical conflicts for the United States. And these may well be the wars of the future.

WHAT NEEDS TO BE DONE?

The fundamental problem in designing strategy considering the use of military force is captured in the phrase 'New World Order: It Ain't Pretty'.[15] While it is difficult to design comprehensive strategy and guidelines for the use of force in an uncertain landscape, at the least, reference points can be defined. This is based on the proposition that the United States cannot simply wait until the world order is defined and the strategic landscape clarified. Doubts and uncertainties cannot be used as a cover for doing nothing. Neither should these be used to rationalize the 'do something syndrome'.

Rethinking Strategy and Force Posture

Current strategic thinking and the notions about US operations reflect the uncertainty and contradictions of the transition period into the next century.

> As we look ahead, the threat is more diffuse, the institutions more varied, and the roles and missions of the players more diverse, while the consensus in the American public over what the primary issues really are, at least, for the near term, will be much looser.[16]

Uncertain as to the shape of future adversaries, unclear as to strategic guidelines, perceiving the world order through conventional lens, the military as well as many political leaders seem to display some of the schizophrenia of the new world order and 'delicatessen' approach to conflicts and military contingencies. At the same time, the military is faced with diminished resources and a changing domestic political and social environment.

In this environment, a difficult and complex issue facing the United States is identifying threats and the nature of political–military challenges. In contrast to threats, the notion of challenge tends to be a longer-term matter rather than a compelling need to respond immediately. Threats, however, may require immediate response either to deter or to negate the threat. Thus, for example, the former Soviet Union posed both a threat and a challenge – a threat of military confrontation, a challenge in its long-term expansion of Communist doctrine. In the long term, China and possibly a resurgent Russia may be seen as a challenge to the United States.

But threats and challenges in the post-Gulf War era, particularly those in the Third World, are more likely to be shaped by unconventional characteristics. Further, threats and challenges are not necessarily limited to state-to-state confrontations. They can encompass a variety of groups within states and some transnational in scope. Most of these are not of an immediate threat to US national interests or security. However, many can be in long term. And it is this that makes it difficult to identify with any degree of confidence when and where the next threat or challenge may emerge that will require some type of response by the United States.

> It is clear that the Cold War structure of international politics has been irreversibly and fundamentally changed. The view or sense of what kind of replacement structure, if any, will fill this vacuum is not only unclear, it is opaque … Only time will tell whether US military might in the new century is the best and most formidable in the world or whether it is consigned to a fate of 'in irons'.[17]

The Conflict Spectrum

The Conflict Spectrum (see Figure 9.1) shows the range of missions, contingencies, and wars to which the US military must be prepared to respond. Given the prime purpose of the military, conflicts of a conventional nature and beyond are those in which the military is most capable. It is in such categories of the spectrum that there is little question about the utility of military force. As one moves to the lower end of the intensity scale, however, the utility of military force becomes increasingly questionable. This is not to suggest that military force may not be important in a variety of such contingencies. But what must also be considered is the fact that involvement at the lower end of the intensity scale is particularly affected by political objectives and non-Western cultures. The utility of such force may be dissipated by the ill-defined or unclear political objectives. Further, questions about American national interest – vital interests, may also be ill-defined. Such questions translate into questions about the proper use of the military. Moreover, this opens the door to more questions and debate about overstretching of military resources and the impact this may have on the military's raison d'être.

Figure 9.1: The Conflict Spectrum

Operations Other Than War ————————————▶

*Non-Combat	Unconventional	Conventional	Nuclear
Military Assistance	Revolution	Limited/Major	Limited/Major
Peacekeeping	Nationalistic, Ethnic,		
Peace-Enforcement	and Religious Conflicts		
Peacemaking	Terrorism, Counter-		
Humanitarian	terrorism		
Domestic Missions			
Shows of Force			

US Effectiveness

◀——— Good—Fair—Poor ————————▶◀——————— Excellent ————————▶

Threats

◀----- Most Likely -------------------------- Least Likely ----------▶

Note: *There is rarely a clear distinction between non-combat contingencies and unconventional conflicts. Virtually all operations other than war have the potential of developing into unconventional conflicts of one type or another. This category includes a variety of humanitarian and peacekeeping operations as well as coalition strategies and military support for UN operations.

The debate over the use of the US military is highlighted by the exchange between Madeleine Albright who was at that time US ambassador to the UN and General Colin Powell, Chairman, Joints Chief of Staff. General Powell has written,

> My constant unwelcome message at all meetings on Bosnia was simply that we should not commit military forces until we had a clear political objective ... The debate exploded at one session when Madeleine Albright, our ambassador to the UN, asked me in frustration, 'What's the point of having this superb military that you're always talking about if we can't use it?' I thought I would have an aneurysm.

American GIs were not toy soldiers to be moved around on some sort of global game board.[18]

As some authorities argue, the military is the instrument of 'hard power', best employed in clear conflict situations according to clear policies aimed at protection of US national interests. Given the lack of an adversary that is a clear threat to the survival of the United States and its core national interests, combined with the changing international landscape, realists point out that there is no threat to American core national interests in the short term.

THE AMERICAN WAY OF WAR

All of this raises questions about the American way of war in the new strategic landscape. These concerns have been discussed in earlier chapters. In brief, one view is that little has changed. The American way of war is rooted in such concepts as the moral high ground, clear objectives, a clear beginning and end to any conflict, short duration, and focused on clearly defined adversaries. The irony is that the diminished threat of major wars, and with it considerably diminished threats to US national interests, has eased American fears. Also, there is a prevailing presumption that peacekeeping in all of its various forms, humanitarian assistance, and a variety of military contingencies short of war are relatively easy and cheap operations. In turn, it is presumed that these can be undertaken for moral reasons and because they are the 'right thing to do'.

The ambiguous strategic landscape of today combined with the focus on the military's primary mission have turned attention to the Weinberger Doctrine.[19] This doctrine, spelled out by the then Secretary of Defense Caspar Weinberger in 1984, identified six criteria for committing US armed forces.[20] In brief, these comprised the following:

1. The issue must be of vital interest to the United States.
2. US troops should be committed wholeheartedly to the intention of winning.
3. There must be clearly defined political and military objectives.
4. Relationships between forces and objectives must be continually reassessed and adjusted.
5. There must be reasonable assurance that US involvement will have the support of the American people and Congress.
6. Commitment of US forces should be a last resort.

But it is not clear that the American public, in general, and elected officials, in particular, fully understand the military dimensions and applicability of the Weinberger doctrine in the use of military force. Again, the Vietnam experience is at the root of this concern. Or, if it is understood, any number of nationally elected officials ignore it for fear that its application would prevent virtually any use of the military except in clear combat operations.

In operations other than war (OOTW) however, clear objectives may be elusive and the role of the military shaped by a variety of diplomatic and political considerations falling far short of a decisive force charter. Indeed, overwhelming force may be out of the question; a show of force or token forces may be more appropriate, particularly when there is no overt adversarial military force involved.

Another perspective lies somewhere in between the Weinberger Doctrine and OOTW. Administrative and support forces can be used in OOTW in conjunction with other United Nations forces or with indigenous forces. Combat forces can be committed when it is clear that a military confrontation has developed that is likely to threaten US national interests. A corollary to this view is that privatization of some elements of US involvement may be appropriate.

In sum, the US military is well prepared for conventional conflicts and wars of a lesser order that are configured in a conventional format. But in many respects, the strategic thinking and operational capacity to respond effectively to one type of conflict may be contradictory to effective response to wars of a lesser order – unconventional conflicts.

The above, combined with efforts at designing a defense budget and military structure to fit budget constraints and domestic priorities, mean that the US military is faced with the prospect of doing more with less.

> American political leaders are requiring the military to *contract* in both size and budget, *contribute* to domestic recovery, *participate* in global stability operations, and *retain* its capability to produce decisive victory in whatever circumstances they are employed – all at the same time … Simply put, international and domestic realities have resulted in the paradox of declining military resources and increasing military missions, a paradox that is stressing our armed forces. The stress is significant.[21]

A number of factors must be re-examined and defined to form the basis for interpreting American national interests and translating these into realistic strategic guidelines and operational doctrine (see Chapter 5). These must be placed in a context recognizing that the character of the strategic landscape has prompted the search for alternative instruments and options. These include selective engagement, honest broker, and soft power as spelled out by Brzezinski, Nitze, and Nye, respectively.[22] A close examination of these concepts shows that they are sophisticated arguments linked to the Weinberger Doctrine and can provide the basis for designing strategy. Too often, however, the military becomes the instrument of choice simply because it is there, well-organized and led, and under the control of the national leadership.

THE US ARMY

All of the contingencies and missions across the conflict spectrum place heavy demands on the US military. The Army faces the most difficult task. This is well expressed by the views of a former Army general.

> There is no simple answer or simplifying strategy that will allow the United States to focus on a single or limited election of military capabilities. This is particularly true of the Army, which by its very nature acts as the decisive element in bringing any conflict to a successful conclusion.[23]

In contrast to other military services, 'The Army's raison d'etre is capability to engage in sustained protracted land warfare.'[24] Indeed, 'Armies have a unique ability to control land and people. Navies and air forces cannot do that; they can coerce and threaten, but they cannot control.'[25] In brief, the US Army's mainstream force structure is aimed at the employment of hard power – the least likely of contingencies.

In the immediate future, most military contingencies will require something other than the hard power capability of the US military in general, and of the Army in particular. This means the selection of a variety of non-combat options, the use of non-military instruments, or a mix of military and non-military instruments. According to Bacevich,

> Armies will deploy only in discrete amounts and for specific achievable purposes, with commanders held accountable for needless collateral damage; force will constitute only one venue among many that states will employ to achieve their aims, with military means integrated with and even subordinated to these other means.[26]

Yet it is important for the Army as well as the military in general, to maintain a hard power capability, if for no other reason than to be able to deter by signaling potential adversaries of the military's capability. However, most contingencies are likely to be in categories that do not require the military to exploit its most effective capability. Rather, these are contingencies that are likely to place the military, particularly the Army, in a decidedly subordinate role and position. Paradoxically, the character of conflict and military contingencies expand the scope of operations other than war, demanding a broad capability.

But it is also the case that the US military may become spread particularly thin – the hollow military syndrome – in trying to respond effectively to all contingencies and conflicts across the spectrum. This also has some impact on the various views of 'jointness', where each service seems to view the conflict environment in terms best supporting their own capabilities. It is important that the issue of military costs be placed in terms of the overall military system and placed in the public realm.

CONCLUSIONS

The United States remains the so-called 'lone superpower' as the world moves into the new century. Many nations look to the United States as the leading economic power and the primary military power. Moreover, any number of Americans consider US national interests to be global in scope. Again, NATO involvement in Kosovo reflects such sentiments. Obviously, this 'global' view affects US military missions and contingencies. Yet, many military professionals view such involvement with trepidation because it must be done with fewer resources and less manpower. In a word, the earlier British concept of the 'thin red line' has been replaced by an American version of the 'thin green line'.

As has been pointed out, military professional issues go beyond reduction of manpower, redeployment to the United States, and budgetary considerations. While these are clearly important issues for the military profession, it is also clear that the conduct and capability of those in the National Security Establishment, including the President and his close advisors, to establish and clearly articulate American national interest, and to understand and be sensitive to military culture and purpose have a primary impact on *esprit de corps* and military cohesiveness.

The questions raised about the Clinton administration's attitude and use and misuse of the military, exacerbated by the Chinese connection and Kosovo, raise to new heights the issues addressed in this study. Indeed, the American public seemed to be increasingly troubled by US policy and President Clinton's leadership. By mid-1999 there was a significant drop in the President's job-approval rating and in the degree of satisfaction with America's current state.

From the military professionals' perspective, all of these matters place them in a difficult position. They must offer competent, political–military perspectives to civilian decision makers and to the American people regarding strategies and force structures for the new security landscape. At the same time, the reshaping of the military must take place while maintaining military *esprit de corps*, coherency, and sense of purpose. And all of this must be done within the bounds of acceptable civil–military norms.

This effort should be guided by the views of General Weyand expressed in the immediate aftermath of the Vietnam War. Focusing on the role of Army professionals, General Weyand wrote,

> As military professionals we must speak out, we must counsel our political leaders and alert the American public that there is no such thing as a 'splendid little war'. There is no such thing as a war fought on the cheap ... The Army must make the price of involvement clear *before* we get involved, so that America can weigh the probable costs of involvement against the dangers of noninvolvement.[27]

The military will survive this difficult period. But it is not clear at this juncture in time what costs the military will have to bear to avoid falling into the 'hollow army' syndrome. It is the military profession that should, and must, know best what the military needs are to serve the nation properly. And it should be the military profession that, even under the most critical oversight and control from the nation it serves, ensures that its views and advice are placed into the political arena, regardless of consequences. In the process, society must try to understand that the prime purpose of the military is to kill and break things. But there is a deeper psychological issue. The military profession is committed to society-sanctioned killing that links the American people directly to the collective killing of adversaries.

In this period of uncertainty, it is best that both the military and political leaders take a page from Sun Tzu. If the US military tries to do everything well, it may end up doing nothing well. And it is time that military professionals told elected leaders and the American public that there are any number of things that the military has difficulty doing – in some cases extreme difficulty in doing. As George Wilson has argued 'A "can't do" attitude is better'.[28]

10

Force Structure and Doctrine: Mainstream Military and Special Operations Forces

The way in which the US military is organized, trained, and operates is determined by military doctrine. For all practical purposes, doctrine and force structure are intermixed. Doctrine refers to the acceptable way in which the military operates; it is the modus operandi of the military. Doctrinal principles are the guidelines for force structure. Force structure refers to the organization of units, command system, and force composition. All of this is driven by the military's primary purpose. Each service designs its doctrine under the umbrella of 'grand' military doctrine which in turn is shaped by military strategy.

As pointed out in previous chapters, the uncertain environments evolving since the end of the Cold War extending into the twenty-first century make it extremely difficult for the military to 'fix' doctrine and force structures with any degree of certainty. These remain, more or less, a version of those of the Cold War period. To be sure, there is much debate within the military as well as in some civilian circles regarding military structure and doctrine, particularly in terms of their relevancy into the twenty-first century. Much of this debate has its roots in the lone superpower concept and world hegemon perspective. These, in turn, affect American efforts to shape appropriate doctrine and force structure such as those reflected in the Base Force, Bottom Up Review, the Quadrennial Defense Review (QDR), the Report of the National Defense Panel, *Joint Vision 2010*, as well as reports from various think-tanks. Nonetheless, questions remain about doctrine and force structure. The military drawdown and levels of defense spending are integral parts of this debate. Complicating these matters is the fact that the force structure is affected by personnel and recruiting matters, issues of gender, homosexuality, and women in combat roles – assignment of women to ground combat units – as well as lingering issues of race. These matters have created controversy about combat cohesion and unit effectiveness. While there is less controversy over women serving as pilots in combat units and serving on certain combat vessels, there is controversy about women in infantry and special operations units. Part of this spills over into the type of force structure and organizational doctrine established by the various services and by the military in general. Many of these issues were noted in Chapter 6, 'Civil–Military Relations'.

At the same time, the focus of the 1990s military appeared to be on preparing, among other things, for what has been called the revolution in military affairs.[1] This has led to the struggle over defense dollars and another round of inter-service rivalries and battles over 'turf'.

FORCE STRUCTURE

As discussed in Chapter 8, military personnel are organized into various units. Also, personnel are divided into major categories identifying support, adminis-trative, and operational units and personnel. This provides a broad view of the force structure in terms of personnel assignments. For example, in the US Army 'Most of the active Army is divided between operational (63 per cent) and institutional forces (25 per cent), with the remainder of the force in temporary status, such as students (12 per cent).'[2] Thus, in discussing the total number of personnel in each of the services it is important to consider the distinctions between those who are in operational areas and those in other categories, and how all of this relates to doctrine.

Force Composition: Gender and Race

The assignment and role of women in the military is a continuing issue in all of the military services, particularly the Army. Earlier, the question of race seemed to occupy the center stage. At the same time, homosexuals in the military continue to be a troubling, if somewhat less dominant issue. In any case, gender seems to now drive the debate about force composition.

In Chapter 6, it was pointed out that the issue of democratization is important in the relationship between the military and society. It is also an important consideration in force structure. Part of the notion of democratization is the integration of genders into the military system. That is, to what parts of the force structure should women be assigned? Should they be assigned to combat units? There is a great deal of literature on these subjects, including published reports by official commissions.[3] Controversy remains over integrated basic training and separate living quarters. And in operational units, women are not assigned to ground combat units. This has most impact on the Army, the Marines, and special operations units.

The *Presidential Commission on the Assignment of Women in the Armed Forces* established the basic tenets regarding assignment of women.[4] These generally remain in effect now. This is the case, even though there has been and remains much debate about the role of women in the military. The report, however, does not exclude women from all combat roles. This is in particular reference to women's roles in the Navy and Air Force.[5]

Department of Defense Data on personnel in the military are shown in Table 10.1.[6] The debate over women in the military has also been aimed at the public at large. For example, the *Chicago Tribune* published a front page article on 'The unknown military', focusing partly on the role of women in the military and the shrinking armed forces.[7] This was particularly aimed at the Army.

Table 10.1: Military Personnel Data

	Officers (%)									
	Army		Navy		USMC		Air Force		DoD	
	1977	1997	1977	1997	1977	1997	1977	1997	1977	1997
Blacks	6.1	11.0	1.8	5.8	3.5	5.9	3.2	5.9	3.9	7.5
Hispanics	0.9	3.4	0.6	3.8	0.7	4.1	1.1	2.2	0.9	3.1
Women	6.7	14.2	6.3	14.2	2.3	4.2	5.6	16.2	5.9	14.2
	Enlisted (%)									
Blacks	26.3	29.7	8.6	19.5	17.4	16.8	14.6	17.4	17.8	22.1
Hispanics	3.7	7.0	3.0	8.5	5.6	11.6	3.1	4.8	3.5	7.5
Women	6.8	15.1	4.2	12.4	2.0	5.4	7.4	17.8	5.8	13.7

	Married (%)		Education (High school diploma) (%)	
	1977	1997	1977	1997
Civilian population, 18–44	64.3	53.0	79.1	78.7
Total Department of Defense (enlisted)	49.7	55.4	71.5	93.8

Note: Adapted from Jack Weible, 'The New Military: It's a Far Different Force Than a Generation Ago', *Army Times*, 13 July 1998, p. 13.

The report indicated that in the Army of 480,00 in 1999, the breakdown by race and gender would be as follows:

Race: Whites – 60.5 per cent; Blacks – 26.8 per cent; Hispanic – 6.4 per cent; Others – 6.3 per cent.

Gender: Male – 418,934 (85.2 per cent); Female – 72,773 (14.8 per cent).

Racial issues remain important, but the military has done much to respond positively. Indeed, one can argue that the military has shown society what can be done to diminish racial friction. This is clearly the view of two prominent military sociologists analyzing the Army.[8] The authors argue that in the military it is an accepted procedure to advance individuals on the basis of merit, not preference. 'Race relations can best be transformed by an absolute commitment to nondiscrimination, coupled with uncompromising standards of performance.'[9] In the Army, black soldiers are routinely in command positions over white soldiers. The Army, according to David Gergen, has succeeded not because of racial preference or being race blind, but on race savvy.[10] Much of the same can be said of all the military services.

Nonetheless, some concern has been raised about the possibility of racial issues shaping promotions in the officer ranks. This issue was raised by *US News and World Report* and in the *Chicago Tribune*. Under the title 'Camouflaging racial differences: 50 years of progress, now slipping', Richard J. Neuman writes 'More pressure will be put on selection boards to ensure that minority candidates get fair treatment. And senior officers will be encouraged to pick more minorities for jobs as aides, staff officers, and other high-profile positions.'[11]

In an op-ed piece in the *Chicago Tribune*, Moskos and Butler appeared to be responding to some of the criticism about race relations in the military, particularly the US Army.[12] Pointing out that, among other things, at the enlisted level the Army has established the largest continuing educational program in the world, the authors conclude,

> The road from the Truman desegregation order of 1948 has not been smooth. Still, the Army experience has proved that race relations can be transformed by a commitment to raising people to meet uncompromised standards of performance. Will American society at large come to the same realization?

Regardless of views to the contrary, the US armed forces have led the way in racial integration.

For most military professionals, issues of force composition are subordinate to unit cohesion and combat effectiveness. Accordingly, the overriding principle should be cohesion and effectiveness, not race or gender. As Martin Binkin points out, 'The concerns relating to the possible effect women would have on combat unit cohesion are the most difficult to dismiss ... [T]he link between male bonding and ground combat performance is strongly rooted in tradition.'[13] Others argue that effectiveness must be attuned to the demands of American society and concern for equality and equal opportunity. This changes the notion of unit cohesion and effectiveness. For some the concept of unit cohesion is especially critical in ground combat units, while democratization is best accomplished in other than ground combat units.

Conflict Characteristics

Force structure is shaped by doctrine, and doctrine is shaped by strategy and policy about the nature and characteristics of conflict. Recalling the conflict spectrum described in Chapter 9, characteristics of conflicts indicate that not only must the military be prepared for conventional conflicts, those of hi-tech/third-wave warfare, and those of an asymmetrical variety, but also those of an 'old-fashioned' type of unconventional conflict, operations other than war, and a variety of ground-intensive ethnic conflicts. Can the existing force structure and operational doctrine respond effectively to the entire range of the conflict spectrum?

An insightful study of this problem is Douglas A. Macgregor's *Breaking the Phalanx: A New Design for Landpower in the 21st Century*.[14] The author argues that

> America cannot afford to enter the new millennium as a nostalgic posthegemon with expensive industrial age armed forces that simply do not fit the new strategic environment. In practical terms, this involves replacing old military structures and concepts – the contemporary equivalent of the Phalanx – with new structures: the modern American military equivalent of the Roman Legion.[15]

Macgregor offers a well-argued reorganization of the military. For example, he advocates the restructuring of Army divisions into more versatile combat groups. He has similar views for other services. Focusing on all of the services he states that 'The nation does not need and cannot afford to maintain two more air forces as well as an amphibious army at sea. Salami slicing must end in favor of reform, reorganization, and jointness.'[16]

However, others note that a capability to perform a variety of missions ranging from traditional conventional-type conflicts to information-age warfare require a great deal of caution in any restructuring of the military. For some, operational doctrine still has its roots in Clausewitz, Jomini, Mahan, Douhet, and Mitchell. If so, the existing force structure is not likely to change greatly.[17] Nonetheless, the Air Force argues that it is the decisive element in the new strategic landscape.[18] Obviously, those in the ground forces point out that historically and into the twenty-first century, the soldier on the ground is what makes the ultimate difference in war.

PLANNING IRRELEVANCE?

The prevailing mind-set within high-level political–military circles seems to focus on the revolution in military affairs, the acquisition of electronic warfare gadgetry, and hi-tech weaponry. This effort has led to debates about appropriate plans and doctrine for responding to the most likely conflicts now and into the next century. These issues were studied in Chapters 8 and 9, but need to be revisited here in terms of force structure and doctrine.

What seems to be lost in the political–military maze that infects the doctrine and force structure posture are the challenges posed by unconventional conflicts as well as other activities associated with operations other than war. These are the most likely type of conflicts now and into the next century. Jeffrey Record has focused on such issues.

> The challenge for the Pentagon is not to adjust doctrine and force structure to a new strategic environment dominated by small wars and military operations other than war (MOOTW), while at the same time continuing to maintain the conventional military supremacy necessary to discourage major interstate aggression against US security interests. The risk is that of carrying too much Clausewitzian baggage into a neo-Jominian world.[19]

However, it seems that the US military is primarily concerned with the revolution in military affairs and doctrines and force structures that are conventional in nature. This is part of the general attitudes of members of Congress and the American people.

According to one account,

> Public support for military intervention has been greater when the main objective has been to coerce foreign policy restraint by an aggressor state, when there has been a clear military strategy, and when the policy has been made a priority by the president and Congress.[20]

It is also the case that, regardless of the military's involvement in a variety of non-combat missions, the mind-set remains towards conventional-type operations.

> As might be expected, the cultural orientation remains focused on the upper end of the conflict spectrum, and the ability to rapidly project overwhelming combat power from the United States for a regional conflict. The fundamental aspects of the Pentagon's warfighting strategy, although reoriented from a global strategy to a regional level, remain fixed on the application of firepower and technology against a conventional opponent in a major regional contingency.[21]

To be sure, military plans for all the services include operations other than war. According to Hoffman, even though the doctrines of each of the military services focus primarily on deterring regional aggression and fighting conventional-type wars, there is attention to operations other than war: 'the concept operations other than war has become an ingrained part of the doctrine of each of the military services'.[22]

Conventional contingencies and major power security relationships remain serious concerns. Taken to their logical conclusions, however, post-Cold War missions assigned to the US military may require involvement in a variety of operations that have little to do with national interests. Further, the operational doctrine and the mind-set appropriate for operations other than war differ from the primary purpose of the US military – success in combat. This places considerable pressure on the military to balance the skills, operational techniques, and mind-sets required for success in combat with those required for peace-keeping and humanitarian missions, including unconventional conflicts.

But, as Snow concludes, 'The style of warfare prevalent in much of the Third World is simply not practiced by the US military, which may explain why the United States has never shown any marked appetite for non-European-style warfare.'[23] It is also important to note that the instigators of unconventional conflicts may not necessarily fight like 'barbarians', that is without skilled leadership, modern weaponry, or hi-tech equipment.[24] Indeed, such groups may have all of these; they also may have a clear advantage because the conflict will be in their own geographic area and they will also have deep knowledge of the political–social landscape in which the conflict takes place.

For a better understanding of doctrine and force structure, it is necessary to review the purpose and organizational features of the various services. Much discussion in previous chapters has been on the mainstream military, its primary purpose, and its characteristics. The increasingly important role of the National Guard and Federal Reserves has focused attention on their force structure. This has revealed continuing friction in the relationship between active and reserve forces. This is especially the case with the active Army forces and their reserve components. In the remainder of this chapter, a brief overview of these issues is discussed. But in terms of doctrine and structure, the greatest differences are between mainstream military and special operations forces. In this respect, doctrine and force structure within the military differ contingent upon military purpose. While there is an overarching military purpose, there are doctrinal differences between mainstream and special operations military units. And it is the latter aspect that is the main focus of subsequent sections. Before we examine the different military services and units, it is important to review the numbers in each category as shown in Table 10.2.

THE NATIONAL GUARD AND FEDERAL RESERVES

The history of the Republic shows reliance on a small standing Army and on citizen-soldiers. This has usually been accompanied by some degree of friction between the standing military and the militia. Much of this evolves from the command structure, perceived capabilities, and civilian versus military professional mind-sets, among other things. A notable historical reference point is the view of Emory Upton. In his book *The Military Policy of the United States*, Upton argued that American military policy was defective.[25] 'Excessive civilian control was a fundamental flaw, since most congressmen, presidents, and secretaries of war were inexperienced in military matters.' The basic problem was that '... America relied upon unreliable citizen-soldiers.' For all practical purposes, Upton based military policy on regulars – professional military men, 'denigrating militiamen and volunteers'.[26]

Table 10.2: End Strength: Active and Reserve Forces

Service	FY 1998 authorization	Fiscal Year 1999		Change from Fiscal Year	
		Request	*Conference report*	*1999 request*	*1998 authorization*
Army	495,000	480,000	480,000	0	−15,000
Navy	390,802	372,696	372,696	0	−18,106
USMC	174,000	172,200	172,200	0	−1,800
Air Force	371,577	370,882	370,882	0	−695
Total	1,431,379	1,395,778	1,395,778	0	−35,601
ARNG	361,516	357,000	357,223	223	−4,293
USAR	208,000	208,000	208,003	3	3
USNR	94,294	90,843	90,843	0	−3,451
USMCR	42,000	40,018	40,018	0	−1,982
ANG	108,002	106,991	106,992	1	−1,010
USAFR	73,447	74,242	74,243	1	796
USCGR	8,000	8,000	8,000	0	0
Total	895,259	885,094	885,322	228	−9,937

Source: adapted from Floyd D. Spence, Chairman, House National Security Committee, *Summary of Major Provisions, HR 3616: National Defense Authorization Act for Fiscal year 1999 (Conference Report)*.

This was in stark contrast to Major John McAuley Palmer's concept of a citizen Army. 'Palmer continued through the 1920s and 1930s as an articulate champion of a "democratic army" of citizen-soldiers with citizen-soldier officers in National Guard and Reserve formations ...'[27]

In the modern period, the Uptonian argument has been overshadowed by Palmer's concept of a citizen–soldier system having a major role in the military policy of the United States. Nonetheless, today there are still debates concerning the role of the reserves that hint at the differences between Upton and Palmer. That is, there has been (and is) dissent and disagreement about the role of the reserves and their relationship to the professional military. This increased to a crescendo as the 'Total Force' concept became the driving force of the US military. The reliance on reserves in operations other than war as well as in conventional operations such as the Gulf War raised more questions about the role and the missions of the various components of the 'Total Force' doctrine.

The debates and discussions about the use of reserve forces in the Gulf War is detailed in Duncan's excellent book.[28] Long discussions eventually led to decisions which effectively and smoothly activated the reserves for the Gulf War. The author also notes that one impressive aspect of the war was the 'responsiveness of citizen warriors in every military to the nation's call to arms'.[29]

Duncan also devotes considerable attention to the roles and missions of the reserves in the post–Gulf War era. He writes that 'Any force planning process must ... begin with clear political strategy and policy guidance.'[30] He recognizes that there is uncertainty in strategic planning and the use of military force. But he stresses that certain principles need to be established and followed in considering the use of the reserves.[31] These range from the concept of Total Force policy, the visibility of the reserve forces, and quality of life issues, to greater participation of reserve forces officers in professional military education.

Stating the critical role played by the reserve forces in the security of the United States, Duncan argues, however, that:

> Their public service must not ... be taken for granted. Reduced defense budgets and the absence of a clear global threat do not justify a mindless use of reservists for unimportant military missions or nonmilitary work that can be performed by others. When danger to the nation has passed, they must be permitted to lay aside the warrior and return to the citizen.[32]

The debates and discussions about the proper role and missions for the National Guard and Federal Reserves continues today. While progress has been made in clarifying these issues, disagreements remain. At the national level various commissions and task forces have attempted to come to grips with these issues.

For example, the Report of the National Defense Panel states, 'While the other services have continued to increase the integration of their active and reserves forces, the Army has suffered from a destructive disunity among its components, specifically between the active Army and the National Guard.'[33] Indeed, the National Guard and the active Army have been feuding over cuts in the strength of the National Guard as well as the end strength of the reserves.[34]

Among a number of recommendations, the National Defense Panel stated the following:

> Some portion of the Army National Guard's divisional combat (including combat support) units should become part of the active divisions and brigades. Infantry and mechanized battalions, for example, would be integrated as organic units of the active divisions and would deploy with them. The active component commander would be responsible for their combat readiness and training.[35]

In 1998 and into 1999 serious efforts were made to develop a more effective force structure in the National Guard and reserves. For example, the National Guard developed enhanced brigades to respond to integration with the active Army. Yet in a September 1998 article in *Armed Forces Journal International*, reference is made to the continuing fragile relationship between the National Guard and the active military.

In the 12 months since the last National Guard conference, the big guns on both sides of a fundamental divide over the Army National Guard's proper role in national security generally have fallen silent ... at least for the time being, factions on both sides of the rift are using the pause to give earlier inflicted wounds time to heal.[36]

The point is that the conflict spectrum in the remainder of the twentieth and into the twenty-first century requires a much more active and integrated role of the National Guard and Federal Reserves in the active military. It is also important to clarify the roles and missions of the various components. This is particularly the case with the downsizing of the military and the tempo of operations (OPTEMPO) and impact on personnel morale (PERSTEMPO). It is probably the case that there will always be some degree of friction between active and reserve forces, stemming from disagreements spelled out here. But in the long run, when there is commitment to an active military mission, these disagreements are likely to disappear, even if only temporarily. The commitment to service to the nation seems to be the overpowering drive whether one speaks of active or reserve forces. This has been the case throughout American history.

SPECIAL OPERATIONS COMMAND

The United States Special Operations Command was created in 1986 by Congress (Public Law 99-661) and strengthened by subsequent legislation (Public Law 100-180 and 100-456).[37] The legislation included provisions for an Assistant Secretary of Defense for Special Operations and Low-Intensity Conflict (SO/LIC), and for a unified command for special operations forces, and prescribed a Board for Low-Intensity Conflict within the National Security Council (NSC). In 1987 other legislation provided for, among other items, the publication of a charter for the Assistant Secretary of Defense for Special Operations and Low-Intensity Conflict and designated the Secretary of the Army as acting Assistant Secretary of Defense for SO/LIC until the office was formally filled for the first time. In addition provisions were made for a separate special operations forces (SOF) budget. The Special Operations Command is the primary organization designed to respond to unconventional conflicts.

The command and control system for the United States Special Operations Command (USSOCOM) is shown in Figure 10.1. While much has been done to strengthen and improve the special operations system, much remains unresolved. Some of this has to do with the distinction between mainstream military and special operations forces, a distinction that places career special operation forces officers almost on the periphery of the military system – this is particularly true of officers who have their own career branch. Moreover, plans and their implementation as well as relationships within the highest levels of

Figure 10.1: United States Special Operations Command

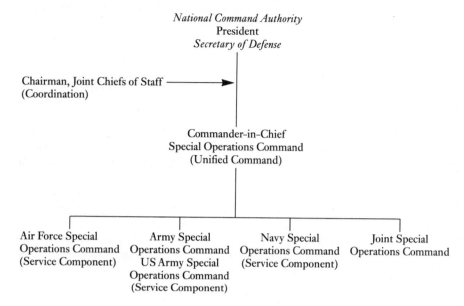

government involving special operations reflect problems and misconceptions of the role of special operations.

As Collins observes, 'Conflicts with the JCS Chairman, the Joint Staff, and USSOCOM over planning responsibilities remain unresolved. Successive Secretaries of Defense have declined to correct such conditions.'[38]

Problems also remain regarding the employment of special operations forces and their relationship to mainstream military forces. These include the commitment of special operations forces and continuing problems of an institutional nature.

> ... military 'cultures' are changing more slowly. Mutual distrust and misunderstandings still separate conventional forces from SOF, because not many of the former fully understand SOF capabilities and limitations. Too few special operations specialists have enough Pentagon experience to make 'The System' work for them instead of against them. SOF constituencies on Capital Hill, among US military services, and in industry remain scant and tenuous; consequently, appropriate acceptance of Special Operations Forces will come only after all parties concerned complete a learning process and put doctrine into practice.[39]

Questions also exist regarding the scope and form of US involvement, should such involvement become necessary. As a last resort, mainstream military forces may become involved in such conflicts. It must be recalled, however, that the major effort rests in a variety of non–military efforts. The commitment of visible mainstream military forces to a Third World unconventional conflict may exacerbate the conflict and may not lead to success. To repeat, the analogy of Vietnam remains the reference point.[40]

However, it is also the case that the use of special operations forces – particularly special forces – is the best means of developing a 'preventive maintenance' strategy, that is, the effort to support an indigenous system or those fighting against an indigenous system while minimizing the American presence in order to prevent the enlargement of the conflict. Indeed, the commitment of such forces, with their ability to minimize US presence, may be the best strategy short of 'Americanizing' the effort; this would create a situation eroding American support of the military effort and engulfing US forces in a Vietnam-type environment. The Americanization of the effort should be considered only if such involvement is clearly necessary to protect American national interests (see Chapter 5).

Unfortunately, there is a tendency in the public as well as in segments of the US military to misread the training, skills, and focus of special forces within the Special Operations Command. In the public realm, too often many Americans view special forces as they are seen in the *Rambo* and *Rambo II* movies. Some in the military view the role of special forces through conventional lenses rather than as individuals who must meld into the political–social milieu of an indigenous system and prepare to remain over the long term. Moreover, the training and education of special forces remains distant from the mainstream career paths. As suggested earlier, this causes friction between special forces and some special-operations personnel as well as for many in mainstream military units.

This is one of the major issues addressed by Susan L. Marquis. She writes,

> Special operators fight a different kind of 'war' than conventional forces. To put it simply, armies take and hold ground. Air forces conduct strategic bombing operations and engage enemy fighters. Navies operate carrier battle groups in the open ocean, conduct offshore attacks on enemy targets, or strike from boats beneath the sea. The traditions of the conventional units are, in many respects, shared histories.[41]

She goes on to describe the differences between conventional operations and special operations forces and concludes,

> This unconventional often indirect, warfare has long been unappreciated or even disdained by conventional forces ... The special operations forces (SOF) are a unique community within the US military. Their organizational culture is separate and distinct from the conventional military.[42]

It is clear that force structures and doctrines driving special operation forces differ from conventional forces. It is also the case that the cultures between mainstream and special operations forces differ – this is true in all of the military services, for example, Navy SEALs and the mainstream Navy. It is also the case that the preparations for war in the twenty-first century pose different problems for the special operations forces than conventional forces. For special operations forces, the focus on unconventional operations is critical. While this may be affected by hi-tech weaponry and third wave warfare, the fact is that operations within the populace and the political–social milieu of society will require the same skills that have been necessary in the twentieth century.

US ARMY SPECIAL FORCES

Most of the skills and specialized training in operations other than war and unconventional conflict are in the special operations forces, particularly US Army Special Forces.[43] The organization of Army Special Forces is shown in Figure 10.2.

Figure 10.2: US Army Special Operations Command

US Army Special Operations Command

| US Army J. F. Kennedy Special Warfare Center/School | US Army Special Forces Command–Airborne | US Army Civil Affairs and Psychological Operations Command | 75th Ranger Regiment | 160th Special Aviation Regiment (Airborne) |

⊢ 1st SFG (Airborne)
⊢ 3rd SFG (Airborne)
⊢ 5th SFG (Airborne)
⊢ 7th SFG (Airborne)
⊢ 10th SFG (Airborne)

US Army National Guard

19th SFG (Airborne)
20th SFG (Airborne)

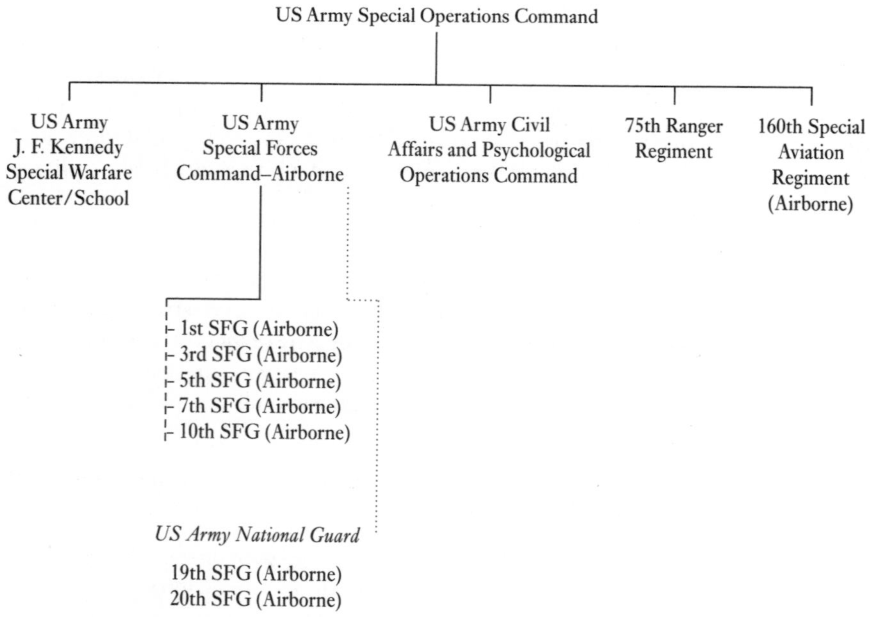

Legend:
SFG   Special Forces Group
– and ⊢ Command and Control
....   Coordination

Although the Special Operations Command was not created until 1986, special forces were first organized in the early 1950s at Fort Bragg, North Carolina. The first ten detachments of the 10th Special Force Group were organized at Fort Bragg in 1952 under the command of Colonel Aaron S. Bank.[44] The primary mission was 'To seek out, train, and support men capable of becoming effective guerrillas. To seek out, engage, and neutralize guerrillas.'[45] More specifically, it was to organize 'stay behind' guerrilla units in Europe to counter the possible Soviet invasion of western Europe. Training included sabotage, hit-and-run raids, and assassinations, and learning to deal with indigenous people. Some individuals who had recently left from behind the Iron Curtain, such as Czechoslovakians and Georgians, were recruited as part of 'A' teams. The initial cadre for the special forces was mainly from the Office of Strategic Services (OSS) of World War II fame. The Navy SEALs and Army Rangers also owe their modern roots to the World War II period.

During the organizational period, special forces were not allowed to display any distinctive uniform such as berets or unique identification, for fear of appearing too 'foreign' to the mainstream US military and the public at large. It was also the case that special forces were viewed with disdain and distrust by most elements of the mainstream US military.

A small group of special forces officers from the 10th Special Forces Group was recruited for service in Korea during the latter part of the war. They served in various unconventional capacities, some in special-mission units on the coasts of both North and South Korea. Some also served with the United Nations Partisan Infantry Korea (UNPIK). Some of the missions included attempts to infiltrate agents into North Korea and in trying to establish a search-and-rescue network for downed American airmen. Yet little has been written about such service.[46]

It was during the Kennedy presidency that 'green berets' were authorized and the special forces given credibility by the president. This began an effort to move special forces into a more legitimate relationship with the American public and the mainstream military.

> President Kennedy himself made a visit to the Special Warfare Center in the fall of 1961 to review the program, and it was by his authorization that special forces troops were allowed to wear the distinctive headgear that became the symbol of Special Forces, the Green Berets.[47]

Nonetheless, the problem of understanding the role of special forces and lingering suspicions of them remain in both the American public and the military.

The special forces came into real prominence during the Vietnam War. Special forces were the driving force in establishing and operating civilian irregular defense groups (CIDG) and in advising Vietnamese Regional and Popular

Forces. The activities and missions of special forces have been studied in a number of publications.[48] Suffice it to say here that there were debits as well as credits associated with special forces operations in Vietnam. In the broadest sense, special forces proved their worth in Vietnam in conducting operations that the mainstream military could not effectively undertake. Moreover, 'Despite the successful accomplishment of its role ... the Special Forces troops were continually conscious of mistrust and suspicion on the part of many relatively senior field grade US military men.'[49] Some of this suspicion and mistrust lingers today. A similar environment persists in the Air Force and the Navy regarding Air Force Special Squadrons and Navy SEALs. It is also the case that 'jointness' has become institutionalized, more or less in the mainstream military, but seems to be lacking in special operations forces.

While efforts have been made to relate special operations doctrine to mainstream military doctrine, the differences are clear: the purposes of mainstream military and special operations forces are also clear. The former is guided by Clausewitzian concepts of war, the latter by Sun Tzu. This shapes the force structure. Army Special Forces, for example, are structured quite differently than the mainstream forces, regardless of the efforts to label special forces units with traditional names such as 'company' and 'battalion'. The basic operational elements of the special forces is the 'A' Team consisting of a 12-man team led by a captain. Second in command is a warrant officer. Two non-commissioned officers are trained in each of the five special forces functional areas comprising weapons, medicine, operations and intelligence, communications, and engineering and demolitions. All team members are special forces qualified, are cross-trained in the different skills, and are multilingual. Women are not assigned to 'A' teams or to the field operating units in special forces, nor are they assigned to Navy SEALs, contrary to the portrayal in the Hollywood film *GI Jane*. Also, women are not assigned to ground infantry combat units.

CONCLUSIONS

The US military must develop doctrines and force structures that are attuned to the uncertainties of the strategic landscape characteristic of the twenty-first century. While the posture and structures cannot be set in concrete, they must have a degree of relevancy to the contours of the new security environment. At the same time, the military must be prepared for present and near term contingencies. Thus there must be a serious analysis of the philosophical and intellectual bases for doctrine and force structures, an analysis that is linked to the realities as well as uncertainties of the security landscape and American domestic imperatives. Such imperatives include force composition and how this reflects American society. Adding to the difficulty is the fact that the concept of national security has broadened and the military has been drawn into a variety of contingencies that may have little to do with its primary purpose. And all of this must be embraced with fewer resources and less manpower.

> While no one can predict the kinds of conflicts the United States may face in the coming decade, it is reasonably clear that instability and internal conflicts in the Third World are likely ... The most difficult challenges ... are those posed by unconventional conflicts ... [these] pose complex and difficult policy questions for the United States, involving Third World cultures, different levels of growth, and different types of political systems. The United States has yet to learn how to deal with the driving forces in these non-Western cultures.[50]

When US involvement becomes necessary because of its national interests, those in the political and military realms need to understand the characteristics of unconventional conflicts and what operations other than war mean in terms of such conflicts. In addition, if such involvement is a matter of national necessity, then it may require the Americanization of the involvement, with all that this may mean in terms of the American way of war. In many such cases the use of special operations forces – particularly Army Special Forces – is likely to be the most appropriate. This is a preventive maintenance strategy and makes American withdrawal less difficult, should circumstance dictate. Surely it is incumbent upon the military profession to explain to the national leaders and the American public the differences between the mainstream military and special operations forces? It is also important that they be informed of the differences between unconventional and conventional wars and the impact these differences have on the US military. Moreover, the military profession must make it clear that special operations forces – particularly Army Special Forces – are not simply a militarized peace corps. Perhaps the most important factor is the need for military professionals themselves to recognize the clear distinctions between mainstream military and special operations forces – and the fact that those in special operations are as professional and committed to their tasks as those in the mainstream military. Finally, it is clear that the military profession has a critical role in ensuring that national elected leaders and the American people are informed of the challenges of various types of conflicts and how these affect doctrines and force structures. And, equally important, the American public must be told of the costs, not only in terms of financial and physical resources, but in human terms and military effectiveness.

PART IV
CONCLUSIONS

11

Constructive Political Engagement

The principal theme of this book is that the changed and changing domestic and international landscapes pose complex and difficult challenges for the US military profession in particular and the military in general. The dilemma facing the military profession is how to respond to these landscapes while maintaining its raison d'être – ensuring that the military remains effective in its primary purpose to engage in war. The most effective way to respond to this dilemma is for the military profession to adopt the doctrine of constructive political engagement. Such a doctrine will provide the basis for insuring that the military perspective is made an integral part of the political decision-making process and that appropriate political considerations are made part of the military perspective. And this can be done within the constitutional principles of civilian supremacy over the military. In sum, in the 'orbit' of the American system, politics and military issues are inextricable.

This chapter sums up the major points in the two major areas: American society and the military, and the utility of force in the international arena. However, all of the issues and factors examined in the previous chapters will not be repeated. The purpose here is to build on the major reference points and use them as the basis to focus on the twenty-first century. We begin by reviewing the major characteristics of the military profession.

THE MILITARY PROFESSION

The military professional ethos has its roots in the purpose of the military. In the most simple terms it is 'to kill and break things'. In more sophisticated terms, it is to manage violence in the service of the state. That translates into education, training, and the development of skills focused specifically on eliminating the nation's enemies as quickly and economically as possible, within the purview of the political directives of the nationally elected leadership. To do this, the military profession must ensure that the military system responds effectively, that is, weaponry, training, organization, doctrine, and strategy must all be aimed at achieving the military's primary purpose. This means that force structure, force composition, command, leadership, and lifestyle must be attuned to the primary purpose. At the individual level, this means that the unit mission and unit effectiveness comes before individual considerations.

In personal terms, the words of Sir John Hackett are revealing.

> The essential basis of the military life is the ordered application of force under an unlimited liability. It is the unlimited liability which sets the man who embraces this life somewhat apart. He will (or should be) always a citizen. So long as he serves he will never be a civilian.[1]

Translating this into the broader military professional system and the military system, we can see that the military cannot be equated to a social institution, corporate business venture, a bureaucratic structure, or political interest group. As pointed out in this study, the military profession has some attributes of all of these, but what clearly distinguishes it from such groups or any other profession is its primary purpose and ethos.

Society must understand that the military profession, by its very nature, does not base itself on the ideals of an egalitarian society. To expect a military professional to be imbued with such principles is to make him or her a non-professional, at least within the American context. To expect the military profession and the military institution to reflect an exact picture of society is to make the profession and institution another civilian organization shorn of the organizational fiber with which it can carry out its unique purpose. For it is one thing to say the profession must be more than a killing business, and it is quite another to say that it need never get involved in the killing business.

Although all desire that nations 'beat their swords into plowshares', only the most naïve believe that this will happen in the foreseeable future. As long as the possibility of conflict exists, in whatever form, across the conflict spectrum there will be need for the military profession, with its competence and understanding of the nature and conduct of war. In that respect, the military and the military profession will stand apart from society, regardless of how the notion of military profession is modified. The military can never be a true replica of society, nor can the military profession ever be just another profession. By necessity, there will always be a gap between the military profession and society, and between the military and society.

The challenges of the twenty-first century are formidable to the military profession. This is the case, not only in terms of the revolution in military affairs, but the changing domestic system, and the changing shape of the international landscape. No one can set the specific direction with any sense of accuracy. At this point in time, all that can be said is that the search for answers goes on. The greatest hope for our society and for the military is the existence of professional men and women who are moved by compassion, troubled by injustice, and are still able to take pride in their professional commitment.

Those responsible for committing military forces must first consider the political-social environment in which these forces will operate including domestic and international dimensions. Therefore, 'Military leaders must be willing to tell their superiors what they need to know ...' not necessarily what civilian decision-makers would find comforting or supportive of their own views.[2] This means that the military profession is not just another job. It is a commitment and a way of life that separates the profession and the military from society and other professions. It is this notion of commitment that is critical if the military is to maintain the moral, ethical, and political cement to maintain its professional culture and serve society.

In sum, the military profession is driven by a special purpose that requires a distinct culture. This must be the basis for military professionals to engage in the political realm when policies are discussed that have a direct bearing on the role and commitment of the military. The corollary is that there must be a serious effort by the profession to ensure that the American public and elected officials and all in the national security system develop a realistic understanding of military culture and what it means to be a military professional.

AMERICAN SOCIETY AND THE MILITARY

There is much debate in the United States about the changing nature of domestic society and the impact of information technology on families and communities. While some argue about the divisions within society and the possible balkanization of society, others stress the enduring values of belief in God, their own family, and in notion of Americanism. Yet it does appear that multiculturalism, diversity, political correctness, gender, race, and homo-sexuality remain troubling issues. At one level, one wonders about the meaning of Americanism if primary emphasis is on multiculturalism and diversity, for example. In addition, the issue of gender and the meaning of sexual harassment have become a complicating and troubling issue, particularly highlighted by the allegations against President Bill Clinton in 1998. These domestic issues and debates about the meaning of 'America' make it difficult for the US military to define a particular relationship with society that is harmonious and yet supportive of the military's raison d'être.

Much of the current debate about the relationship between the military and society revolves around convergence or divergence. The roots of this debate owe their inception to the earlier views of Huntington and Janowitz. While convergence presumes that domestic pressures and democratic requirements are causing convergence of military and civilian value systems, divergence presumes a relatively separate military revolving around its set of values leading to isolation from the mainstream civilian system.

The issue is the degree to which the military should reflect society and still maintain its professional character to carry out its primary mission. The fact that there is serious debate within the United States about the meaning of 'America' and its culture, presents a difficult problem for the military. The need for cohesion and a salient core value system is critical for the military to perform its primary role. This must be fixed on the meaning of America and loyalty to the nation-state. Striving for such a focus, the military may be pursuing one set of values that may incrementally move it towards the notion of divergence. Yet, it is clear that the military in a democratic system cannot remain at a *great* distance from the society it serves. The values of society must have a visible and meaningful connection with the values within the military. While these are not new issues facing the military, they have become increasingly visible, highlighted by the role of women in the military and the sharpened debate about American culture. But the question is how can the military maintain a set of core values and remain within the orbit of society, a society in which there is disagreement about the meaning of America?

This question has led to a great deal of military professional ambivalence regarding the relationship between the military and society. There is recognition that there must be a degree of convergence between the military and society, yet this stops short of accepting a close linkage that would dilute the uniqueness of the profession and the profession's military focus. In any case, the uniqueness of the military profession and the character of the military lifestyle and military community, tend to make the military and the military profession distinct from society in general. The fact that a decreasing number of elected officials in particular, and of members of society in general, will have had any military experience tends to foster a professional view that there is little civilian understanding of the military and the military profession.

> Civilian officials need to spend a greater amount of time studying the military, understanding its challenges as a profession, and wrestling with the intricacies of its employment. The strong attitudes, culture, and capabilities of the military must be fully understood by those elected to make policy decisions.[3]

The convergence and divergence theories seem to permeate much of the debate about the relationship between the military and society. Regardless of the pros and cons of such debates, the historical patterns of the American political system and the evolution of the military profession cannot be separated. The intent of the Founding Fathers and the requisites of a democratic system do not provide a separate sub-system removed from society. The legitimacy and credibility of the military rests with its linkages with society and societal values. This can not be a perfect reflection of society. At the same time, the military profession cannot be like other professions. Nevertheless there is both a political–psychological as well as a formal link between the military and society.

What kind of model best represents this relationship? In its ideal form, the model presumes that the military profession – the officer corps, is an educated elite whose role in society is the organization, control, and application of force in pursuit of democratic values, as determined by the nationally elected leadership. Complementing this is the view that the profession not only controls and supervises the military instrument in accord with established policy, but that professional morals and ethics require a commitment to democratic ideals. This requires a role in the political process for the achievement of goals that best serve the American system. This leads to an active role – constructive political engagement in those policy issues affecting the military's purpose and military professional raison d'être.

Rather than issues of convergence and divergence, or debate about 'gaps' between the military and society, the more appropriate approach is one based on equilibrium. Equilibrium requires that there be open debate between all segments of the public, those in the national security establishment, and military professionals. From this, adjustments can be made and understanding reached about military perspectives and civilian concerns.[4]

In brief, there is no 'fixed' relationship between military and society other than the principle of civilian supremacy. Rather there must be a constant and mostly harmonious relationship based on changing domestic and international landscapes and the need for the military to maintain its capability to win wars, regardless of the changing environments. Civilian authority has the primary power over budgets and the career management of the military, regardless of what may be the military professional position. This is further reinforced by the fact that to function effectively, the military must have the support of the American people.

There are a number of other considerations in the equilibrium model. First, the model is based on a concept of friendly adversaries. This presumes that although adversaries may disagree with one another at times and use their political power to pursue their own priorities, they must function in accord with the democratic rules of the game. For example, the military profession as a political actor (among other things) pursues its priorities through a variety of informal and formal channels and processes, legitimately and credibly. However, the military profession's latitude in the official policy sphere is limited to those policies that have a direct bearing on the military.

Second, the relationship between the military and society is symbiotic. The relationship between the military profession and other political actors in the American system, although at times adversarial, is mutually advantageous in the pursuit of goals and in the perpetuation of the American system. Conflict and give-and-take relationships are not antithetical to democracy. On the contrary, it can be argued that such relationships are a sign of a healthy democracy as long as all political actors understand their proper role.

Third, the relationships between the military and society are asymmetrical. That is, although committed to defend the state, the military does not have the critical role in determining the norms or boundaries of the political power of those making the decisions on military commitment. This is the power of civilian institutions where public debate can legitimately occur – the military profession must be part of this public debate. Policies regarding the limits of dialogue and dissent are primarily formulated through civilian institutions and by elected officials, not by military professionals. Thus, while the military cannot be isolated from the impact of policies, nor from the influence of political dialogue, it is the critical instrument (and in this sense isolated) when it comes to per- forming its primary role in war. Further, the professional ethos accepts without qualification the fact that civilian policymakers are pre-eminent in the American system, even with respect to matters concerning the military profession and the military in general.

Fourth, military and civilian institutions parallel each other; that is, while they are not the same, they are interconnected by a variety of relationships, values, and norms. This parallelism occurs at every level of the military institution and between various elites. There is a multiplicity of relationships, but each political actor maintains its own identity and integrity. This is done within the context of a democratic value system and ideology, and provides the direction and basis of legitimacy for the operation and existence of each sub-system.

Fifth, equilibrium envisions a relationship which is dynamic, interacting, and self-adjusting. Both society and the military are seen as seeking the same goals – the reinforcement and perpetuation of the democratic political system – although they vary in the pursuit of these goals. There are no absolutes in such relationships, except the absolute required to maintain and perpetuate the political system and the notion that the elected national leadership is supreme over the military.

In the final analysis, the equilibrium model of civil–military relations rests on the notion of constructive political engagement. The military profession cannot be a passive and neutral cog in the political system. The military professional must be able to exercise common sense judgement and to articulate views based on an understanding of military and civilian priorities and the intermix between politics and the military profession. The military profession must accept the notion that it is a political instrument, and being political is a necessity, not for partisan purposes and blatant advocacy, but in the sense of sophisticated and enlightened perspectives regarding the military perspective.

It would seem, therefore, that there is a pressing need to review the prevailing views about the relationship of the military and American society, civil–military relations, and military professionalism in order to identify the relevance of various approaches to these matters. The evidence suggests that there is ample cause to question various approaches and what seems to be an intellectual and military tradition.

Any philosophical redirection of the military must come from open, reasoned, and multisided public dialogue.

> As a start toward re-establishing this dialogue, we would all do well to learn a good deal more about our past civil–military relationships and about impressions and distortions they have left. We also need to chart our present position by sociological as well as historical and political triangulation, sighting on as many points as possible. In short, we need to examine the *entire* record.[5]

UTILITY OF MILITARY FORCE

The commitment of the US military in the existing strategic landscape and that likely to evolve in the twenty-first century are largely determined by America's perception of its role in the world and, indeed, by the perception of other nations. The notion of world hegemon has become an increasingly apt characteristic. This is not a notion limited to policy-making and academic circles. In 1998 a front-page article in the *Chicago Tribune*, for example, the United States as world hegemon was a major theme.[6] 'The word is hegemon. Get used to it. It means Numero Uno. Mr Big, the 800-pound gorilla. If you're an American, it means you.' The article points out that the American presence and its impact is on virtually every part of the globe. While any number of nations welcome the American presence, others decry it. 'Militarily, politically, culturally, economically, the US dominates the globe, though it doesn't always get its way – and often is resented as arrogant.'[7] Yet the fact is that grand strategy remains unclear and elusive. At the same time, the US military must be prepared to respond to any number of contingencies ranging from conventional and unconventional conflicts to operations other than war, encompassing peacekeeping, peace enforcement, and peace making as well as humanitarian contingencies. The driving force is that the military is capable across the conflict spectrum.

Yet any number of authorities decry the expanding commitment of the military worldwide while the military has been reduced, and is being reduced in numbers and given limited resources. Not only has this placed great stress on the military, it has caused significant problems in personnel retention and in maintaining effectiveness. Equally troubling to many military professionals as well as to some in civilian circles is that the use of the military for contingencies in operations other than war (OOTW) detracts considerably from the military's ability to maintain its combat readiness. While it is recognized that the military is an important instrument in OOTW and armed diplomacy, the commitment of the military in such missions must first be carefully examined in terms of the priority of national interests. And if committed, the military should be the instrument of last resort.

'The American Army is really a people's Army in the sense that it belongs to the American people who take a jealous proprietary interest in its involvement ... the American Army is not so much an arm of the Executive Branch as it is an arm of the American people.'[8] The support of the American people for military involvement rests primarily on military contingencies conforming to the American way of war, diminishing support for involvement in various forms of operations other than war and unconventional conflict.

While the superpower era demanded a particular global political–military capacity and strategic thinking, the strategic landscape of the new world order demands a different strategic mind-set and operational capacity. The transition from one to the other has resulted in an ad hoc mixture of strategic and operational guidelines, and political–military capacity. Complicating the dilemma, there has emerged in the United States a notion of wars of conscience, policy driven by moral indignation, and the 'do something' syndrome.[9] The US military is well prepared for conventional conflicts or missions that are con-figured in a conventional format. But in many respects the strategic thinking and operational capacity required to respond effectively to such conflicts and missions may have little to do with effective response in OOTW and unconventional conflicts.

In sum, the United States remains ill disposed and ill prepared to respond to unconventional conflicts. Not only is the American way of war contrary to the characteristics of unconventional conflicts, but mainstream US military forces are neither disposed nor doctrinally oriented to engage effectively in such conflicts. Yet the strategic landscape is replete with situations that are within the scope of operations other than war and unconventional conflicts. And in the long run some of these may develop into serious threats to American national interests. There is a serious need, therefore, to clarify the meaning of 'national interests' with respect to Third World instability, to rethink strategic orientation, and to reconsider the utilization of the US military. It may be best that the United States does not become involved in any number of operations other than war or unconventional conflicts, lest such involvement change the dynamics of the situation to the disadvantage of American interests. Moreover, given the nature of the American domestic setting, the Weinberger Doctrine may be the best guide to the commitment of military forces.

The military profession has not been clear or persuasive in the public airing of these problems. The cue should be taken from General Powell's response to Secretary of State Madeleine Albright's view that since we have a superb military it should be used. This 'Albright syndrome' seems to afflict many in civilian circles, particularly those with little if any military experience. Indeed, it is the obligation of military professionals to alert national leaders and the public of the costs and consequences of military involvement. Unless those in the civilian realm understand such costs and consequences, the military will remain 'stressed' by the possibility of dire future consequences.

TIME FOR A POLITICS–SAVVY MILITARY[10]

It has been an article of faith in the military profession to erect a wall between the military and 'politics' – a wall that has little basis in fact. But most in military and civilian circles have accepted the wall as a fact of life. Such a wall, mythical or otherwise, is an anachronism. The domestic and strategic landscapes of the remaining year of the twentieth century and into the next have inextricable political and military ingredients. To respond effectively to this environment, the concept of the military profession must be *philosophically* broadened and encompass a more prominent political dimension; the military profession must adopt a doctrine of constructive political engagement – framing and building a judicious and artful involvement in the policy arena. This is a first step in responding to the uncertainties of the remaining year of the twentieth century, nurturing a proper relationship with society, retaining the military's raison d'être, and transition to the next century.

Constructive political engagement is not a radically new approach. Generals Matthew Ridgway, Fred Weyand, and more recently, former General Colin Powell have pointed to the need for military professionals to tell the American people and political leaders the costs of involvement, before the United States gets involved.

The US military belongs to the American people, and military professionals have a duty and obligation to ensure that the people and its political leaders are counseled and alerted to the needs and necessities of military life. But this cannot be done by adhering to a military profession that is isolated from the political realm. It cannot be done by adhering to the view held by any number of political leaders that military professionals are paid to do, not to think or speak out. Nor can it be done by adhering to a notion of the military profession as a silent order of monks isolated from the political realm.

Too often military professional passivity in politics in general, has lead to difficulties in responding effectively to missions and contingencies, and in maintaining a high degree of readiness and modernity. This has also contributed to the notion that military professional involvement in politics in any form is contrary to democratic principles. This reinforces what seems to pervade the military today – extreme defensiveness in light of criticism from the public and Congress. To be sure the behavior of some military professionals has shaken public confidence in the military. But the military professional response often borders on apologetics, rather than on careful articulation of the disciplinary demands of the military and the ability of the military to correct internal problems, and that improper behavior reflects on only a handful of those in the military and is not characteristic of the profession as a whole.

To be sure, there are those who have adopted the notion that the US military has become politicized; some have accepted this view because more military personnel now vote! Others take refuge in the view that there must be a *clear* separation between the military and politics, while never clarifying what they mean by a clear separation. Such views connote a negative view of the meaning of 'politics'. Yet politics in its most neutral sense means a legitimate and credible effort by individuals, groups, and institutions within the United States, to pursue political goals. Politics is an essential ingredient of American democracy.

The US military has passed through difficult times in the past. From such experiences at least one lesson should be clear: the military profession cannot withdraw into an ethical cocoon and take on a defensive posture. Prudent and positive response to those issues affecting the military, publicly articulated and aired, with the senior leaders of the military profession leading the way, is the most important lesson to be learned.

In light of the current political–military environment, the military profession must offer an intellectually and philosophically sound view of the capability of the military and those policies and strategies that offer the best path for achieving success. This means that the military profession cannot remain distant from the American political process. It must become involved in that part of the political process that concerns national security, defense policies, and the functioning of the military system. This is to ensure that military concerns and perspectives are well integrated into the policy area that affects military life. The reverse is also true – to ensure that political perspectives are well integrated into the military dimension.

This is not to suggest that the military become embroiled in partisan politics. Yet it is also the case that to remain passive and allow misjudgments and misguided policies and strategies to emerge from the political arena without a thorough debate and airing of the military perspective is a major step in eroding the military's legitimacy and effectiveness. Once a decision is made to commit the military, however, political engagement regarding the decision must then be carefully articulated through professional channels to those at the highest levels of the National Command Authority, including the commander-in-chief. Yet it is important that changes in the strategic and operational situations as viewed 'from the ground' be effectively articulated and incorporated into the policy making machinery throughout the national command system. Even in such circumstances, the American people cannot be isolated from the military perspective. This is no mean task.

In simple terms, what is advocated here is a version of Charles Moskos and John Sibley Baker's 'race-savvy' approach – that is, to show neither race blindness nor race preference.[11] The military profession must develop a mind-set that is gender-savvy and politics-savvy. This means that gender roles must be driven by the purpose of the military and the need for combat cohesion, not by gender blindness nor gender preference. Military professional political-savvy is neither political blindness nor political preference; it means alerting and counseling national leaders and the American public about the costs of committing the military, the substance of military culture, and military life. Political-savvy recognizes that the military is an arm of the American people, that military and political objectives and environments are in most cases inextricable, necessitating a public airing and political discourse of the military perspective.

And it is a politics-savvy military profession that can best counsel and alert the public and elected officials that the military's prime purpose is society-sanctioned killing – to kill and break things. And only by political-savvy and political engagement can the military profession effectively make it clear that there is a difference between military and civilian life, and between the military profession and other professions.

There is no 'fixed' relationship between the military and society other than the uncompromising principle of civilian supremacy. This also means that American civilians and elected leaders must develop a deep understanding of the military, its primary purpose, and how all of this affects the military culture.

INTO THE TWENTY-FIRST CENTURY

Each chapter in this study concluded with some attention focused on the military profession posture and its role in the political realm. The purpose in this concluding section is to highlight the most important efforts needed to ensure that the military profession operates within the orbit of the American system and yet retain its effectiveness in carrying out America's policies and strategy.

The fundamental conclusion in this study is that the military profession must adopt the doctrine of constructive political engagement, framing and building a judicious and artful involvement in the policy arena. A politics-savvy military profession is the basic ingredient for constructive political engagement. This is essential in both the military's relationship to American society and in the utility of military force in the new world order. There are a number of elements in both areas that need to be considered in adopting constructive political engagement.

But first there are internal matters that must be addressed by the military profession. The military profession should consider doing the following to govern its drive for the next century:

1. Reinforce the concept of leadership as the primary driving force in maintaining the trust and honor of the military system.

2. Ensure uncompromising moral and ethical principles and commitment as part of the professional ethos.

3. Recognize and reinforce the pivotal role of enlisted professionals.

4. Reinforce the interaction of the three professional tiers and develop a close bond and trust at all levels.

5. Ensure that trust and devotion to duty remain essential characteristics of the military profession.
6. Adopt a military education system that includes a healthy dose of American politics.

From these internal efforts, a number of principles evolve to establish the military professional role in the political realm. These are placed under each of the two major parts of this study.

American Society and the Military

The broad challenge for the military profession is to define the meaning of devotion to duty to include constructive political engagement. Devotion to duty is not simply to 'salute and do one's duty'. That is an anachronistic and distorted notion. Devotion to duty encompasses devotion to the American public and insuring that all understand the military perspective. The military profession cannot function as a 'silent order of monks'. It is an arm of the American people and the people must be informed of the state and posture of their military.

It follows that the considerations listed below should govern the military profession.

1. Constructive political engagement means that military perspectives must be clearly presented to the commander-in-chief, members of Congress, those in the national security system, the media, and the American public.
2. Constructive political engagement means that the American public and those in the national security system including the commander-in-chief and members of Congress must develop a more realistic understanding of what it means to be a military professional and of the essence of military culture.
3. The relationship between the military and society must be one of trust and understanding. While the military must operate within the orbit of society, it is clear that its prime purpose and the nature of the military profession preclude it from being another societal institution or becoming 'democratized' to the extent of eroding its combat cohesion and unit effectiveness.
4. The meaning of devotion to duty needs to be re-examined. Devotion to duty is not simply an acceptance of orders, saluting and going on. To be sure, it means that the profession carries out its duties and policies as decided by civilian leadership. But it also means that the military profession must not stand by silently and allow misplaced strategies and policies to erode military capability and increase military costs. The profession must ensure that its views are heard, not on a one-time basis, but by constant input into the decision-making process.

The New World Order and the Utility of Military Force

The following are considerations that should govern the use of military force and shape constructive political engagement.

1. Domestic and international landscapes now and into the next century are driven by globalization and technological advancements. This will erode the ability of a state to control matters within its territory and those affecting the international environment. This may also mean that the concept of state sovereignty will become increasingly diminished.

2. In the conflict environment emerging from these changes, conflicts of a lesser order (unconventional conflicts and operations other than war) will be likely to characterize conflicts.

3. The nature of conflicts and the intertwining of domestic and international landscapes highlight the need to develop strategies and policies that are based on the notion that politics and the military are inextricable. That is, the commitment of military forces will always involve political objectives and political considerations.

4. US strategies and policies for conflicts into the twenty-first century must clearly delineate national security and national interests. All conflicts and turmoil in the world are not matters of national security or national interests. The United States cannot presume that it is the world hegemon and that all things must be met unilaterally.

5. The military perspective must be clearly projected into those strategies and policies that are based on military commitment, defense policy, and military strategy. And the costs of committing the military must be made clear.

THE RELEVANCE OF CLAUSEWITZ

While many debate the relevance of Clausewitz to the new security landscape, in our view the Clausewitzian notion of war and politics remain valid. Carl von Clausewitz theorized 150 years ago that 'War is merely the continuation of policy by other means.'[12] Victimized by the modern American penchant for converting the profound into platitude, this product of the Prussian general's genius has, sadly, become a bromide. We tend to lose sight of the thought that caused the statement, that surrounds it and that gives it meaning. 'Policy, then, will permeate all military operations, and, in so far as their violent nature will admit, it will have a continuous influence on them.'[13] Clausewitz insists that war 'is not a mere act of policy but a true political instrument, a continuation of political activity by other means'.[14] Wars, therefore, are political acts that must be initiated, ended and defined from start to finish by the political leadership of the state. This process described by Clausewitz is intensified in a republic such as the United States. It behooves senior military leadership to be able to interact constructively with the political leadership in the formulation of strategic and national security policy that, by logical extension, is the preparation for war. And, conversely, it is important that the national civilian leadership understand the need for senior military leadership involvement in the political process – those areas that deal with military effectiveness, and military professionalism, and military culture. The same holds true with respect to the American people in general. In modern states such has always been the case and today, in the light of the shifting domestic and strategic landscapes, it is even more vital that this civilian–military and military–political interaction become the standard.

A FINAL WORD

In the final scheme of things, only a doctrine of constructive political engagement and a politically savvy military profession can remind the public and its elected officials that the military's prime purpose is to 'kill and break things' in the defense of the American way of life. This means that the military is part of the American political system and the American people, but it can never be the same as civilian society.

Perhaps John Keegan said it best:

> Soldiers are not as other men – that is the lesson I have learned from a life cast among warriors. The lesson has taught me to view with extreme suspicion all theories and representations of war that equate it with other activity in human affairs ... War is fought ... by men whose values and skills are not those of politicians and diplomats. They are those of a world apart, a very ancient world, which exists in parallel with the everyday world but does not belong to it. Both worlds change over time, and the warrior adapts in step to the civilian. It follows it, however, at a distance. The distance can never be closed.[15]

12

The President and Civilian and Military Cultures

It is a legal and political fact that in the American system there is absolute civilian control of the military. While this may be a well-established fact, how this is done is often shrouded in misperceptions and legal abstractions. As pointed out in earlier chapters, there are any number of civilian–military linkages and many inextricable intertwining of political–military institutions and policies. At the apex of all of these linkages and connections is the president as commander-in-chief. How the president performs this role and his commitment of the military to various missions and contingencies are key to addressing military stature and *esprit de corps*. It follows that the political and cultural issues raised by the President Clinton impeachment episode in late 1998 and into 1999, in retrospect, need to be addressed.

Though civilian and military cultures were examined in Chapter 4, the impeachment issue and military culture were only briefly noted. There is some deliberate repetition here on cultures and characteristics of the international landscape as background for this chapter. In retrospect, we believe that the whole impeachment episode and its aftermath deserve a more detailed look, one that connects to Chapter 4 but more specifically focuses on presidential character, and civilian and military cultures. While we cannot anticipate what will result in the aftermath of the impeachment trial and the 'not guilty' verdict of the Senate, we believe that the issue of presidential character and conduct has a decided impact on military culture.

Constructive political engagement is a difficult proposition for the military profession, because it treads a fine line between politics and the military. Within the military and in the civilian world, the tendency is to avoid this problem by trying to impose a clear line of separation between the military and politics. But, realistically, politics and the military cannot be separated. As has been the constant theme here, the military is not only a military institution but also a political one. Politics in this sense has to do with the political objectives of military commitment; the understanding of the costs and consequences of military involvement; the need for readiness and effectiveness prior to such commitments, and the ability clearly to articulate the impact of all of this unequivocally to elected leaders and the American public.

Much of this political dimension revolves around the notion of military culture and its distinction from civilian culture. At the same time, it has been stressed that the military must operate within the orbit of the US political system and be congruent with civilian cultures. Civilian cultures, in turn, must provide reference points for military culture. These reference points emanate from elected national leaders, the general sense of moral values, and the values reflected in the principal governmental institutions. In this respect, the perceptions of the conduct and character of the commander-in-chief are critical reference points.

The events that took place in late 1998 and into 1999 – Operation Desert Fox (the missile and bomb attack on Iraq in 1998), the continuing confrontation with Iraq, Kosovo, and the impeachment of President Bill Clinton – raise questions about civilian and military cultures. At another level, questions are raised about personal political motivations and the use of the military. These events need to be examined and related to civilian and military cultures.

THE PRESIDENT AND THE MILITARY

The role of President Clinton as commander-in-chief became disturbing to many military men and women. While some brush aside such views, increasing evidence seems to indicate a 'gap' between the president and the military. There has never been a comfortable relationship between President Clinton and the military, owing to perceptions about his anti-Vietnam war activities, his avoidance of military service, and his negative views on military service. Clearly however, those in the military are constrained from speaking out against presidential conduct. Nonetheless, there is sufficient concern expressed in various ways to indicate that President Clinton's character and conduct is troubling to many in the military. This is particularly disturbing when presidential character and conduct is seen as reflecting prevailing civilian culture.

The concern regarding the impact of presidential character on the military has recently been expressed in a number of ways. For example, two retired military officers who testified at the Clinton impeachment hearings pointed out that the president's actions and the apparent double standard displayed have had a negative impact on military morale.[1]

An editorial in the *Armed Forces Journal International* criticized US policy and strategy in committing military forces into Bosnia.[2] These criticisms in turn were linked to questions about the president's character and judgment:

> As the lurid saga of President Bill Clinton's trysts unfolds, he's the object of little sympathy in military quarters ... Although the majority of the American public has only recently come to realize that their president plays loose with the truth

and has a proclivity for inducing others to follow his lead with hair-splitting, semantical obfuscation, America's military forces have long seen evidence of those traits in their commander-in-chief. The US military involvement in Bosnia provides abundant illustrations of both points.[3]

In assessing the decision to implement Operation Desert Fox, Ralph Peters writes in the *Wall Street Journal*: 'Even now, I want to believe that the president is making his decisions based upon the nation's needs. But it is very difficult to maintain that belief.'[4] Addressing the trust and honor that is supposed to exist between the military and the commander-in-chief, Peters concludes that, in the main, US military men and women 'do not respect Mr Clinton – but they are ready to die for their president'.

According to opinion polls in early 1999, however, a majority of Americans gave President Clinton a job-approval rating hovering around 70 per cent, although this dropped sharply in mid-July. Polls also show that the great majority of Americans felt that President Clinton was not trustworthy. For most in the military profession, performance in an official capacity is inseparable from the 'whole' man or woman, encompassing character, conduct, honor, trust, and loyalty. While this relationship was addressed earlier, it is important to review it in light of recent events.

THE MEANING OF CULTURE

Despite its abundant usage and currency, the meaning of culture seems to defy concise definition. Even in the academic disciplines of anthropology and sociology where such a definition rightfully belongs, one finds ambiguity and senses frustration. Walter Wallace laments, 'And never having established a common definition ... culture ... it is no wonder that the catalog of sociological laws remain so empty.'[5] Alan Bernard and Jonathan Spencer do not even attempt to articulate such a definition for anthropology, stating rather, 'What makes a word like culture so important for anthropologists is precisely the argument it generates ...'.[6] As Samuel Gilmore points out, 'there is no current, widely accepted composite resolution of the definition of culture'.[7] When all the variables that can influence the definition of a concept like culture are contemplated, and the demands placed on the term by commentators from all quarters are considered, one can well understand the ambiguity and sympathize with the frustration.

The *Encyclopedia of Anthropology* states that 'The difficulty stems from the fact that the concept is used to label various states of awareness occurring at different levels of abstraction.'[8] Emphasizing this idea, Christopher Clausen comments: 'Much journalistic use of the term has to do with intermediate "cultures"' and, therefore, 'the term has come to be used indiscriminately for the very large ..., the very small ..., and the merely silly'.[9] The *Encyclopedia of*

Anthropology proposes that the different levels of usage be recognized (the authors do not recognize Clausen's 'silly' category) and be labeled 'accordingly'.[10]

According to this approach, culture is an idiosyncratic, personal culture; culture comprises 'aspects of culture held in common ... by at least two people'; and culture reflects a national culture.[11] Recognizing the possible multiple uses of the word but searching for a singular, governing concept, T. S. Eliot said that definition of culture was dependent upon 'whether we have in mind the development of an individual, of a group or class, or of a whole society'. He went on to explain, 'It is part of my thesis that the culture of the individual is dependent on the culture of the group or class, and the culture of the group or class is dependent upon the whole society to which that group or class belongs.'[12]

This does not mean that there is no agreement on the general meaning of culture. Nor do we mean to imply that academia evades tackling this elusive concept. 'Culture refers to the comprehensive change in the individual and social life, due to the continued and systematic influences of mental improvement and refinement. Whatever affects the intellectual status ... may be said to be an element in culture.'[13] Similarly, anthropologist Clifford Geertz wrote, 'man is an animal suspended in webs of significance he himself has spun, I take culture to be those webs'.[14] What many commentators find disturbing about such definitions is that they are too inclusive.

Regardless of the variety of approaches, there are at least two fundamental areas of agreement. One is that culture is exclusively human and the other is that culture is learned and therefore subject to change. The second concept is important to many commentators today because if culture is learned then it can be unlearned.

According to Johnston,

> despite variations in terminology found in definitions of culture, there are nonetheless a number of more-or-less shared elements. Culture consists of shared decision rules, recipes, standard operating procedures, and decision routines that impose a degree of order on individual and group conceptions of their relationship to their environment.[15]

Unfortunately, rarely in the literature is there an effort to prescribe how the term culture is to be used. It may be that the numerous ways the concept is used leads to the difficulty in arriving at a precise definition. As expected, this issue causes problems when addressing military culture and its relationship to civilian culture.

In the present environment, the United States may well be in a 'cultural war'. As pointed out in Chapter 4, there are any number of issues in this cultural war, ranging from immigration, diversity, multiculturalism, to the notion of Americanism. All of this has been sharpened by perceptions, rightly or wrongly, about economic prosperity and peace in the world. But, for some, the real issues go much deeper, to issues of morality, ethics, and the meaning of American values. This is reflected in the book by William Bennett, *The Death of Outrage*, and the sharp debates and conflicting statements emerging from President Clinton's impeachment and subsequent trial.[16] Is there any wonder that civilian understanding of military culture and its place in America's cultural system has been blinded by acrimonious debates about the meaning of America?

MILITARY CULTURE

We define military culture in the broadest sense, taking a cue from Johnston.[17] Culture is a way of life including norms of behavior, systems of belief, lifestyle, language, symbols, manners, and expectations. This applies both to the institution and to the individual. Military culture establishes the shape of the military 'world'. Moreover, it is this all-consuming cultural world that underpins military doctrine and the military's primary purpose. The military profession stands and falls according to its ability to maintain and reinforce this military culture.

Military culture cannot stand by itself, however. In the United States, military culture must be congruent with civilian culture. For the most part, this means that military culture must be within the 'orbit' of the American political–social system. At the same time, the military profession reasonably expects those who order the military into harm's way not only to understand military culture but to use this as a basis for shaping policy and strategy.

Almost from the time he took office President Clinton's perceived character flaws had an impact on the military. Publicity about Clinton's avoiding military service, 'loathing' of the military, and anti-Vietnam War activities deviated considerably from military culture. This led to the perception of any number of military men and women that 'duty, honor, country' had little resonance in the president's character. However, few if any presidential historians, media commentators, or members of Congress have taken time to address seriously the apparent disjuncture between the military and President Clinton. Prominent military sociologist Charles Moskos has stated, 'there has always been a kind of tone-deafness on the administration's part with regard to military culture'.[18]

In examining the views of service members about President Clinton's behavior, one writer concluded:

> No matter what Clinton has done or is accused of doing, service members said they know they still have to obey him and treat him with respect as long as he remains in office – even if the only respect some troops have left is for themselves as disciplined members of the armed forces.[19]

To reiterate, the 'gap' between the military and President Clinton does not seem to have affected civilian support for the president, at least into early 1999. For many of the president's supporters, his conduct is seen as simply reflecting the new culture. If this is true, then it is fair to ask: is military culture out of tune with civilian culture?

Fragmentation of society, balkanization of America, multiculturalism, and diversity, are common labels for American culture into the twenty-first century. Some see these developments as part of the cultural wars characterizing the changes in American society; that is, the changes brought about by the 1960s generation, characterized by a more accommodating and less stringent moral and ethical code of personal behaviour and conduct. This leads to questions about the concept of Americanism and its moral underpinning. Given the disagreements and debates over the meaning of American culture, it is difficult for the military to maintain its culture and reinforce its place in the US system. But in the military culture, it seems clear. A notion of *one* United States firmly rooted in the Declaration of Independence and the Constitution is the driving force for the military system. At the individual level, this means personal responsibility and accountability, trust, loyalty, commitment, and ultimate liability.[20]

There are military sub-cultures; that is, cultures associated with each individual service. These stem from the services' views of war fighting and their roles in various missions and contingencies.[21] Indeed, as we have stressed in this work, the military profession is not a monolith, nor do the military services agree on appropriate delineation of roles and missions. But there is no question in our view that in its primary focus, the culture of all the services is aimed at defense of the nation and is shaped by the primary mission of war fighting. Moreover, this culture has its roots in the view that killing the adversary that is a threat to the United States is a 'just' effort for the nation and the end results are morally justified. Duty, honor, and country have meaning to the military profession. This has added to the questions about the congruence between military and civilian cultures.

What further complicates the notion of military culture is the debate and disagreement about the role of the military in the world order. This is further exacerbated by changing notions about the probability of war, the concept of asymmetric wars, and the view that there is no current serious threat to the United States' vital interests. In short, the military is being affected by its involvement in a variety of missions and contingencies – operations other than war on the lower end of the conflict spectrum. Declining military readiness and 'hollow army' syndrome are increasingly becoming characteristics of the US military. Reduced resources and the problem of acquiring recruits, in both number and quality, is beginning to plague military readiness.[22] This remains the case even as proposals are made for an increase in the 1999 military budget.

In broad terms, the military is seen as an institution-in-being, well organized and equipped for the twenty-first century. Thus, it is presumed that it is ready for virtually any mission or contingency in the foreign arena. Moreover, there are those who are convinced that the military needs to move closer to society congruence. This is prompted by those who, on the one hand, acknowledge that the military is a prime fighting force, but on the other see the military as an arm of diplomacy and foreign policy – in any number of instances as the *primary* arm of foreign policy. From this it follows that the military must develop the mind-set and training to serve in a variety of non–combat missions – operations other than war. Earlier, we referred to such notions as the 'Albright syndrome'.

THE WORLD ORDER AND STRATEGIC LANDSCAPE

Another dimension of military culture and its connection with presidential leadership has its roots in strategy, policy, and political considerations. To examine this matter in somewhat more detail, there is a need to review the broader issue of world order, strategic landscape, and utility of military force.

There is an abundance of literature studying, examining, and analyzing the shape of the new world order and strategic landscape. One common view is that there is little to threaten US national interests, at least over the first two decades of the twenty-first century. Another is that the world is becoming an increasingly hostile arena and there are likely to be any number of threats to the US national interest into the first years of the next century. There are a variety of views combining elements of both these assessments.

Thus, while there is no fixed view, there appears to be some consensus that there are areas of peace, such as western Europe, and North America, surrounded by areas of turbulence, such as the Middle East, and parts of Africa and Asia. It seems clear that turmoil and turbulence in certain parts of the world will continue and is likely to increase. While there is a possibility of the rise of regional hegemons and major world powers, the more likely prospect is the emergence of large weak states. Not only are such states vulnerable to intra–state turmoil and international non–state intrusion, but they may come under the control of a small group determined to overcome weakness by resorting to a military response to internal turmoil and international intrusion.

In such a world order, the strategic landscape is likely to be an amalgam of a variety of unconventional conflicts, encompassing ethnic and religious conflicts, secessionist movements, terrorism, a combination of these, as well as asymmetric conflicts. This includes continuing threats of weapons of mass destruction.

In terms of the strategic landscape and the probability of wars, Mandelbaum concludes:

> What is increasingly unlikely is a war fought by the most powerful members of the international system ... A major war is unlikely but not unthinkable ... it is obsolete in the sense that it is no longer in fashion. It is obsolete in the sense that it no longer serves the purpose for which it was designed.[23]

However, in his study of war Kagan does not see any major change from historical behavior.[24] He concludes:

> The evidence provided by the experience of human beings living in organized societies for more than five millennia suggests ... [that] war has been more common than peace, and extended periods of peace have been rare in a world divided into multiple states. The cases we have examined indicate that good will, unilateral disarmament, the avoidance of alliances, teaching and preaching of the evils of war by those states who, generally satisfied with the state of the world, seek to preserve peace, are of no avail.[25]

There is little to suggest, however, that major wars are likely to occur in the foreseeable future. As two scholars note, 'There is no threat to America as long as the most powerful nations on the planet remain democracies.'[26] Wars of a lesser order are likely to continue. In any case, the expectations are that the military must be prepared to respond across the conflict spectrum – from unconventional conflicts to major wars and wars involving weapons of mass destruction.

> It is reasonable, and indeed necessary, for American policymakers to act on what is known about people rather than rely on a hope for a betterment of behavior. Based on this, the old Roman maxim 'si vis pacem, para bellum – if you wish peace, be prepared for war' still holds true.[27]

The strategic landscape reflects the uncertainty of the world order. This makes it extremely difficult for the military to shape force posture and doctrine for effective response to the new conflict environment. In such circumstances, the use of the military in operations other than war and in a variety of United Nations efforts challenge some basic precepts of military culture. This has caused serious misgivings within the military profession, and is likely to continue to do so.

Such matters were increasingly sharpened during the Vietnam War. In a particularly revealing and moving book about the war, Moore and Galloway show the gap between military and civilian cultures that developed.[28]

> Many of our countrymen came to hate the war we fought. Those who hated it the most – the professionally sensitive – were not, in the end, sensitive enough to differentiate between the war and the soldiers who had been ordered to fight it. They hated us as well, and we went to ground in the cross fire, as we had learned in the jungles ...
>
> We knew what Vietnam had been like, and how we looked and acted and talked and smelled. No one in America did. Hollywood got it wrong every damned time, whetting twisted political knives on the bones of our dead brothers.

CONSTRUCTIVE POLITICAL ENGAGEMENT

All of these matters – the relationship between the president and the military, the utility of military force, and presidential character and conduct – are crystallized in the debates and disagreements about divergence or congruence between civilian and military cultures. Further, these matters are essential ingredients in constructive political engagement.

We also add another consideration – these same concerns must be addressed within the military system. That is, it must constantly be stressed by training, education, and motivation, that the purpose of the military remains to defend the country and 'kill and break things' in the name of democracy; that the military requires ultimate liability in the defense of the state; that the military is not primarily a social-service organization nor an instrument for the environment or refugees. While there are commitments of the military to other operations, these should not be allowed to detract from the training, skills, and motivations for war fighting. It is vital that those in the National Command Authority, nationally elected leaders, the general public, and members of the media be aware of these issues. And, one hopes, this should lead to reasoned debate and discussion of the most acceptable and appropriate use of military force. But this cannot be done if senior military professionals, in particular, remain silent.

It must be stressed again that military culture must remain focused on war fighting and all of those matters that diminish this culture must be clearly stated, aired in public, and the American people made aware of the costs and consequences. Those who argue that such matters and actions are not in the province of the military profession, are again reminded to heed the words of General Matthew Ridgway. In looking at the role of the Army in the post-Korean era, he concluded:

> Reduction in force levels which have sorely weakened our power to meet the threat of aggression were accompanied by actions which adversely affected the spirit of the forces that remain. For reason of economy the Army was repeatedly threatened with the loss of many of those small perquisites which help maintain *esprit*, the soldier's confidence that he has the support of the people at home, that he is not the Tommy Atkins of Kipling's song, idolized in war, ignored and kicked around in peace.[29]

The analogy to the current period for all of the armed services seems clear.

General Ridgway's advice on speaking out remains the cornerstone of constructive political engagement.

> The professional soldier should never pull his punches, should never limit himself for one moment, be dissuaded from stating the honest estimates his own military experience and judgement tell him will be needed to do the job required of him.

No factor of political motivation could excuse, no reason of 'party' or political expediency could explain such an action.[30]

After serving for two years as Army Chief of Staff, General Ridgway resigned.

Constructive political engagement requires that the military profession make it clear to the United States' elected leaders and the American public the meaning of US military culture and its importance in responding to the twenty-first century. Equally important, it must make clear that military culture cannot be an exact replica of society – not if the military is expected to be effective in its primary mission. It is also clear that the commander-in-chief is a critical reference point for the military; he/she must epitomize the character and conduct expected of military professionals. One cannot expect less from those who send military men and women into harm's way. The military profession must stress that as long as the United States expects the military to defend the nation's system and way of life, it cannot expect the military to deviate from its war-fighting culture. Nor can the military profession ignore the motivations of those that are prepared to send military men and women into harm's way. However, these principles cannot be simply those that are maintained within the military profession following the notion of a 'silent order of monks'. The American public and elected officials must be made aware that such principles are essential ingredients of military culture. It is essential that senior members of the military profession take the lead in telling it like it is to the American public.

Notes

PREFACE

1. Sam C. Sarkesian, *Beyond the Battlefield: The New Military Professionalism* (New York: Pergamon Press, 1981), p. 15.

1: WAR, PEACE, POLITICS, AND THE US MILITARY

1. An excellent study of civil–military relations is Don M. Snider and Miranda A. Carlton-Carew (eds), *US Civil–Military Relations in Crisis or Transition?* (Washington, DC: Center for Strategic and International Studies, 1995).
2. The study of military profession and civil–military relations takes its cue from graduate education and military professionalism as reported in Sam C. Sarkesian, John Allen Williams, and Fred B. Bryant, *Soldiers, Society, and National Security* (Boulder, CO: Lynne Rienner, 1995).
3. For a particularly penetrating view of the historical issues associated with military professionalism see C. Robert Kemble, *The Image of the Army Officer in America: Background for Current Views* (Westport, CT: Greenwood Press, 1973). See also Maurice Matloff (ed.), *American Military History, Vol. 2, 1902–1996* (Conshohocken, PA: Combined Books, 1996); and H. R. McMaster, *Dereliction of Duty: Lyndon Johnson, Robert McNamara, the Joint Chiefs of Staff, and the Lies that Led to Vietnam* (New York: HarperCollins, 1997).
4. Alfred de Vigny, *The Military Condition*, trans. and notes Marguerite Barnett (London: Oxford University Press, 1964), p. 14. See also Maxwell Taylor, *Swords and Plowshares* (New York: W. W. Norton, 1972), pp. 254–5.
5. See, for example, Kemble, *Army Officer*, p. 127; Russell F. Weigley, *The American Way of War: A History of United States Military Strategy and Policy* (Bloomington: Indiana University Press, 1977), pp. 167–71; and Samuel P. Huntington, *The Soldier and the State: The Theory and Politics of Civil–Military Relations* (New York: Vintage Books, 1964 [1957]), p. 229, note 3.
6. Kemble, *Army Officer*, p. 127.
7. Allan R. Millett and Peter Maslowski, *For the Common Defense: A Military History of the United States of America*, revised and expanded edn (New York: Free Press, 1994), p. 259.
8. Kemble, *Army Officer*, p. 120.
9. Millett and Maslowski, *Common Defense*, p. 316. The authors examine the change in American military policy, the image of the military, and civil–military relations in Chapter 10, 'Building the Military Forces of a World Power 1899–1917'.

10. Marshall Smelser, *American History at a Glance* (New York: Barnes & Noble, 1963), p. 189.

11. John A. Garrity, *The American Nation: A History of the United States* (New York: Harper & Row, 1966), p. 698.

12. This period also included America's extension into various colonial-type ventures using Marines and Army units, such as in Nicaragua and the Panama Canal Zone. In addition Army, Marine, and Navy personnel, as well as reserve officers, were instrumental in administering the Civilian Conservation Corps (CCC) in the 1930s, following the Great Depression.

13. Richard Harwood, 'Troubled Times for the Military', *Chicago Sun-Times*, 19 July 1970, Section Two, p. 1. According to the *Chicago Sun-Times*, 9 August 1970, Section Two, p. 12, a Gallup poll found that nearly 30 per cent of those surveyed gave the Pentagon a 'highly unfavorable' rating.

14. See, for example, William Proxmire, *Report from the Wasteland* (New York: Praeger Publishers, 1970); Robert Sherrill, *Military Justice is to Justice as Military Music is to Music* (New York: Harper & Row, 1970); Seymour Hersh, *My Lai 4* (New York: Random House, 1970); and Townsend Hoopes, *The Limits of Intervention* (New York: David McKay, 1970).

15. Sam C. Sarkesian, 'The Military Image: Myths and Realities: A Political Perspective'. Paper prepared for delivery at the sixty-sixth annual meeting of the American Political Science Association, Los Angeles, California, 8–12 September 1970.

16. Gen. H. Norman Schwarzkopf with Peter Petre, *The Autobiography: It Doesn't Take a Hero* (New York: Linda Grey Bantam Books, 1992), pp. 181, 201. See also pp. 186–7. See also Lt-Gen. Harold G. Moore (Ret.) and Joseph L. Galloway, *We Were Soldiers Once ... and Young: Ia Drang: The Battle that Changed the War in Vietnam* (New York: Random House, 1992).

17. Moore and Galloway, *We Were Soldiers Once*, p. xv.

18. Mark J. Eitelberg and Roger D. Little, 'Influential Elites and the American Military after the Cold War', in Snider and Carlton-Carew (eds), *US Civil–Military Relations*, p. 35.

19. McMaster, *Dereliction of Duty*, pp. 300–34. See also Lewis Sorley, *Honorable Warrior General Harold K. Johnson and the Ethics of Command* (Lawrence: University of Kansas Press, 1998).

20. McMaster, *Dereliction of Duty*, pp. 333–4. In the most recent period, the issue of the silence of the most senior military professionals surfaced again. See Rick Maze, 'Congress Hears Readiness Woes: Top Military Brass Takes Tongue Lashing', *Army Times*, 12 October 1998, p. 4. Maze writes,

> As the Joint Chiefs warned of growing readiness problems, one big question loomed over the Senate hearings. What took them so long to be candid? The Chiefs took a tongue lashing from Sen. John McCain, R.-Ariz ... The chiefs never mentioned readiness problems, the pay gap or retired pay during the February hearings where they defended the 1999 budget request ... 'The fact is, with the exception of the Marine Corps, you were not candid', McCain said.

21. Jeffrey Record, *The Wrong War: Why We Lost in Vietnam* (Annapolis, MD: Naval Institute Press, 1998), p. 67.

22. Ibid., p. 67.

23. See Robert S. McNamara with Brian VanDeMark, *In Retrospect: The Tragedy and Lessons of Vietnam* (New York: Times Books, 1995).

24. See, for example, Charles W. Kegley Jr, and Eugene R. Wittkopf, *World Politics: Trends and Transformations*, 6th edn (New York: St Martin's Press, 1997); Michael T. Klare and Yogesh Chandran (eds), *World Security: Challenges for a New Century*, 3rd edn (New York: St Martin's Press, 1998); Bruce Russett and Harvey Starr, *World Politics: The Menu*

for Choice (New York: W. H. Freeman, 1996); and David W. Zeigler, *War, Peace, and International Politics*, 7th edn (New York: Longman, 1997).

25. See, for example, US House of Representatives, Committee on Armed Services, *Women in the Military: The Tailhook Affair and the Problem of Sexual Harassment* (Washington, DC: US House of Representatives, September 1992). See also David Evans, 'Tailhook Report Rips Navy', *Chicago Tribune*, 24 April 1993, pp. 1, 4. See also Paul M. Maubert. In an op-ed piece, 'Don't Blame Personnel Drain on the Economy', *Army Times*, 22 June 1998, p. 62. The author cites his extensive contacts with active-duty personnel in the Army, and argues that what is lacking is leadership by those in the senior military ranks. For example, he writes that many junior officers and noncommissioned officers feel that 'Starting at basic training, leadership is chosen for its willingness to espouse correct party line rather than any warlike qualities.' See also David McCormick, *The Downsized Warrior: America's Army in Transition* (New York: New York University Press, 1998).

26. See, for example, Katherine Boo, 'Universal Soldier: What Every Woman Can Learn from the Heroine of Tailhook', *Washington Monthly*, September 1992, pp. 37–40. See also Elisabetta Addis, Valeria E. Russo, and Lorenza Sebesta (eds), *Women Soldiers: Images and Realities* (New York: St Martin's Press, 1997), and Christopher Jehn, 'Women in the Military', SSP Seminar, Security Studies Program, Massachusetts Institute of Technology, 19 February 1997.

27. Lt-Col. Robert L. Maginnis, 'A Chasm of Values', *Military Review*, 73, 2 (February 1993), p. 11.

28. See McMaster, *Dereliction of Duty*.

29. 'The Starr Report', *Chicago Tribune*, 13 September 1998, pp. 2–29 and the 'Clinton Response', pp. 30–5.

30. Bradley Graham, 'Military Leaders Consider Impact of Clinton Affair', Washington-post.com Special Report: 'Clinton Accused', 15 September 1998, p. A10.

31. Col. Harry G. Summers Jr, 'Clinton betrayal imperils us all', *Army Times*, 14 September 1998, p. 62.

32. George Melloan, 'Costs to America of an Embarrassing Leader', *Wall Street Journal*, 15 September 1998, p. A23.

33. See, for example, 'Clinton's Warrior Woes: Can a Man Who Avoided the Draft Ever Prove Himself as America's Commander in Chief?', *US News and World Report*, 15 March 1993, pp. 22–4.

34. The phrase 'fog of peace' is taken from John T. Fishel, *The Fog of Peace: Planning and Executing the Restoration of Panama* (Carlisle, PA: US Army War College Strategic Studies Institute, 1992).

35. Hon. John F. Lehman Jr, and Dr Harvey Sicherman, *The Demilitarization of the Military*, Report of a Defense Task Force (Philadelphia, PA: Foreign Policy Research Institute, 1997). See also Eliot Cohen, 'Are US Forces Overstretched? Civil–Military Relations', *Orbis: A Journal of World Affairs*, 41, 2 (Spring 1997), pp. 177–86.

36. Lehman and Sicherman, *Demilitarization*, p. 177.

37. Cohen, 'Are US Forces Overstretched?', p. 186.

38. John D. Steinbruner, 'Reluctant Strategic Realignment: The Need for a New View of National Security', *Brookings Review* (Winter 1995), p. 4.

39. Millett and Maslowski, *Common Defense*, p. 263.

40. Robert D. Kaplan, 'Fort Leavenworth and the Eclipse of Nationhood', *Atlantic Monthly*, 278, 3 (September 1996), pp. 75–8, 80–6, 88–90.

41. See Patrick Pexton, 'Future Seizes Operations Other Than War', *Army Times*, 25 November 1996, p. 8, in which the reporter writes that 'Vision 2010 embraces humanitarian, peacekeeping missions.'

42. Col. Robert Killebrew, 'Why War is Still War: Operations Other Than War Are Proving Awfully Warlike', *Armed Forces Journal International* (January 1995), p. 35. See also his

article, 'Deterrence With a Vengeance; Combat Infantrymen Remain the Best Choice for Peace Enforcement Operations', *Armed Forces Journal International* (October 1998), pp. 76, 78, 80–1.

43. See Glenn W. Goodman Jr, 'The Green Berets – Still the Best', *Armed Forces Journal International* (December 1996), pp. 42–5.
44. John T. Fishel, *Civil Military Operations in the New World* (Westport, CT: Praeger, 1997).
45. Ibid., p. 235.
46. For an excellent analysis of this issue see Lawrence Freedman, *The Revolution in Strategic Affairs*, Adelphi Paper 318 (New York: Oxford University Press, 1998).
47. Chairman of the Joint Chiefs of Staff, *Joint Vision 2010* (Washington, DC: Department of Defense, 1996).
48. This includes the publication, *The Army Enterprise Strategy* (Washington, DC: Department of the Army, August 1994), which appears to have anticipated *Joint Vision 2010*. Subsequently, the Army published *Vision 2010* (see Note 41).
49. Jeffrey B. White, 'Some Thoughts on Irregular Warfare', *Studies in Intelligence*, 39, 5 (1996), p. 51.
50. Ibid.
51. See Mark T. Clark, 'The Continuing Relevance of Clausewitz', *Strategic Review* (Winter 1998), pp. 54–61. The author examines the ongoing debate about the relevance of Clausewitzian theory in future wars and concludes that core elements of Clausewitz's theory are still useful for understanding most, if not all, forms of conflict and suggests areas for further research (p. 54). See also Col. Robert B. Killebrew, 'The Army After Next; TRADOC's Crystal Ball Eyes Service's Shape Beyond Force XXI', *Armed Forces Journal International* (October 1966).
52. A reference to the five Joint Chiefs of Staff of the US military during the Vietnam War.

2: THE MILITARY PROFESSION

Many of the ideas and assessments in this chapter are based on an earlier work, Sam C. Sarkesian, *Beyond the Battlefield: The New Military Professionalism* (New York: Pergamon Press, 1981).

1. Lt-Col. (Ret.) Lawrence P. Crocker, *Army Officer's Guide*, 45th edn (Harrisburg, PA: Stackpole Books, 1990), p. 59. The same author notes that officers should 'Avoid the Political. Be somewhat guarded in your political comments … Soldiers must be nonpolitical and serve each [political party] with equal zeal' (p. 55).
2. Gen. Sir John Hackett, *The Profession of Arms* (New York: Macmillan, 1983), p. 9.
3. Samuel P. Huntington, *The Soldier and the State*, p. 19.
4. Ibid., p. 20.
5. Sam C. Sarkesian, *The Professional Army Officer in a Changing Society* (Chicago, IL: Nelson-Hall, 1975).
6. Ibid., p. 36. See also Sam C. Sarkesian and Thomas M. Gannon, 'Introduction: Military Professionalism', in Sam C. Sarkesian and Thomas M. Gannon (eds), 'Military Ethics and Professionalism', special issue of *American Behavioral Scientist*, 19, 8 (May/June 1976), p. 36.
7. Sarkesian, *Beyond the Battlefield*, p.36.
8. This and the following quote are from Hackett, *The Profession of Arms*, p. 202.
9. McCormick, *The Downsized Warrior*, pp. 162–3.
10. Paul Christopher, 'Unjust War and Moral Obligation: What Should Officers Do?', *Parameters: US Army War College Quarterly*, 25, 3 (Autumn 1995), p. 86.
11. Walter Millis, 'Puzzle of the Military Mind', *New York Times*, 18 November 1972, p. 144.

12. Orville D. Menard, *The Army and the Fifth Republic* (Lincoln: University of Nebraska Press, 1967), p. 5, in which the author writes:

> An Army is an emanation of the nation it serves, reflecting social, political, and technological foundations ... An army is not a mirror image of the nation, nor a microcosm – the nation writ small; it is in organization, purposes, attitude, and behavior conditioned by the sustaining state.

13. Sam C. Sarkesian, John Allen Williams, and Fred B. Bryant, *Soldiers, Society, and National Security* (Boulder, CO: Lynne Rienner, 1995), p. 16.
14. Sarkesian and Gannon, 'Introduction: Military Professionalism', p. 503.
15. Lt-Col. (Ret.) Lawrence P. Crocker, *Army Officer's Guide*, 47th edn (Harrisburg, PA: Stackpole Books, 1996), pp. 29, 30.
16. Ibid., p. 30.
17. The characteristics of professions are discussed in a number of publications including Walter Millis, *Arms and Men* (New York: Putnam, 1956); Sam C. Sarkesian, *The Professional Army Officer in a Changing Society* (Chicago: Nelson-Hall, 1975); Huntington, *The Soldier and the State*; Morris Janowitz, *The Professional Soldier: A Social and Political Portrait* (Glencoe, IL: Free Press, 1960); and Franklin D. Margiotta (ed.), *The Changing World of the American Military* (Boulder, CO: Westview Press, 1978). For a particularly insightful look at the Navy, see John Allen Williams, 'The NEW Military Professionals', *US Naval Institute Proceedings*, 122/5/1,119 (May 1996), pp. 42–8.
18. Huntington, *The Soldier and the State*, and Janowitz, *The Professional Soldier*. See also Samuel E. Finer, *The Man on Horseback: The Role of the Military in Politics* (New York: Praeger, 1962).
19. See, for example, A. M. Carr-Saunders and P. A. Wilson, *The Professions* (Oxford: Clarendon Press, 1933); Arthur A. Ekirch Jr, *The Civilian and the Military* (New York: Oxford University Press, 1956); Louis Smith, *American Democracy and Military Power: A Study of Civil Control of the Military Power in the United States* (Chicago: University of Chicago Press, 1951).
20. Huntington, *The Soldier and the State*, p. 11.
21. Ibid., p. 13.
22. Ibid., p. 464.
23. Samuel P. Huntington, 'The Soldier and the State in the 1970s', in Margiotta (ed.), *The Changing World of the American Military*, p.16.
24. The quotes in this paragraph are from Huntington, 'The Soldier and the State in the 1970s', p. 33 (italics in the original).
25. Huntington, *The Soldier and the State*, p. 456.
26. Janowitz, *The Professional Soldier*, pp. 264–5.
27. Ibid., p. xi.
28. Ibid., p. 418.
29. This and the following quote are from Janowitz, *The Professional Soldier*, p. 440.
30. Charles C. Moskos, 'The Emergent Military', *Pacific Sociological Review*, 16 (1973), pp. 255–80.
31. Sarkesian, *Beyond the Battlefield*, p. 188. See also James Clotfelter, *The Military in American Politics* (New York: Harper & Row, 1973); Gene M. Lyons and John W. Masland, *Education and Military Leadership* (Princeton, NJ: Princeton University Press, 1959); and John W. Masland and Laurence I. Radway, *Soldiers and Scholars* (Princeton, NJ: Princeton University Press, 1957).
32. Snider and Carlton-Carew (eds), *US Civil–Military Relations*.
33. Sarkesian, Williams, and Bryant, *Soldiers, Society, and National Security*.
34. Ibid., p. 153.

35. F. G. Hoffman, *Decisive Force: The New American Way of War* (Westport, CT: Praeger, 1996).
36. Ibid., p. 6.
37. Ibid., p. 14.
38. See Janowitz, *The Professional Soldier*.
39. See, for example, Moskos, 'The Emergent Military', and Lt-Col. William Hauser, *America's Army in Transition: A Study in Civil–Military Relations* (Baltimore, MD: Johns Hopkins University Press, 1973), pp. 202–12.
40. Sarkesian, Williams, and Bryant, *Soldiers, Society, and National Security*, p. 161. See also the following: Huntington, 'The Soldier and the State in the 1970s', pp. 32–3; and Maj. Steve Eden, 'Preserving the Force in the New World Order', *Military Review*, 74, 6 (June 1994), pp. 2–7. The winner of the 1993 *Military Review* writing contest, this article argues that the army must be prepared for challenges in the new world order by establishing three training priorities.

> Certain units – we will call them Class A units – would be 'fenced off' from operations other than war, solely dedicated to conventional combat. Class B units would train primarily for conventional warfare, though sustaining a minimum level of expertise in more mundane aspects of operations other than war. Class C units … would prepare for missions other than high-intensity maneuver warfare. (pp. 4–5)

41. See, for example, Sean D. Naylor, 'Two Wars, Two Opinions', *Army Times*, 20 January 1997, p. 3, in which the author notes the disagreements between the Army and the Air Force regarding the two-war strategy.
42. See Mackubin Thomas Owens, 'Organizing For Failure: Is The Rush Toward "Jointness" Going Off Track?', *Armed Forces Journal International* (June 1998), pp. 12–13. Also see Senator Dan Coats (R., Indiana), 'Joint Experimentation: Anything But Strategic Monism', *Armed Forces Journal International* (August 1998), pp. 46–7.
43. Keith D. McFarland, 'The 1949 Revolt of the Admirals', in Lloyd J. Matthews and Dale E. Brown (eds), *The Parameters of War: Military History from the Journal of the US Army War College* (Washington, DC: Pergamon-Brassey's, 1987), pp. 149–63.
44. Ibid., p. 149.
45. Lt-Col. (Ret.) Ralph Peters, 'Wasting Talent the Army Way', *Army Times*, 16 March 1998, p. 35.
46. McCormick, *The Downsized Warrior*, p. 121.
47. Ibid., pp. 121–2.
48. Frederick C. Thayer, 'Professionalism: The Hard Choice', in Frank Trager and Philip S. Kronenberg (eds), *National Security and American Society: Theory and Process, and Policy* (Lawrence, KS: University of Kansas Press, 1973), p. 568.

3: POLITICS AND THE MILITARY: A HISTORICAL INTRODUCTION

1. Huntington, *The Soldier and the State*.
2. Russell F. Weigley, 'The American Military and the Principle of Civilian Control from McClellan to Powell', *Journal of Military History*, 57 (October 1993), p. 36.
3. Huntington, *The Soldier and the State*, p. 206.
4. Ibid., p. 207.
5. The first military secretary in American history was Maj.-Gen. Benjamin Lincoln who was named Secretary of War in 1781. After the Constitutional Convention had done its work, Henry Knox became the first Secretary of War and head of the newly established War Department in August 1789. See William Gardner Bell, *Commanding Generals and Chiefs of Staff, 1775–1983* (Washington, DC: Center of Military History United States

Army, 1983), p. 7.

6. Bell, *Commanding Generals*, p. 5.
7. Douglas Southall Freeman, *George Washington, A Biography*, V, *Victory with the Help of France* (New York: Charles Scribner's Sons, 1952), p. 387.
8. It has been established that the two anonymous Newburgh addresses were, in fact, written by Maj. John Armstrong. See Trevor Dupuy and Gary M. Hammerman, *People and Events of the American Revolution* (New York: R. R. Bowker, 1974), p. 272.
9. See Dupuy and Hammerman, *People and Events of the American Revolution*.
10. James Kirby Martin and Mark Edward Lender, *A Respectable Army: The Military Origins of the Republic, 1763–1789* (Arlington Heights, IL: Harlan Davidson, 1982), p. 188.
11. Ibid.
12. Ibid.
13. Millett and Maslowski, *Common Defense*, p. 89.
14. Remonstrance of the Army. On 20 November 1647, after the end of the English Civil War, a delegation of Army officers laid before the House of Commons a political manifesto which, while aiming at bringing Charles I to trial, called for a fundamental change in the government and an expansion of powers of the representative body. The remonstrance also dealt with due compensation for the Army. When presented to Parliament it was entitled the 'Declaration of the army' and as such became part of the constitutional tradition. Pride's Purge: Fearful that the peace faction in Parliament would reach an accommodation with Charles, Colonel Thomas Pride's infantry regiment entered the House and prevented those members whose views were 'inimical to the army' from taking their seats. Between 80 and 90 were so treated, thus producing the 'Rump parliament'. See Ian Gentles, *The New Model Army in England, Ireland and Scotland, 1643–1645* (Oxford: Blackwell, 1992), pp. 272–83. For the full text of the Declaration of the Army, see John P. Kenyon, *The Stuart Constitution, 1603–1688*, 2nd edn (Cambridge: Cambridge University Press, 1986), pp. 263–8. After assuming the title of Lord Protector in December 1653, Oliver Cromwell appointed 11 'Major generals in the late summer of 1655 to supervise the government of the English provinces ...', thus creating something akin to a military dictatorship. See Barry Coward, *Oliver Cromwell: Profiles in Power* (London: Longman, 1991), p. 131.
15. Dupuy and Hammerman, *People and Events*, p. 272.
16. Bell, *Commanding Generals*, p. 7.
17. Ibid.
18. Ibid.
19. Millet and Maslowski, *Common Defense*, p. 126.
20. Ibid. This was far different than the Prussian General staff of 1816. See US Army Center for Military History, *American Military History, Army Historical Series*.
21. Huntington, *The Soldier and the State*, pp. 195–203.
22. Bell, *Commanding Generals*, p. 26.
23. Winfield Scott, *The Memoirs of Lieutenant General Winfield S. Scott, LL.D.* (Freeport, NY: Books for Libraries Press, 1970), vol. I, p. 35.
24. Ibid.
25. Donald R. Hickey, *The War of 1812: A Forgotten Conflict* (Urbana, IL: University of Illinois Press, 1989), p. 76.
26. Bell, *Commanding Generals*, p. 157.
27. See Martin and Lender, *Respectable Army*, pp. 110–13.
28. Bell, *Commanding Generals*, p. 10, and Millet and Maslowski, *Common Defense*, p. 127.
29. Scott, *Memoirs*, p. 12.
30. Ibid., p. 38.
31. Ibid.
32. John S. D. Eisenhower, *Agent of Destiny: The Life and Times of General Winfield Scott*

(New York: Free Press, 1997). The quotes in this paragraph are from p. 205.

33. James M. McPherson, *Battle Cry of Freedom* (New York: McGraw-Hill, 1989), p. 48.
34. Eisenhower, *Agent of Destiny*, p. 226.
35. Ibid., p. 229.
36. Scott, *Memoirs*, p. 399.
37. Ibid., p. 400.
38. As quoted in Millet and Maslowski, *Common Defense*, p. 156.
39. Eisenhower, *Agent of Destiny*, p. 307.
40. Ibid., p. 357.
41. Scott, *Memoirs*, II, p. 627.
42. Russell F. Weigley, 'The American Military and the Principle of Civilian Control from McClellan to Powell', *Journal of Military History,* 57 (October 1993): 36.
43. Ibid.
44. Bruce Catton, *Mr Lincoln's Army* (Garden City, NY: Doubleday, 1951), p. 80.
45. Ibid., p. 81.
46. Ibid.
47. Bruce Tap, *Over Lincoln's Shoulder: The Committee on the Conduct of the War* (Lawrence, KS: University Press of Kansas, 1998), p. 101.
48. T. Harry Williams, *Lincoln and His Generals* (New York: Alfred Knopf, 1952), p. 46.
49. Ibid.
50. See Weigley, *The American Way of War*, p. 133.
51. Williams, *Lincoln and His Generals*, p. 66.
52. Tap, *Over Lincoln's Shoulder*, p. 102.
53. Catton, *Lincoln's Army*, p. 324.
54. McPherson, *Battle Cry*, p. 414.
55. Ibid., p. 510.
56. As quoted in Bruce Catton, *Grant Takes Command* (Boston, MA: Little, Brown, 1968), p. 111.
57. William S. McFeely, *Grant, A Biography* (New York: W. W. Norton, 1981), p. 96.
58. R. Ernest Dupuy and Trevor Dupuy, *The Harper Encyclopedia of Military History: From 3500 BC to the Present* (New York: HarperCollins, 1993), pp. 977–9.
59. McFeely, *Grant*, p. 78.
60. Ibid., pp. 263–4.
61. Ibid., p. 271.
62. Robert M. Utley, *Frontier Regulars, the United States Army and the Indian 1866–1891* (New York: Macmillan, 1973), p. 15.
63. Robert G. Athern, *William Tecumseh Sherman and the Settlement of the West* (Norman, OK: University of Oklahoma Press, 1956), p. 233.
64. Stanley Hirshon, *The White Tecumseh* (New York: John Wiley, 1997), p. 346.
65. As quoted in Athearn, *Sherman and the West*, p. 262.
66. Ibid., p. 240.
67. Ibid., p. 16.
68. Bell, *Commanding Generals*, p. 20.
69. Weigley, 'American Military and Civil Control', p. 36.
70. Stephen Ambrose, *Duty Honor Country: A History of West Point* (Baltimore, MD: Johns Hopkins University Press, 1966), p. 181. (Note that General Scott was a staunch supporter of the Academy.)

4: CIVILIAN AND MILITARY CULTURES

1. See, for example, Fred Whitehead (ed.), *Culture Wars: Opposing Viewpoints* (San Diego, CA: Greenhaven Press, 1994); Arthur M. Schlesinger Jr, *The Disuniting of America: Reflections on a Multicultural Society*, revised edn (New York: W. W. Norton, 1998); Deborah Tannen, *The Argument Culture: Moving from Debate to Dialogue* (New York: Random House, 1998); Alan Wolfe, *One Nation, After All: What Americans Really Think About God, Country, Family, Racism, Welfare, Immigration, Homosexuality, Work, The Right, The Left and Each Other* (New York: Viking Press, 1998); John T. Miller, *Americans No More? The Unmaking of Americans: How Multiculturalism Has Undermined America's Assimilation Ethic* (New York: Free Press, 1998); and Michael Desch, 'Culture and Society', presentation at the SSP Seminar, Center for International Studies, Massachusetts Institute of Technology, 9 October 1996.
2. See Note 1 and Georgie Ann Geyer, 'Dictators, Democrats, and Demagogues', speech at the National Strategy Forum, Chicago, Illinois, 4 December 1996. See also Georgie Ann Geyer, *Americans No More: The Death of Citizenship* (New York: Atlantic Monthly Press, 1996).
3. Geyer, 'Dictators, Democrats, and Demagogues'.
4. Clinton Rossiter, *The Political Thought of the American Revolution: Part Three of Seedtime of the Republic* (New York: Harcourt, Brace, 1963).
5. See, for example, Charles W. Kegley Jr, and Eugene R. Wittkopf, *American Foreign Policy: Patterns and Process*, 5th edn (New York: St Martin's Press, 1996).
6. Dennis L. Bark, 'Europe: America's Heritage', *The United States Institute of Peace Journal* (May 1989), p. 1.
7. Stephen E. Ambrose, *Citizen Soldiers: The US Army from the Normandy Beaches to the Bulge to the Surrender of Germany June 7, 1944–May 7, 1945* (New York: Simon & Schuster, 1997), p. 472.
8. See, for example, Raymond C. Taras and Rajat Ganguly, *Understanding Ethnic Conflict: The International Dimension* (New York: Longman, 1998), pp. 48–53.
9. David Gress, 'The Idea of the West', Internet, Foreign Policy Research Institute, FPRI@AOL.COM. This and the previous quote are from David Gress, *From Plato to NATO: The Idea of the West and Its Opponents* (New York: Free Press, 1998).
10. See, for example, Kenneth D. Wald, *Religion and Politics in the United States*, 2nd edn (Washington, DC: CQ Press, 1992).
11. See, for example, John Mearsheimer, 'Why We Will Soon Miss the Cold War', *Atlantic Monthly* (August 1990), pp. 23–30.
12. Colin Powell with Joseph E. Persica, *My American Journey* (New York: Random House, 1995), p. 610.
13. Wald, *Religion and Politics*, p. 338.
14. Thomas E. Ricks, *Making the Corps* (New York: Scribner, 1998).
15. Ibid., p. 20.
16. John Hillen, 'No Keepin'em on the Farm Once They've Seen Paris', *American Enterprise* (May/June 1998), p. 82.
17. The importance of primary groups (buddy system) in the military, unit cohesion and effectiveness is studied in W. Darryl Henderson, *Cohesion: The Human Element in Combat* (Washington, DC: National Defense University Press, 1985). See also Edward A. Shils and Morris Janowitz, 'Cohesion and Disintegration in the Wehrmacht in World War II', *Public Opinion Quarterly* (Summer 1948), pp. 280–315, and Morris Janowitz and Roger Little, *Sociology and the Military Establishment*, revised edn (New York: Russell Sage Foundation, 1965), pp. 77–99. See also Ambrose, *Citizen Soldiers*, pp. 22–3.
18. John Hillen, 'The Military Culture Wars', *Weekly Standard*, 12 January 1998, p. 11.

19. The ideas in this paragraph are from Sarkesian, *The Professional Army Officer*, p. 7.
20. Russell B. Reynolds, *The Officer's Guide* (Harrisburg, PA: Stackpole Books, 1970), p. 87.
21. Sam C. Sarkesian, 'The US Military Must Find Its Voice', *Orbis* (Summer 1998), p. 437.

5: THE NATIONAL SECURITY SYSTEM

1. Donald M. Snow, *National Security: Defence Policy in a Changed International Order*, 4th edn (New York: St Martin's Press, 1993), p. 6.
2. Adapted from Sam C. Sarkesian, *US National Security: Policymakers, Processes, and Politics*, 2nd edn (Boulder, CO: Lynne Rienner, 1995), p. 81.
3. Robert Holzer, 'Marine Corps Turns to Academia and Industry for Experts', *Navy Times*, 13 July 1998, p. 26.
4. Michael T. Klare and Daniel C. Thomas (eds), *World Security: Challenges for a New Century* (New York: St Martin's Press, 1991), p. 3.
5. Sun Tzu, *The Art of War*, trans. and introduction Samuel B. Griffith (New York: Oxford University Press, 1971).
6. Hillen, 'The US Role in Global Security', p. 3.
7. Carnes Lord, 'Strategy and Organization at the National Level', in James C. Gaston (ed.), *Grand Strategy and the Decisionmaking Process* (Washington, DC: National Defense University Press, 1992), pp. 141–59.
8. Gordon A. Craig and Alexander L. George, *Force and Statecraft: Diplomatic Problems of Our Time*, 3rd edn (New York: Oxford University Press, 1995), p. 258.
9. Robert Ellsworth, 'American National Security in the Early 21st Century', in David Jablonsky *et al.*, *US National Security: Beyond the Cold War* (Carlisle, PA: US Army War College, Strategic Studies Institute, 1997), p. 93.
10. National interests can be defined in a variety of ways. However, there are certain reference points that need to be included in any definition. These are included here. For other definitions see, for example, Jablonsky *et al.*, *US National Security*.
11. Ray S. Cline, *World Power Assessment: A Calculus or Strategic Drift* (Washington, DC: Center for Strategic and International Studies, 1975), p. 11.
12. Adda Bozeman, *Strategic Intelligence and Statecraft: Selected Essays* (Washington, DC: Brassey's, 1992).
13. Craig and George, *Force and Statecraft*, p. 273.
14. Hoffman, *Decisive Force*, p. 131.

6: CIVIL–MILITARY RELATIONS

This is a revised version of a paper presented at the Mershon Center Conference on Civil–Military Relations, The Ohio State University, Columbus, Ohio, 3–6 December 1992.

1. Sam C. Sarkesian, 'Military Professionalism and Civil–Military Relations in the West', *International Political Science Review*, 2, 3 (1981), p. 285.
2. James Alden Barber Jr, 'The Military Services and American Society: Relationships and Attitudes', in Stephen E. Ambrose and James A. Barber Jr (eds), *The Military and American Society: Essays and Readings* (New York: Macmillan, 1967), p. 160. See also Allan R. Millett, *The American Political System and Civilian Control of the Military: A Historical Perspective* (Columbus: Ohio State University Press, 1979).
3. See, for example, Andrew J. Bacevich, 'Absent History: A Comment on Dauber, Desch, and Feaver', *Armed Forces and Society*, 24, 5 (Spring 1998), pp. 447–53.
4. Thomas R. Dye, *Politics in America*, 3rd edn (Upper Saddle River, NJ: Prentice-Hall,

1999), p. 598. In analyzing events up to March 1997, the International Institute for Strategic Studies, *Strategic Survey 1997–98* (London: Oxford University Press, 1998), pp. 73–4, concluded: 'the US basked in an extraordinary glow of good fortune. The economy was roaring along at some of the highest levels of growth and employment since the 1970s.'

5. Huntington, *The Soldier and the State*, and Janowitz, *The Professional Soldier*. See also Finer, *The Man on Horseback*.

6. See, for example, Carr-Saunders and Wilson, *The Professions*, Ekirch, *The Civilian and the Military*, and Louis Smith, *American Democracy and Military Power*.

7. Don M. Snider and Miranda A. Carlton-Carew, 'The Current State of US Civil–Military Relations: An Introduction', in Snider and Carlton-Carew (eds), *US Civil–Military Relations*, pp. 8–14.

8. James Burk, 'The Logic of Crisis and Civil–Military Relations Theory: A Comment on Desch, Feaver, and Dauber', *Armed Forces and Society*, 24, 3 (Spring 1998), p. 462.

9. Sarkesian, *Beyond the Battlefield*, p. 188. See also Clotfelter, *The Military in American Politics*, Lyons and Masland, *Education and Military Leadership*, and Masland and Radway, *Soldiers and Scholars*.

10. Joseph Ellis and Robert Moore, *School for Soldiers: West Point and the Profession of Arms* (New York: Oxford University Press, 1974), p. 180.

11. Moore and Galloway, *We Were Soldiers Once*, p. xv.

12. Michael I. Handel, *Masters of War: Classical Strategic Thought*, second revised and expanded edn (London: Frank Cass, 1996).

13. Ibid., p. 9, and the following quote from p. 246.

14. Ibid., p. 247.

15. Peter Braestrup, *Big Story: How the American Press and Television Reported and Interpreted the Crisis of Tet 1968 in Vietnam and Washington*, I (Boulder, CO: Westview Press, 1977), p. 184.

16. *Reporting the Next War*, Cantigny Conference Series, Robert R. McCormick Tribune Foundation, report of a conference held at Cantigny, Wheaton, Illinois, 23–24 April 1992, pp. 9–10.

17. See, for example, 'CNN retracts Tailwind coverage' from Internet CNN.COM, 8 July 1998; Paul Glastris, 'Are Press Standards Slipping?', *US News & World Report*, 13 July 1998, p. 22; News Briefs, *Army Times*, 3 August 1998, p. 2; and Neil Creighton, 'War Stories that Never Happened', *Chicago Tribune*, 2 August 1998, sec. 1, p. 17.

18. See, for example, William Matthews, 'Generals Side with Clinton: But Critics Say Retired Officials Have Ax to Grind', *Army Times*, 26 October 1992, p. 19.

19. Clifford Krauss, 'Foley to Oust House Panel Chief over Jockeying to Join Cabinet', *New York Times*, 9 January 1993, p. 1.

20. See, for example, the commentary by Charles Moskos, 'Don't Ignore Good Reasons for Homosexual Ban', *Army Times*, 16 March 1992, p. 31.

21. See, for example, Greg Seigle, 'Boys will be Boys, Tailhook, Gulf War Assaults Spotlight Army Attitudes', *Army Times*, 27 July 1992, pp. 12–14.

22. James McHugh, 'McKinney Guilty on One Count', *Army Times*, 23 March 1998, p. 16.

23. Steven F. Rausch, 'America, the Army and the Buffalo Soldiers', *Military Review*, 72, 7 (July 1992), p. 2.

24. Sarkesian, *Beyond the Battlefield*, p. 285.

25. Sam C. Sarkesian, John Allen Williams, and Fred C. Bryant, 'Civilian Graduate Education and the US Military Profession', paper prepared for presentation at the American Political Science Association Convention, Chicago, Illinois, 3–6 September 1992.

26. See, for example, 'Darts and Laurels', *Armed Forces Journal International* (February 1998), p. 48. The staff of the journal gave a 'dart' to the 'Commander-in-Chief Clinton for continuing to cloud the issue of US military involvement in Bosnia'.

27. David Callahan, *Unwinnable Wars: American Power and Ethnic Conflict*, Twentieth Century Fund Book (New York: Hill and Wong, 1997), p. 188. See also Col. (Ret.) Robert B. Killibrew, 'Deterrence With a Vengeance: Combat Infantrymen Remain The Best Choice For Peace Enforcement Operations', *Armed Forces Journal International* (October 1998). On p. 76, the author states, 'The US Army has begun using "stability operations" to refer to the broad range of peace activities, that fall short of actual conflict, but where the possibility of a transition to full-scale fighting exists.'

28. Alan Ned Sabrosky and Robert L. Sloane (eds), *The Recourse to War: An Appraisal of the "Weinberger Doctrine"* (Carlisle, PA: US Army War College Strategic Studies Institute, 1988).

29. Powell, *My American Journey*, p. 434.

30. Huntington, 'The Soldier and the State in the 1970s', p. 31.

31. Ibid., p. 33 (italics in the original).

32. Herbert Garfinkel, 'Introduction', in Andrew J. Goodpaster and Samuel P. Huntington *et al.* (eds), *Civil–Military Relations* (Washington, DC: American Enterprises Institute for Public Policy, 1977), p. 2.

33. Sam C. Sarkesian and John Allen Williams, 'Civil–Military Relations in the New Era', paper presented at the US Army War College/National Strategy Forum Workshop on 'US Domestic and National Security Agendas: Into the 21st Century', Cantigny, Illinois, 17–19 September 1992.

34. Gerald E. Miller, 'The Future Demands of Military Professionalism: The views of a Retired Navy Vice Admiral', in Margiotta, *The Changing World of the American Military*, pp. 385–94.

35. Ibid., p. 388.

36. Douglas Johnson and Steven Metz, 'American Civil–Military Relations: A Review of the Recent Literature', in Snider and Carlton-Carew (eds), *US Civil–Military Relations In Crisis or Transition?*, p. 217.

37. The temper of this debate is seen in articles appearing in *Armed Forces and Society*. See especially the issue on 'A Symposium on Civil–Military Relations', 24, 3 (Spring 1998). See also the following: Peter D. Feaver, 'The Civil–Military Problematique: Huntington, Janowitz and the Question of Civilian Control', 25, 2 (Winter 1996), pp. 149–78; Andrew J. Bacevich, 'Absent History: A Comment on Dauber, Desch, and Feaver', 24, 3 (Spring 1998), pp. 447–54; Michael C. Desch, 'A Historian's Fallacies: A Reply to Bacevich', 24, 4 (Summer 1998), pp. 589–94; in the same issue, Peter D. Feaver, 'Modeling Civil–Military Relations: A Reply to Burk and Bacevich', pp. 595–602.

38. See William Tecumseh Sherman, *Memoirs of General W. T. Sherman* (New York: The Library of America, 1990), p. 879, where Sherman writes, 'There is a soul to an army as well as to the individual man, and no General can accomplish the full work of his army unless he commands the soul of his men, as well as their bodies and legs.' Written after the American Civil War, General Sherman's words are as relevant now as they were then. The soul of an army reaches both into the military as well as the civilian system. However, society has yet to understand what this means in terms of civil–military relations, while in the new era, the military has yet to translate this into a meaningful political and social engagement with society.

7: THE NEW WORLD ORDER

1. Kegley and Wittkopf, *World Politics*, p. 10. See also Russett and Starr, *World Politics*, p. xi.

2. John Mearsheimer, 'Why We Will Soon Miss the Cold War', *Atlantic Monthly* (August 1990), pp. 23–30.

3. Dan Cordtz, 'War in the Twenty-First Century: The Streetfighter State', *Financial World*, 29 August 1995, p. 42.
4. Gordon R. Sullivan and Anthony M. Coroalles, *Seeing the Elephant: Leading America's Army into the Twenty-First Century* (Cambridge, MA: Institute for Foreign Policy Analysis, 1995), p. 3.
5. Samuel P. Huntington, 'The Clash of Civilizations', *Foreign Affairs*, 72, 3 (Summer 1993), pp. 22–49.
6. Ibid., p. 35.
7. Ibid., p. 40.
8. Shireen T. Hunter, *The Future of Islam and the West: Clash of Civilizations or Peaceful Coexistence?* (Westport, CT: Praeger, 1998), published with the Center for Strategic and International Studies (Washington, DC). See also 'Comments: Responses to Samuel P. Huntington's "The Clash of Civilizations?"', *Foreign Affairs*, 72, 4 (September/October 1993), pp. 1–26.
9. Ibid., p. 28.
10. Joseph S. Nye Jr, *Understanding International Conflicts: An Introduction to Theory and History*, 2nd edn (New York: Longman, 1997), p. 181. The references to Nye in the remainder of this paragraph are from pp. 181–3. Although the author has written this book for college undergraduates, there are important insights for analyzing international politics and conflicts that go far beyond undergraduate considerations.
11. Martin van Creveld, 'The Fate of States', *Parameters: US Army War College Quarterly*, 26, 1 (Spring 1996), p. 4. The author bases his conclusions on four dimensions: 'The Declining Ability to Fight; The Rise and Fall of the Welfare State; Modern Technology, Economics, and the Media; and Maintain Public Order.' He discusses each of these, concluding that the '... fate of the state appears sealed ... it is coming to an end' (pp. 16–17).
12. Ronald Steel, 'The New Meaning of Security', in Jablonsky *et al.*, *US National Security*, p. 65.
13. Paul M. Kennedy, *The Rise and Fall of the Great Powers: Economic Change and Military Conflict from 1500 to 2000* (New York: Random House, 1987).
14. K. R. Dark and A. L. Harris, *The New World and the New World Order: US Relative Decline, Domestic Instability in the Americas and the End of the Cold War* (New York: St Martin's Press, 1996), p. 70.
15. For a particularly insightful view of information technology see Michael L. Dertouzos, *What Will Be: How the New World of Information Will Change Our Lives* (New York: HarperEdge, 1997).
16. See, for example, Freedman, *Revolution in Strategic Affairs*.

8: US STRATEGY AND CONFLICT CHARACTERISTICS

1. Carl von Clausewitz, *On War*, ed. Annotal Rappoport (Baltimore, MD: Penguin Books, 1968), p. 243.
2. Bruce Palmer Jr, 'Strategic Guidelines for the United States in the 1980s', in Bruce Palmer Jr (ed.), *Grand Strategy for the 1980s* (Washington, DC: American Enterprise Institute for Public Policy Research, 1978), p. 73.
3. Klaus Knorr, 'National Security Studies: Scope and Structure of the Field', in Trager and Kronenberg (eds), *National Security and American Society*, p. 6.
4. Barry R. Posen and Andrew L. Ross, 'Competing Visions for US Grand Strategy', *International Security*, 21, 3 (Winter 1996/97).
5. Ibid., p. 5.
6. See Stephen John Stedman, 'The Interventionists', in Eugene R. Wittkopf (ed.), *The*

Future of American Foreign Policy (New York: St Martin's Press, 1994), pp. 318–28.

7. Schwarzkopf, *Autobiography*, pp. 181, 188. See also Moore and Galloway, *We Were Soldiers Once*.

8. See, for example, Record, *The Wrong War*.

9. See William R. Peers, *The My Lai Massacre and Its Cover-Up: Beyond the Reach of Law?* (New York: Free Press, 1976), and by the same author, *The My Lai Inquiry* (New York: Norton, 1978).

10. McMaster, *Dereliction of Duty*, Timothy J. Lomperis, *From People's War to People's Rule: Insurgency, Intervention, and the Lessons of Vietnam* (Chapel Hill, NC: University of North Carolina Press, 1997), and Record, *The Wrong War*.

11. Record, *The Wrong War*, pp. xvii–xix.

12. George Bush, President of the United States, 'Reshaping Our Forces', delivered at the Aspen Institute, Aspen Colorado, 2 August 1990, *Vital Speeches of the Day*, 1990, p. 677. The concept of peacetime engagements was also detailed in the White House, *National Security Strategy of the United States* (Washington, DC: US Government Printing Office, January 1993).

13. Secretary of Defense Dick Cheney, 'US Defense Strategy and the DoD Budget Request', in a prepared statement to the House Armed Services Committee, *Defense Issues*, 6, 4 (1991), p. 3. The quotes related to the new strategy are from this source. See also Lewis Libby, 'Remarks on Shaping US Defence Strategy: Persistent Challenges and Enduring Strengths', *America's Role in a Changing World, Part II, Adelphi Papers 257*, Winter 1990/91, pp. 64–75, and Paul D. Wolfowitz, 'The New Defense Strategy', in Joseph Kruzel (ed.), *American Defense Annual, 1990–1991* (Lexington, MA: Lexington Books, 1990), pp. 176–95.

14. Michael P. W. Stone, Secretary of the Army, in a speech delivered at the National Strategy Forum, Chicago, Illinois, 20 February 1992.

15. See James Schlesinger, 'Quest for a Post-Cold War Foreign Policy', *Foreign Affairs*, 72, 1 (1993), p. 28.

16. Schwarzkopf, *Autobiography*, p. 460.

17. The White House, *A National Security Strategy for a New Century* (Washington, DC: US Government Printing Office, May 1997).

18. Ibid., p. 29.

19. Harry Summers, 'Clinton Should Practice What His Book Preaches', *Army Times*, 12 September 1994, p. 63.

20. *US Intervention Policy for the Post-Cold War World: New Challenges and New Responses*, Final Report of the Eighty-Fifth American Assembly, 7–10 April 1994 (New York: Harriman, 1994), p. 5.

21. See *FY 1994 Defense Budget Begins New Era*, news release (Washington, DC: Office of the Assistant Secretary of Defense – Public Relations, March 1994). See also Jim Tice, 'Drawdown Accelerates', *Army Times*, 12 April 1993, p. 4. See also Harlan K. Ullman, *In Irons: US Military Might in the New Century* (Washington, DC: National Defense University, 1995), particularly Ch. 1.

22. See Les Aspin, Chairman, Committee on Armed Services, House of Representatives, Memorandum, 'Sizing US Conventional Forces', 22 January 1992. Also see charts by Representative Aspin on 'The New Security: A Bottom-Up Approach to the Post-Cold War Era'.

23. Aspin, 'Sizing US Conventional Forces'.

24. *FY 1994 Defense Budget*.

25. Floyd Spence, Chairman, House National Security Committee, *National Security Report*, 2, 3 (Washington, DC: House National Security Committee, May 1998). See also Floyd D. Spence, Chairman, *National Security Committee Reports Defense Bill out of Committee*, press release (Washington, DC: House National Security Committee, 6 May 1998).

26. Tom Donnelly, '100,000 More Troops Could Be Cut by 2000', *Army Times*, 19 April 1993, p. 26.
27. Peter G. Peterson and James K. Sebenius, 'The Primacy of the Domestic Agenda', in Graham Allison and Gregory F. Treverton (eds), *Rethinking America's Security: Beyond Cold War to New World Order* (New York: W. W. Norton, 1992), p. 61.
28. Rick Maze, 'Clinton: Military Needs More Money', *Army Times*, 5 October 1998, p. 3. See also Rick Maze, '99 Defense Authorization Bill is "Band Aid" Compromise', *Army Times*, 5 October 1998, p. 3.
29. Michael Kilian, 'America's Needy Military: The High Cost of Neglect', *Chicago Tribune*, 18 October 1998, Section 2, p. 3.
30. Michael R. Gordon, 'Aspin Overhauls Pentagon to Bolster Policy Role', *New York Times*, 28 January 1993, p. A17. See also John Lancester, 'White House Outlines Vision of New Military', *Washington Post*, 30 January 1992, p. A-10.
31. See Tom Donnelly, 'Services Outline their Futures in High-stakes Era', *Army Times*, 26 April 1993, p. 25. See also Molly Moore, 'War Exposed Rivalries, Weaknesses in Military', *Washington Post*, 10 June 1991, pp. A-1–17.
32. Gen. Gordon R. Sullivan and Lt-Col. James M. Dubik, *Land Warfare in the 21st Century* (Carlisle, PA: US Army War College, Strategic Studies Institute, February 1993).
33. Secretary of the Air Force, *Global Reach – Global Power* (Washington, DC: Pentagon, n.d.); Department of the Air Force, *A Report, Reaching Globally, Reaching Powerfully: The United States Air Force in the Gulf War* (Washington, DC: US Government Printing Office, 1991). See also US Navy, Office of Chief of Naval Operations, *The United States Navy in 'Desert Storm'* (Washington, DC: Department of the Navy, 1991).
34. Earl H. Tilford Jr, *Halt Phase Strategy: New Wine in Old Skins … With Powerpoint* (Carlisle, PA: US Army War College, Strategic Studies Institute, 1998).
35. Ibid. This quote and the following quotes are taken from pp. 1, 16, 15, 29, 32, respectively.
36. Ibid., p. iii.
37. R.-Adm. James B. Hinkle, 'Influencing Global Events', *Armed Forces Journal International*, May 1997, pp. 33–4.
38. Ibid., p. 34. See also Colin S. Gray, *The Navy in the Post-Cold War World: The Uses and Value of Strategic Sea Power* (University Park: Pennsylvania State University Press, 1994).
39. Donald C. F. Daniel and Bradd C. Hayes, *The Future of US Sea Power* (Carlisle, PA: US Army War College, Strategic Studies Institute, 1993). This and the following quote are from p. 39.
40. Mackubin Thomas Owens, 'Organizing For Failure: Is The Rush Toward "Jointness" Going Off Track?', *Armed Forces Journal International* (June 1998), pp. 12–13.
41. Senator Dan Coats (R., Indiana), 'Joint Experimentation: Anything But Strategic Monism', *Armed Forces Journal International* (August 1998), pp. 46–7.
42. See, for example, Douglas W. Craft, *An Operational Analysis of the Persian Gulf War* (Carlisle, PA: US Army War College, Strategic Studies Institute, 1992).
43. Samuel W. Lewis, 'Point of View: The Decade of the 1990s', *United States Institute of Peace Journal*, 3, 1 (March 1990), p. 2.
44. For a detailed discussion of the characteristics of unconventional conflicts see Sam C. Sarkesian, *America's Forgotten Wars: The Counterrevolutionary Past and Lessons for the Future* (Westport, CT: Greenwood Press, 1984).
45. See Bush, 'Reshaping Our Forces'.
46. Millett and Maslowski, *Common Defense*, p. 334.
47. Callahan, *Unwinnable Wars*, p. 239.
48. James M. Smith, *USAF Culture and Cohesion: Building an Air and Space Force for the 21st Century*, INSS Occasional Paper 19 (US Air Force Academy, CO: Institute for National Security Studies, 1998), p. 15.

49. See, for example, Col. (Ret.) Lloyd J. Matthews (ed.), *Challenging the United States Symmetrically and Asymmetrically: Can America be Defeated?* (Carlisle, PA: US Army War College, Strategic Studies Institute, 1998).
50. Department of the Army, *FM 100–5 Operations* (Washington, DC: Government Printing Office, 1993), pp. 13–20.
51. Ibid., pp. 13–18.
52. Ibid., pp. 13–20.
53. Cheney, 'US Defense Strategy and DoD Budget Request', p. 3.
54. See, for example, Sam C. Sarkesian, *Unconventional Conflicts in a New Security Era: Lessons from Malaya and Vietnam* (Westport, CT: Greenwood, 1993).
55. Major Eduardo Aldunate, 'Observations on the Theory of LIC and Violence in Latin America', *Military Review*, June 1991, pp. 80, 86. See also Freedman, *Revolution in Strategic Affairs*, particularly p. 76, in which the author focuses on the apparent disconnection between information-age warfare and those within the political–social milieu of society.
56. Mao Tse-tung, *Guerrilla Warfare*, trans. and introduction Samuel B. Griffith (New York: Praeger, 1961), p. 7.
57. Samuel P. Huntington, 'The Clash of Civilizations', *Foreign Affairs*, 72, 3 (Summer 1993), p. 25.
58. For an excellent analysis of Clausewitz and Sun Tzu see Handel, *Masters of War*.
59. Hoffman, *Decisive Force*, p. 4.
60. *US Intervention Policy in the Post-Cold War World*, pp. 6–7.
61. Sullivan and Dubik, *Land Warfare in the 21st Century*, p. 11.
62. Sarkesian, *Unconventional Conflicts in a New Security Era*, pp. 188–9.
63. See, for example, Steven Metz and James Kievit, *Strategy and the Revolution in Military Affairs: From Theory to Policy* (Carlisle, PA: US Army War College, Strategic Studies Institute, 1995) and Freedman, *The Revolution in Strategic Affairs*.
64. Chairman, Joint Chiefs of Staff, *Joint Vision 2010*.

9: MILITARY FORCE AND OPERATIONAL PARAMETERS

1. Chairman, Joint Chiefs of Staff, *Joint Vision 2010*, p. 1.
2. See, for example, 'The Pentagon's Quadrennial Review', in ROA National Security report, May 1997, and George C. Wilson 'Cohen's Game Plan: Two Wars at Once, But Critics Argue that Two Major Regional Conflict Plan is Outdated', *Army Times*, 26 May 1997, p. 4. See also George C. Wilson, 'QDR Arrives to Favorable Reviews', *Army Times*, 2 June 1997, pp. 16–17, and Jack Weible, 'Panel: Good Points, but Where's the Money?', *Army Times*, 2 June 1997, p. 18. See also criticism of the two-war concept in William Matthews, 'Second Simultaneous War Would Cost Many Lives', *Army Times*, 19 October 1998. On p. 11, the author writes, 'The Army is ready to fight and win one major theater war, but is likely to suffer massive casualties if it tries to also fight and win a second one, according to Gen. Dennis Reimer [Army Chief of Staff].'
3. See, for example, Jeffrey Record, *The Creeping Irrelevance of US Force Planning* (Carlisle, PA: US Army War College, Strategic Studies Institute, 1998).
4. *Transforming Defense: National Security in the 21st Century*, Report of the National Defense Panel (Arlington, VA, December 1997).
5. Ibid., pp. ii, iv.
6. Gen. Colin Powell, as quoted in Harry Summers, 'Powell Echoes Grant in Focusing Military', *Army Times*, 27 September 1993, p. 68.
7. Gen. Colin Powell, 'US Forces: Challenges Ahead', *Foreign Affairs*, 72, 5 (Winter 1992/93), pp. 38–9.

8. As quoted in John G. Roos, 'The Perils of Peacekeeping: Tallying Costs in Blood, Coin, Prestige, and Readiness', *Armed Forces Journal International* (December 1993), p. 17.

9. Ibid.

10. House Committee on National Security, Congress of the United States, *Military Readiness 1997: Rhetoric and Reality* (Washington, DC: Superintendent of Documents, 1997), p. 1.

11. John Macartney, 'Weekly Intelligence Notes', *AEP Intelligencer* (Winter 1998), p. 1. The author writes that the CIA Director has changed the

> ... direction in CIA's Operations Directorate ... away from the clandestine operations aimed at influencing foreign governments or attempting to remove foreign political leaders. Covert operations are now aimed at disrupting terrorist plans, stopping narcotics shipments, or fouling up financial transactions of missile makers.

12. David Shukman, *Tomorrow's Wars: The Threat of High-Technology Weapons* (New York: Harcourt Brace, 1996), pp. 255–6.

13. Ralph Peters, 'Our Soldiers, Their Cities', *Parameters: US Army War College Quarterly*, 26, 1 (Spring 1996), p. 43.

14. See Matthews (ed.), *Challenging the United States*. Also in the same publication, Charles J. Dunlap Jr, 'Preliminary Observations: Asymmetrical Warfare and the Western Mindset', pp. 1–15, and Lloyd J. Matthews, 'Part I: Symmetries and Asymmetries: A Historical Perspective, Introduction', pp. 19–23.

15. 'New World Order: It Ain't Pretty; CinC's See Uncertainty, Turmoil Everywhere They Turn', *Army Times*, 3 May 1993, front page.

16. Allison and Treverton (eds), *Rethinking America's Security*, p. 421.

17. Ullman, *In Irons*, pp. 264–5.

18. Powell, *My American Journey*, p. 576.

19. For the major elements of the Weinberger Doctrine see Caspar W. Weinberger, *Annual Report to Congress, Fiscal Year 1987, Budget, FY 1988: Authorization Request and FY 1987–1991, Defense Programs* (Washington, DC, Government Printing Office, 5 February 1986).

20. Ibid. For an examination of this doctrine see David T. Twining, 'The Weinberger Doctrine and the Use of Force in the Contemporary Era', in Sabrosky and Sloane (eds), *The Recourse to War*, particularly pp. 9–38. See also Handel, *Masters of War*, pp. 185–203.

21. Sullivan and Dubik, *Land Warfare in the 21st Century*, p. 8 (italics in original).

22. Zbigniew Brzezinski, 'Selective Global Commitment', *Foreign Affairs*, 70, 4 (Fall 1991), pp. 1–2; Paul H. Nitze, 'America: An Honest Broker', *Foreign Affairs*, 69, 4 (Fall 1990), pp. 1–14; and Roger Nye, 'Soft Power', *Foreign Policy*, 72, 1 (1993), p. 4.

23. Jack N. Merritt, 'The Future of the US Army', in Kruzel (ed.), *American Defense Annual, 1990–1991*, p. 231.

24. Ibid., p. 239.

25. Ibid.

26. A. J. Bacevich, 'New Rules: Modern War and Military Professionalism', *Parameters: US Army War College Quarterly*, 20, 4 (December 1990), p. 22.

27. Gen. Fred C. Weyand, 'Vietnam Myths and American Realities', *CDRS CALL*, July–August 1976, pp. 3, 4. As quoted in Harry G. Summers Jr, *On Strategy: The Vietnam War in Context* (Carlisle, PA: US Army War College, Strategic Studies Institute, 1981), p. 25. Italics in original.

28. George C. Wilson, 'A "Can't Do" Attitude is Better', *Army Times*, 6 July 1998, p. 62.

10: FORCE STRUCTURE AND DOCTRINE: MAINSTREAM MILITARY AND
SPECIAL OPERATIONS FORCES

1. See, for example, Steven Metz and James Kievit, *The Revolution in Military Affairs and Conflict Short of War* (Carlisle, PA: US Army War College, Strategic Studies Institute, 1994); Paul Bracken and Raoul Henri Alcala', *Whiter the RMA: Two Perspectives in Tomorrow's Army* (Carlisle, PA: US Army War College, Strategic Studies Institute, 1994); and Freedman, *The Revolution in Strategic Affairs.*

2. Report to Congressional Committees, *Force Structure: Army Support Forces Can Meet Two-Conflict Strategy With Some Risks* (Washington, DC: General Accounting Office, 1997), p. 2.

3. See, for example, Report to the President, *Presidential Commission on the Assignment of Women in the Armed Forces* (Washington, DC: US Government Printing Office, 1992). Also see the *Kassebaum Report*, referring to Nancy Kassebaum Baker, Chairman of the Federal Advisory Commission on Gender-Related Training and Related Issues (Washington, DC: Department of Defense, 1997). The cover letter is addressed to Secretary of Defense William S. Cohen, dated 16 December 1997. A number of recommendations are made based on the fact that,

   > The Committee strongly supports a gender-integrated volunteer military force. The committee also firmly believes that gender-integrated training must continue to be an important element of the training program. But the committee has concluded that certain organizational changes are required.

   Another commission was established to look at integrated training. This commission's report is to be published in September 1998. See Rick Maze, 'Second Gender Panel ready for Look at Integrated Training', *Army Times*, 16 March 1998, p. 7.

4. *Presidential Commission*, pp. 22–3 spells out this recommendation and pp. 43–8 provide an alternative view that states 'The Armed Forces should not assign women to combat.'

5. Ibid.

6. Adapted from Jack Weible, 'The New Military: It's A Far Different Force Than A Generation Ago', *Army Times*, 13 July 1998, pp. 12–14. See also Ullman, *In Irons*, especially Ch. 1.

7. F. Richard Ciccone and Joesph A. Kirby, 'The Unknown Military', *Chicago Tribune*, 19 April 1998, pp. 1, 12.

8. Charles C. Moskos and John Sibley Butler, *All That We Can Be: Black Leadership and Racial Integration the Army Way*, Twentieth Century Fund Book (New York: Basic Books, 1996).

9. Ibid., p. 13.

10. David Gergen, 'Becoming "Race Savvy"', *US News and World Report*, 2 June 1997, p. 78.

11. Richard J. Newman, 'Camouflaging Racial Differences: 50 Years of Progress, now Slipping', *US News and World Report*, 27 July 1998, p. 27.

12. Charles Moskos and John Sibley Butler, 'Lessons on Race from the Army', *Chicago Tribune*, 26 July 1998. This and the following quote are from section 1, p. 15. See also McCormick, *The Downsized Warrior*, pp. 85–6.

13. Martin Binkin, *Who Will Fight the Next War? The Changing Face of the American Military* (Washington, DC: Brookings Institution, 1993), p. 168. See also Addis, Russo and Sebesta (eds), *Women Soldiers.*

14. Douglas A. Macgregor, *Breaking the Phalanx; A New Design for Landpower in the 21st Century* (Westport, CT: Praeger, 1997).

15. Ibid., p. 4. See also Sean D. Naylor, 'Experimentation Plan Advances Force XXI; Troop

Ready to Test Light Forces, New Strike Force', *Army Times*, 19 October 1998, pp. 4, 6.

16. Macgregor, *Breaking the Phalanx*, p. 214.
17. See, for example, William T. Johnson, Douglas V. Johnson II, James O. Kievit, Douglas C. Lovelace Jr, and Steven Metz, *The Principles of War in the 21st Century: Strategic Considerations* (Carlisle, PA: US Army War College, Strategic Studies Institute, 1995).
18. See, for example, Tilford, *Halt Phase Strategy*.
19. Record, *Creeping Irrelevance*, pp. 1–2.
20. Robert J. Leiber, 'Making Foreign Policy Without the Soviet Threat', in Robert J. Leiber (ed.), *Eagle Adrift: American Foreign Policy at the End of the Century* (New York: Longman, 1997), p. 17.
21. Hoffman, *Decisive Force*, p. 113.
22. Ibid., p. 115.
23. Donald M. Snow, *Distant Thunder: Third World Conflicts and the New International Order* (New York: St Martin's Press, 1993), p. 210.
24. See David Tucker, 'Fighting Barbarians', *Parameters: US Army War College Quarterly*, 28, 2 (Summer 1998), pp. 69–79.
25. This and the following quote are from Allan R. Millett and Peter Maslowski, *For the Common Defense: A Military History of the United States of America*, revised and expanded edn (New York: The Free Press, 1994), p. 272.
26. Ibid., p. 273.
27. Weigley, *American Way of War*, p. 221.
28. Stephen M. Duncan, *Citizen Warriors: America's National Guard and Reserve Forces and the Politics of National Security* (Novato, CA: Presidio Press, 1997).
29. Ibid., pp. 131–2.
30. Ibid., p. 225.
31. Ibid., pp. 226–39.
32. Ibid., pp. 239–40.
33. Report of the National Defense Panel December 1997, *Transforming Defense: National Security in the 21st Century* (Arlington, VA: National Defense Panel, 1997), p. 52.
34. G. E. Willis, 'National Guard Approves Cuts; Deal with Army Leadership Assures Organization Has Voice in Future Decisions', *Army Times*, 7 July 1997, p. 27. As the author notes, however, this is based on the assumption that there would develop and remain 'a good working partnership among the three Army components'.
35. Report of the National Defense Panel, *Transforming Defense*, p. 53.
36. John G. Roos, 'Cease Fire: Fragile Truce Holding in "Total Army"', *Armed Forces Journal International* (September 1998), p. 20.
37. See John M. Collins, *Special Operations Forces: An Assessment 1986–1993, CRS Report for Congress* (Washington, DC: Congressional Research Services, 1993), includes detailed analyses of congressional legislation. The Collins report is one of the best analyses of special operations forces. See also John M. Collins, *Special Operations Forces: An Assessment* (Washington, DC: National Defense University Press, 1994).
38. Collins, *Special Operations Forces: An Assessment*, p. 18.
39. Ibid., p. 149.
40. From a strategic perspective, a different view on Vietnam is provided by Lomperis, *From People's War to People's Rule*. The author argues against using Vietnam as a lesson of war for the United States. He writes that 'Vietnam is a better ghost than a lesson … it can be summoned for any lesson a conjurer wants' (p. 10). The issue of the Vietnam War is defined in terms of political legitimacy and compared with a number of case studies, with Vietnam being the basis for comparison. The two major questions the author examines are what makes for a successful insurgency and what are the most effective method and scope of Western intervention.
41. Susan L. Marquis, *Unconventional Warfare: Rebuilding US Special Operations Forces*

(Washington, DC: Brookings Institution, 1997), p. 6.

42. Ibid., pp. 6, 44.
43. Ibid., pp. 255–70. See also, for example, Lt-Gen. Peter J. Schoomaker, 'Special Operations: Shaping the Future Force', *Army*, 47, 4 (April 1997), pp. 12–15, and Dennis Steel, 'Defining Army Special Ops' Role for the Next Century', *Army* (April 1997), pp. 16–20.
44. For an excellent historical study of special forces see Charles M. Simpson III, *Inside the Green Berets: The First Thirty Years – A History of the US Army Special Forces* (Novato, CA: Presidio Press, 1983). See also Alfred H. Paddock Jr, *US Army Special Warfare: Its Origins* (Washington, DC: National Defense University, 1982).
45. Simpson, *Inside the Green Berets*, p. 1.
46. For some insights into such operations see William B. Breuer, *Shadow Warriors: The Covert War in Korea* (New York: John Wiley, 1997).
47. Col. Francis J. Kelly, *Vietnam Studies: US Army Special Forces, 1961–1971* (Washington, DC: Department of the Army, 1973), pp. 5–6.
48. See, for example, Kelly, *Vietnam Studies*, and Robin Moore, *The Green Berets* (New York: Avon Books, 1965).
49. Kelly, *Vietnam Studies*, p. 172.
50. Sarkesian, *Unconventional Conflicts*, pp. 188–9.

11: CONSTRUCTIVE POLITICAL ENGAGEMENT

1. Hackett, *The Profession of Arms*, p. 202.
2. Hoffman, *Decisive Force*, p. 131.
3. Ibid., p. 131.
4. As noted earlier, the issue of equilibrium is addressed by Johnson and Metz, 'American Civil–Military Relations: A Review of the Recent Literature', in Snider and Carlton-Carew (eds), *US Civil–Military Relations in Crisis or Transition?*, p. 217.
5. Kemble, *Image of the Army Officer*, p. 203.
6. R. C. Longworth, 'Like it or not, US in charge', *Chicago Tribune*, 12 April 1998, pp. 1, 12.
7. Ibid., p. 1.
8. Gen. Fred C. Weyand, as quoted in Harry G. Summers Jr, *On Strategy: The Vietnam War in Context* (Carlisle, PA: US Army War College, Strategic Studies Institute, 1981), p. 7.
9. Donald M. Snow, *Peacekeeping, Peacemaking and Peace-Enforcement: The US Role in the New International Order* (Carlisle, PA: US Army War College, Strategic Studies Institute, 1993), p. 6.
10. Most of this section is based on a version of Sam C. Sarkesian, 'It's Time for a Politically Savvy Military', *Army Times*, 17 November 1997, p. 64.
11. Moskos and Butler, *All That We Can Be*.
12. Clausewitz, *On War*, p. 87.
13. Ibid.
14. Ibid.
15. John Keegan, *A History of Warfare* (New York: Alfred A. Knopf, 1993), p. xvi.

12: THE PRESIDENT AND CIVILIAN AND MILITARY CULTURES

1. Rick Maze, 'Retired Officers Testify at Impeachment Hearings', *Army Times*, 14 December 1998, p. 6.
2. John G. Roos, 'Commander-in-Chief Clinton: The Military Has Already Been Marched

Down The Moniker Road', *Armed Forces Journal International* (November 1998), p. 4.
3. Ibid.
4. Ralph Peters, 'A Question of Leadership', *Wall Street Journal*, 17 December 1998. This and the following quote are from p. A22.
5. Walter L. Wallace, 'Toward a Disciplinary Matrix in Sociology', in Neil J. Smelser (ed.), *Handbook of Sociology* (Newbury Park, CA: Sage Publications, 1988), p. 24.
6. Alan Bernard and Jonathan Spencer, 'Culture', in Alan Bernard and Jonathan Spencer (eds), *Encyclopaedia of Social and Cultural Anthropology* (London: Routledge, 1996), p. 136.
7. Samuel Gilmore, 'The Contemporary Debate on Culture', in Marie L. Borgatta (ed.), *Encyclopedia of Sociology* (New York: Macmillan, 1992), p. 409.
8. David E. Hunter and Phillip Whitten (eds), *Encyclopedia of Anthropology* (New York: Harper & Row, 1976), p. 103.
9. Christopher Clausen, 'The Culture of Culture', *The New Leader* 77 (6–20 June), p. 14.
10. Hunter and Whitten, *Encyclopedia of Anthropology*, p. 103.
11. Ibid.
12. T. S. Eliot, *Christianity and Culture: The Idea of a Christian Society and Notes Toward the Definition of Culture* (San Diego, CA: Harcourt Brace, 1976), p. 93.
13. J. Jastrow and J. Mark Baldwin, 'Culture', in J. Mark Baldwin (ed.), *Dictionary of Philosophy and Psychology* (Gloucester, MA: Peter Smith, 1960), p. 248.
14. Clifford Geertz, *The Interpretation of Cultures: Selected Essays* (New York: Basic Books, 1973), p. 26.
15. See Alastair Iain Johnston, *Cultural Realism: Strategic Culture and Grand Strategy in Chinese History* (Princeton, NJ: Princeton University Press, 1995), p. 35.
16. William J. Bennett, *The Death of Outrage: Bill Clinton and the Assault on American Ideals* (New York: Free Press, 1998).
17. See note 15, above.
18. As quoted in G. E. Willis, 'Service Members Speak up on Clinton's Behavior', *Army Times*, 28 September 1998, p. 4.
19. See, for example, William C. Moore, 'The Military Must Revive Its Warrior Spirit', *Wall Street Journal*, 27 October 1998, p. A22.
20. See Don Snider, 'An Uninformed Debate on Military Culture', *Orbis, a Journal of World Affairs* (Winter 1998). The author provides an excellent overview of military culture and sub-cultures.
21. See 'Culture Wars in the Military', *Orbis, a Journal of World Affairs* (Winter 1998). This issue includes the following four articles: Don M. Snider, 'America's "Multicultural" Military'; Williamson Murray, 'Cultures of Victory and Defeat'; John Hillen, 'The Brave New World of Persons-at-Arms'; and Andrew J. Bacevich, 'Four Uncertain Trumpets of Change'.
22. For example, see Richard Parker, 'Military Losing the Recruiting Battle', *Chicago Tribune*, 13 December 1998, p. 14, section 1. See also Tom Philpott, 'Back on the Edge', *Retired Officer Magazine*, 14, 1 (January 1999), pp. 52–8, 60.
23. Michael Mandelbaum, 'Is Major War Obsolete?', *Survival, The IISS Quarterly* (Winter 1998–99), p. 20.
24. Donald Kagan, *On the Origins of War and the Preservation of Peace* (New York: Doubleday, 1995). See also Jeremy Black, *Why Wars Happen* (New York: New York University Press, 1998).
25. Kagan, *On the Origins of War*, p. 570.
26. Max Singer and Aaron Wildavsky, *The New World Order: Zones of Peace/Zones of Turmoil*, rev. edn (Chatham, NJ: Chatham House Publishers, 1996), pp. 208, 213.
27. Paul J. Best, 'American Force Posture for the Twenty-First Century', in Kul B. Rai, David F. Walsh and Paul J. Best (eds) *America in the 21st Century: Challenges and*

Opportunities in Domestic Politics (Upper Saddle River, NJ: Prentice-Hall, 1998), p. 211.

28. Moore and Galloway, *We Were Soldiers Once*. The quotes are from pp. xv and xvi.
29. General Matthew B. Ridgway (USA, Ret.). As told to Harold H. Martin, *Soldier: The Memoirs of Matthew B. Ridgway* (New York: Harper & Brothers, 1956), p. 305.
30. Ibid., p. 271.

Bibliography

The following journals, periodicals and newspapers have been quoted in this study:

Adelphi Papers
AEP Intelligencer
American Behavioral Scientist
American Enterprise
Armed Forces and Society
Armed Forces Journal International
Army
Army Times
Atlantic Monthly
Brookings Review
Chicago Tribune
Chicago Sun-Times
Financial World
Foreign Affairs
Foreign Policy
International Political Science Review
International Security
Journal of Military History
Military Review
Navy Times
New Leader
New York Times
Orbis, a Journal of World Affairs
Pacific Sociological Review
Parameters: US Army War College Quarterly
Public Opinion Quarterly
Retired Officer Magazine
Small Wars and Insurgencies
Strategic Forum

Bibliography

Strategic Review
Strategic Survey
Studies in Intelligence
Survival, The IISS Quarterly
United States Institute of Peace Journal
US Naval Institute Proceedings
US News and World Report
Wall Street Journal
Washington Monthly
Washington Post
Weekly Standard

Adams, Thomas K., *US Special Operations Forces in Action: The Challenge of Unconventional Warfare* (London: Frank Cass, 1998).

Addis, Elisabetta, Russo, Valeria E. and Sebesta, Lorenza (eds), *Women Soldiers: Images and Realities* (New York: St Martin's Press, 1997).

Allison, Graham and Treverton, Gregory F. (eds), *Rethinking America's Security: Beyond Cold War to New World Order* (New York: W. W. Norton, 1992).

Ambrose, Stephen E., *Duty Honor Country, A History of West Point* (Baltimore, MD: Johns Hopkins University Press, 1966).

——, *Citizen Soldiers: The US Army from the Normandy Beaches to the Bulge to the Surrender of Germany June 7, 1944–May 7, 1945* (New York: Simon & Schuster, 1997).

Ambrose, Stephen E. and Barber, James A. Jr (eds), *The Military and American Society: Essays & Readings* (New York: Macmillan, 1967).

Andrzejewski, Stanislaw, *Military Organization and Society* (London: Routledge & Kegan Paul, 1954).

The Army Enterprise Strategy (Washington, DC: Department of the Army, 1944).

Aspin, Les, Chairman, Committee on Armed Services, House of Representatives, Memorandum, 'Sizing US Conventional Forces' (Washington, DC: Congress of the United States, 22 January 1992).

Athern, Robert G., *William Tecumseh Sherman and the Settlement of the West* (Norman, OK: University of Oklahoma Press, 1956).

Baldwin, J. Mark (ed.), *Dictionary of Philosophy and Psychology* (Gloucester, MA: Peter Smith, 1960).

Bell, William Gardner, *Commanding Generals and Chiefs of Staff, 1775–1983* (Washington, DC: Center of Military History United States Army, 1983).

Bennett, William J., *The Death of Outrage: Bill Clinton and the Assault on American Ideals* (New York: Free Press, 1998).

Bernard, Alan and Spencer, Jonathan (eds), *Encyclopaedia of Social and Cultural Anthropology* (London: Routledge, 1996).

Binkin, Martin, *Who Will Fight the Next War? The Changing Face of the American*

Military (Washington, DC: Brookings Institution, 1993).

Black, Jeremy, *Why Wars Happen* (New York: New York University Press, 1998).

Borgatta, Marie L. (ed.), *Encyclopedia of Sociology* (New York: Macmillan, 1992).

Bozeman, Adda, *Strategic Intelligence and Statecraft: Selected Essays* (Washington, DC: Brassey's, 1992).

Bracken, Paul and Alcala', Raoul Henri, *Whiter the RMA: Two Perspectives in Tomorrow's Army* (Carlisle, PA: US Army War College, Strategic Studies Institute, 22 July 1994).

Braestrup, Peter, *Big Story: How the American Press and Television Reported and Interpreted the Crisis of Tet 1968 in Vietnam and Washington*, vol. I (Boulder, CO: Westview Press, 1977).

Breuer, William B., *Shadow Warriors: The Covert War in Korea* (New York: John Wiley, 1997).

Callahan, David, *Unwinnable Wars: American Power and Ethnic Conflict*, Twentieth Century Fund Book (New York: Hill & Wong, 1997).

Carr–Saunders, A. M. and Wilson, P. A., *The Professions* (Oxford: Clarendon Press, 1933).

Catton, Bruce, *Mr Lincoln's Army* (Garden City, NY: Doubleday, 1951).

——, *Grant Takes Command* (Boston, MA: Little Brown, 1968).

Chairman, Joint Chiefs of Staff, *Joint Vision 2010* (Washington, DC: Department of Defense, 1996).

Clausewitz, Carl von, *On War*, ed. A. Rappoport (Baltimore, MD: Penguin Books, 1968).

Cline, Ray S., *World Power Assessment: A Calculus or Strategic Drift* (Washington, DC: The Center for Strategic and International Studies, 1975).

Clotfelter, James, *The Military in American Politics* (New York: Harper & Row, 1973).

Collins, John M., *Special Operations Forces: An Assessment 1986–1993, CRS Report for Congress* (Washington, DC: Congressional Research Services, 1993).

——, *Special Operations Forces: An Assessment* (Washington, DC: National Defense University Press, 1994).

Coward, Barry, *Oliver Cromwell: Profiles in Power* (London: Longman, 1991).

Craft, Douglas W., *An Operational Analysis of the Persian Gulf War* (Carlisle, PA: US Army War College, Strategic Studies Institute, 1992).

Craig, Gordon A. and George, Alexander L., *Force and Statecraft: Diplomatic Problems of Our Time*, 3rd edn (New York: Oxford University Press, 1995).

Crocker, Lt-Col. (Ret.), Lawrence P., *Army Officer's Guide*, 45th edn (Harrisburg, PA: Stackpole Books, 1990).

——, *Army Officer's Guide*, 47th edn (Harrisburg, PA: Stackpole Books, 1996).

Daniel, Donald C. F. and Hayes, Bradd C., *The Future of US Sea Power* (Carlisle, PA: US Army War College, Strategic Studies Institute, 1993).

Dark, K. R. and Harris, A. L., *The New World and the New World Order: US*

Relative Decline, Domestic Instability in the Americas and the End of the Cold War (New York: St Martin's Press, 1996).

Department of the Air Force, *A Report, Reaching Globally, Reaching Powerfully: The United States Air Force in the Gulf War* (Washington, DC: US Government Printing Office, 1991).

Department of the Army, *FM 100-25, Doctrine for Army Special Operations Forces* (Washington, DC: US Government Printing Office, 1991).

——, *FM 100-5 Operations* (Washington, DC: US Government Printing Office, 1993).

——, *The Army Enterprise Strategy* (Washington, DC: US Dept of the Army, 1994).

Dertouzos, Michael L., *What Will Be: How the New World of Information Will Change Our Lives* (New York: HarperEdge, 1997).

Duncan, Stephen M., *Citizen Warriors: America's National Guard and Reserve Forces and the Politics of National Security* (Novato, CA: Presidio Press, 1997).

Dupuy, Trevor and Hammerman, Gary M., *People and Events of the American Revolution* (New York: R. R. Bowker, 1974).

Dupuy, Ernest R. and Dupuy, Trevor, *The Harper Encyclopedia of Military History, From 3500 BC to the Present* (New York: HarperCollins, 1993).

Dye, Thomas R., *Politics in America*, 3rd edn (Upper Saddle River, NJ: Prentice-Hall, 1999).

Eisenhower, John S. D., *Agent of Destiny: The Life and Times of General Winfield Scott* (New York: Free Press, 1997).

Ekirch, Arthur A. Jr, *The Civilian and the Military* (New York: Oxford University Press, 1956).

Eliot, T. S., *Christianity and Culture: The Idea of a Christian Society and Notes Toward the Definition of Culture* (San Diego, CA: Harcourt Brace, 1976).

Ellis, Joseph and Moore, Robert, *School for Soldiers: West Point and the Profession of Arms* (New York: Oxford University Press, 1974).

Finer, Samuel E., *The Man on Horseback: The Role of the Military in Politics* (New York: Praeger, 1962).

Fishel, John T., *The Fog of Peace: Planning and Executing the Restoration of Panama* (Carlisle, PA: US Army War College, Strategic Studies Institute, 1992).

——, *Civil Military Operations in the New World* (Westport, CT: Praeger, 1997).

Freedman, Lawrence, *The Revolution in Strategic Affairs*, Adelphi Paper 318 (New York: Oxford University Press, 1998).

Freeman, Douglas Southall, *George Washington, A Biography*, V, *Victory with the Help of France* (New York: Charles Scribner's Sons, 1952).

FY 1994 Defense Budget Begins New Era, news release (Washington, DC: Office of the Assistant Secretary of Defense – Public Relations, 1994).

Garrity, John A., *The American Nation: A History of the United States* (New York: Harper & Row, 1966).

Gaston, James C. (ed.) *Grand Strategy and the Decisionmaking Process* (Washington, DC: National Defense University Press, 1992).

Geertz, Clifford, *The Interpretation of Cultures: Selected Essays* (New York: Basic Books, 1973).

Gentles, Ian, *The New Model Army in England, Ireland and Scotland, 1643–1645* (Oxford: Blackwell, 1992).

Geyer, Georgie Ann, *Americans No More: The Death of Citizenship* (New York: Atlantic Monthly Press, 1996).

Goodpaster, Andrew J. and Huntington, Samuel P., *et al.* (eds), *Civil–Military Relations* (Washington, DC: American Enterprises Institute for Public Policy, 1977).

Gray, Colin S., *The Navy in the Post-Cold War World: The Uses and Value of Strategic Sea Power* (University Park, PA: Pennsylvania State University Press, 1994).

Gress, David, *From Plato to NATO: The Idea of the West and Its Opponents* (New York: Free Press, 1998).

Hackett, Gen. Sir John, *The Profession of Arms* (New York: Macmillan, 1983).

Handel, Michael I., *Masters of War: Classical Strategic Thought*, 2nd revised and expanded edn (London: Frank Cass, 1996).

Hauser, Lt-Col. William, *America's Army in Transition: A Study in Civil–Military Relations* (Baltimore, MD: Johns Hopkins University Press, 1973).

Hays, Peter L., Vallance, Brenda J. and Van Tassel, Alan R. (eds), *American Defense Policy*, 7th edn (Baltimore, MD: Johns Hopkins University Press, 1997).

Henderson, W. Darryl, *Cohesion: The Human Element in Combat* (Washington, DC: National Defense University Press, 1985).

Hersh, Seymour, *My Lai 4* (New York: Random House, 1970).

Hickey, Donald R., *The War of 1812: A Forgotten Conflict* (Urbana, IL: University of Illinois Press, 1989).

Hirshon, Stanley, *The White Tecumseh* (New York: John Wiley, 1997).

Hoffman, F. G., *Decisive Force: The New American Way of War* (Westport, CT: Praeger, 1996).

Hoopes, Townsend, *The Limits of Intervention* (New York: David McKay, 1970).

House Committee on National Security, Congress of the United States, *Military Readiness 1997: Rhetoric and Reality* (Washington, DC: Superintendent of Documents, 1997).

Hunter, David E. and Whitten, Phillip (eds), *Encyclopedia of Anthropology* (New York: Harper and Row, 1976).

Hunter, Shireen T., *The Future of Islam and the West: Clash of Civilizations or Peaceful Coexistence?* (Westport, CT: Praeger, 1998).

Huntington, Samuel P., *The Soldier and the State: The Theory and Politics of Civil–Military Relations* (Cambridge, MA: Harvard University Press, 1957; New York: Vintage, 1964).

Jablonsky, David, Steel, Ronald, Korb, Lawrence, Halperin, Morton H. and Ellsworth, Robert, *US National Security: Beyond the Cold War* (Carlisle, PA: US Army War College, Strategic Studies Institute, 1997).

Janowitz, Morris, *The Professional Soldier: A Social and Political Portrait* (Glencoe, IL: Free Press, 1960).

Janowitz, Morris and Little, Roger, *Sociology and the Military Establishment*, revised edn (New York: Russell Sage Foundation, 1965).

Johnson, William T., Johnson, Douglas V. II, Kievit, James O., Lovelace, Douglas C. Jr and Metz, Steven, *The Principles of War in the 21st Century: Strategic Considerations* (Carlisle, PA: US Army War College, Strategic Studies Institute, 1995).

Johnston, Alastair Ian, *Cultural Realism: Strategic Culture and Grand Strategy in Chinese History* (Princeton, NJ: Princeton University Press, 1995).

Jordan, Amos A., Taylor, William J. and Mazarr, Michael J., *American National Security*, 5th edn (Baltimore, MD: Johns Hopkins University Press, 1999).

Kagan, Donald, *On the Origins of War and the Preservation of Peace* (New York: Doubleday, 1995).

Kassebaum Report, referring to Nancy Kassebaum Baker, Chairman of the Federal Advisory Commission on Gender-Related Training and Related Issues (Washington, DC: Department of Defense, 1997).

Keegan, John, *A History of Warfare* (New York: Alfred A. Knopf, 1993).

Kegley, Charles W. Jr and Wittkopf, Eugene R., *American Foreign Policy: Patterns and Process*, 5th edn (New York: St Martin's Press, 1996).

——, *World Politics: Trends and Transformations*, 6th edn (New York: St Martin's Press, 1997).

Kelly, Col. Francis J., *Vietnam Studies: US Army Special Forces, 1961–1971* (Washington, DC: Department of the Army, 1973).

Kemble, C. Robert, *The Image of the Army Officer in America: Background for Current Views* (Westport, CT: Greenwood Press, 1973).

Kennedy, Paul M., *The Rise and Fall of the Great Powers: Economic Change and Military Conflict from 1500 to 2000* (New York: Random House, 1987).

Kenyon, John P., *The Stuart Constitution, 1603–1688*, 2nd edn (Cambridge: Cambridge University Press, 1986).

Klare, Michael T. and Chandran, Yogesh (eds), *World Security: Challenges for a New Century*, 3rd edn (New York: St Martin's Press, 1998).

Klare, Michael T. and Thomas, Daniel C. (eds), *World Security: Challenges for a New Century* (New York: St Martin's Press, 1991).

Kruzel, Joseph (ed.), *American Defense Annual, 1990–1991* (Lexington, MA: Lexington Books, 1990).

Lehman, Hon. John F. Jr and Sicherman, Harvey, *The Demilitarization of the Military*, Report of a Defense Task Force (Philadelphia, PA: Foreign Policy Research Institute, 1997).

Leiber, Robert J. (ed.), *Eagle Adrift: American Foreign Policy at the End of the*

Century (New York: Longman, 1997).

Lomperis, Timothy J., *From People's War to People's Rule: Insurgency, Intervention, and the Lessons of Vietnam* (Chapel Hill: University of North Carolina Press, 1997).

Lyons, Gene M. and Masland, John W., *Education and Military Leadership* (Princeton, NJ: Princeton University Press, 1959).

McCormick, David, *The Downsized Warrior: America's Army in Transition* (New York: New York University Press, 1998).

McFarland, Keith D., 'The 1949 Revolt of the Admirals', in Lloyd J. Matthews and Dale E. Brown (eds), *The Parameters of War: Military History from the Journal of the US Army War College* (Washington, DC: Pergamon-Brassey's).

McFeely, William S., *Grant, A Biography* (New York: W. W. Norton, 1981).

Macgregor, Douglas A., *Breaking the Phalanx: A New Design for Landpower in the 21st Century* (Westport, CT: Praeger, 1997).

McMaster, H. R., *Dereliction of Duty: Lyndon Johnson, Robert McNamara, the Joint Chiefs of Staff, and the Lies That Led to Vietnam* (New York: HarperCollins, 1997).

McNamara, Robert S. with VanDeMark, Brian, *In Retrospect: The Tragedy and Lessons of Vietnam* (New York: Times Books, 1995).

McPherson, James M., *Battle Cry of Freedom* (New York: McGraw-Hill, 1989).

Mahan, Alfred T., *The Influence of Sea Power Upon History, 1660–1783* (Boston, MA: Little, Brown, 1890).

Mao Tse-tung, *Guerrilla Warfare*, trans. and introduction Samuel B. Griffith (New York: Praeger, 1961).

Margiotta, Franklin D. (ed.) *The Changing World of the American Military* (Boulder, CO: Westview Press, 1978).

Marquis, Susan L., *Unconventional Warfare: Rebuilding US Special Operations Forces* (Washington, DC: Brookings Institution, 1997).

Martin, Harold H., *Soldier: The Memoirs of Matthew B. Ridgway* (New York: Harper & Brothers, 1956).

Martin, James Kirby and Lender, Mark Edward, *A Respectable Army: The Military Origins of the Republic, 1763–1789* (Arlington Heights, IL: Harlan Davidson, 1982).

Masland, John W. and Radway, Laurence I., *Soldiers and Scholars* (Princeton, NJ: Princeton University Press, 1957).

Matloff, Maurice (ed.), *American Military History*; II, *1902–1996* (Conshohocken, PA: Combined Books, 1996).

Matthews, Col. (Ret.) Lloyd J. (ed.), *Challenging the United States Symmetrically and Asymmetrically: Can America be Defeated?* (Carlisle, PA: US Army War College, Strategic Studies Institute, 1998).

Matthews, Lloyd J. and Brown, Dale E. (eds), *The Parameters of War: Military History from the Journal of the US Army War College* (Washington, DC: Pergamon-Brassey's, 1987).

Menard, Orville D., *The Army and the Fifth Republic* (Lincoln, NE: University of Nebraska Press, 1967).

Metz, Steven and Kievit, James, *Strategy and the Revolution in Military Affairs: From Theory to Policy* (Carlisle, PA: US Army War College, Strategic Studies Institute, 1995).

Miller, John T., *Americans No More? The Unmaking of Americans: How Multiculturalism Has Undermined America's Assimilation Ethic* (New York: Free Press, 1998).

Millett, Allan R., *The American Political System and Civilian Control of the Military: A Historical Perspective* (Columbus: Ohio State University Press, 1979).

Millett, Allan R. and Maslowski, Peter, *For the Common Defense: A Military History of the United States of America*, revised and expanded edn (New York: Free Press, 1994).

Millis, Walter, *Arms and Men: A Study in Military History* (New York: Putnam, 1956).

Moore, Lt-Gen. (Ret.) Harold G. and Galloway, Joseph L., *We Were Soldiers Once ... and Young: Ia Drang: The Battle that Changed the War in Vietnam* (New York: Random House, 1992).

Moore, Robin, *The Green Berets* (New York: Avon Books, 1965).

Moskos, Charles C. and Butler, John Sibley, *All That We Can Be: Black Leadership and Racial Integration the Army Way*, Twentieth Century Fund Book (New York: Basic Books, 1996).

Nye, Joseph S. Jr, *Understanding International Conflicts: An Introduction to Theory and History*, 2nd edn (New York: Longman, 1997).

Paddock, Alfred H. Jr, *US Army Special Warfare: Its Origins* (Washington, DC: National Defense University, 1982).

Palmer, Bruce Jr (ed.), *Grand Strategy for the 1980s* (Washington, DC: American Enterprise Institute for Public Policy Research, 1978).

Peers, William R., *The My Lai Massacre and Its Cover-Up: Beyond the Reach of Law?* (New York: Free Press, 1976).

——, *The My Lai Inquiry* (New York: Norton, 1978).

Powell, Colin with Persica, Joseph E., *My American Journey* (New York: Random House, 1995).

Proxmire, William, *Report from the Wasteland* (New York: Praeger Publishers, 1970).

Rai, Kul B., Walsh, David F. and Best, Paul J. (eds), *America in the 21st Century: Challenges and Opportunities in Domestic Politics* (Upper Saddle River, NJ: Prentice-Hall, 1998).

Record, Jeffrey, *The Wrong War: Why We Lost in Vietnam* (Annapolis, MD: Naval Institute Press, 1998).

——, *The Creeping Irrelevance of US Force Planning* (Carlisle, PA: US Army War College, Strategic Studies Institute, 1998).

Report to Congressional Committees, *Force Structure: Army Support Forces Can Meet Two-Conflict Strategy With Some Risks* (Washington, DC: General Accounting Office, 1997).

Report of the National Defense Panel December 1997, *Transforming Defense: National Security in the 21st Century* (Arlington, VA: National Defense Panel, 1997).

Report to the President, *Presidential Commission on the Assignment of Women in the Armed Forces* (Washington, DC: US Government Printing Office, 1992).

Reporting the Next War, Cantigny Conference Series, Robert R. McCormick Tribune Foundation, report of a conference held at Cantigny, Wheaton, Illinois, 23–24 April 1992.

Reynolds, Russell B., *The Officer's Guide* (Harrisburg, PA: Stackpole Books, 1970).

Ricks, Thomas E., *Making the Corps* (New York: Scribner, 1998).

Rossiter, Clinton, *The Political Thought of the American Revolution: Part Three of Seedtime of the Republic* (New York: Harcourt, Brace, 1963).

Russett, Bruce and Starr, Harvey, *World Politics: The Menu for Choice* (New York: W. H. Freeman, 1996).

Sabrosky, Alan Ned and Sloane, Robert L. (eds), *The Recourse to War: An Appraisal of the 'Weinberger Doctrine'* (Carlisle, PA: US Army War College Strategic Studies Institute, 1988).

Sarkesian, Sam C., *The Professional Army Officer in a Changing Society* (Chicago, IL: Nelson-Hall, 1975).

——, *Beyond the Battlefield: The New Military Professionalism* (New York: Pergamon Press, 1981).

——, *America's Forgotten Wars: The Counterrevolutionary Past and Lessons for the Future* (Westport, CT: Greenwood Press, 1984).

——, *Unconventional Conflicts in a New Security Era: Lessons from Malaya and Vietnam* (Westport, CT: Greenwood, 1993).

——, *US National Security: Policymakers, Processes, and Politics*, 2nd edn (Boulder, CO: Lynne Rienner, 1995).

Sarkesian, Sam C. and Gannon, Thomas M. (eds), 'Military Ethics and Professionalism', special issue of *American Behavioral Scientist*, 19, 8 (May/June 1976).

Sarkesian, Sam C., Williams, John Allen and Bryant, Fred B., *Soldiers, Society, and National Security* (Boulder, CO: Lynne Rienner, 1995).

Schlesinger, Arthur M. Jr, *The Disuniting of America: Reflections on a Multicultural Society*, revised edn (New York: W. W. Norton, 1998).

Schwarzkopf, Gen. Norman H. with Petre, Peter, *The Autobiography: It Doesn't Take a Hero* (New York: Linda Grey Bantam Books, 1992).

Scott, Winfield, *The Memoirs of Lieutenant General Winfield S. Scott, LL.D.*, I (Freeport, NY: Books for Libraries Press, 1970).

Secretary of the Air Force, *Global Reach – Global Power* (Washington, DC: Department of Defense, 1991).

Sherman, William Tecumseh, *Memoirs of General W. T. Sherman* (New York: The Library of America, 1990).

Sherrill, Robert, *Military Justice is to Justice as Military Music is to Music* (New York: Harper and Row, 1970).

Shukman, David, *Tomorrow's Wars: The Threat of High-Technology Weapons* (New York: Harcourt Brace, 1996).

Simpson, Charles M. III, *Inside the Green Berets: The First Thirty Years – A History of the US Army Special Forces* (Novato, CA: Presidio Press, 1983).

Singer, Max and Wildavsky, Aaron, *The New World Order: Zones of Peace / Zones of Turmoil*, rev. edn (Chatham, NJ: Chatham House Publishers, 1996).

Smelser, Marshall, *American History at a Glance* (New York: Barnes and Noble, 1963).

Smelser, Neil J. (ed.), *Handbook of Sociology* (Newbury Park, CA: Sage, 1988).

Smith, James M., *USAF Culture and Cohesion: Building an Air and Space Force for the 21st Century*, INSS Occasional Paper 19 (US Air Force Academy, CO: Institute for National Security Studies, June 1998).

Smith, Louis, *American Democracy and Military Power: A Study of Civil Control of the Military Power in the United States* (Chicago: University of Chicago Press, 1951).

Snider, Don M. and Carlton-Carew, Miranda A. (eds), *US Civil–Military Relations in Crisis or Transition?* (Washington, DC: Center for Strategic & International Studies, 1995).

Snow, Donald M., *Peacekeeping, Peacemaking and Peace-Enforcement: The US Role in the New International Order* (Carlisle, PA: US Army War College, Strategic Studies Institute, 1993).

——, *Distant Thunder: Third World Conflicts and the New International Order* (New York: St Martin's Press, 1993).

——, *National Security: Defense Policy in a Changed International Order*, 4th edn (New York: St Martin's Press, [1993] 1998).

Sorley, Lewis, *Honorable Warrior General Harold K. Johnson and the Ethics of Command* (Lawrence, KS: University of Kansas Press, 1998).

Spence, Floyd D., Chairman, House National Security Committee, *National Security Report*, 2, 3 (Washington, DC: House National Security Committee, May 1998).

——, *National Security Committee Reports Defense Bill out of Committee*, press release (Washington, DC: House National Security Committee, 1998).

——, *Summary of Major Provisions, HR 3616: National Defense Authorization Act for Fiscal Year 1999* (Conference Report) (Washington, DC: House National Security Committee, 1998).

Sullivan, Gordon R. and Coroalles, Anthony M., *Seeing the Elephant: Leading America's Army into the Twenty-First Century* (Cambridge, MA: Institute for

Foreign Policy Analysis, 1995).

Sullivan, Gen. Gordon R. and Dubik, Lt-Col. James M., *Land Warfare in the 21st Century* (Carlisle, PA: US Army War College, Strategic Studies Institute, 1993).

Summers, Harry G. Jr, *On Strategy: The Vietnam War in Context* (Carlisle, PA: US Army War College, Strategic Studies Institute, 1981).

Sun Tzu, *The Art of War*, trans. and introduction Samuel B. Griffith (New York: Oxford University Press, 1971).

Tannen, Deborah, *The Argument Culture: Moving from Debate to Dialogue* (New York: Random House, 1998).

Tap, Bruce, *Over Lincoln's Shoulder: The Committee on the Conduct of the War* (Lawrence, KS: University Press of Kansas, 1998).

Taras, Raymond C. and Ganguly, Rajat, *Understanding Ethnic Conflict: The International Dimension* (New York: Longman, 1998).

Taylor, Maxwell, *Swords and Plowshares* (New York: W. W. Norton, 1972).

Tilford, Earl H. Jr, *Halt Phase Strategy: New Wine in Old Skins ... With Powerpoint* (Carlisle, PA: US Army War College, Strategic Studies Institute, 1998).

Trager, Frank and Kronenberg, Philip S. (eds), *National Security and American Society: Theory and Process, and Policy* (Lawrence, KS: University of Kansas Press, 1973).

Transforming Defense: National Security in the Twenty-first Century (Report of the National Defense Panel, Arlington, VA, December, 1977).

Trefousse, Hans, *The Radical Republicans: Lincoln's Vanguard for Racial Justice* (New York: Knopf, 1969).

Ullman, Harlan K., *In Irons: US Military Might in the New Century* (Washington, DC: National Defense University, 1995).

Upton, Emory, *The Military Policy of the United States* (Washington, DC: US Government Printing Office, 1904).

US House of Representatives, Committee on Armed Services, *Women in the Military: The Tailhook Affair and the Problem of Sexual Harassment* (Washington, DC: US House of Representatives, September 1992).

US Intervention Policy for the Post-Cold War World: New Challenges and New Responses, Final Report of the Eighty-Fifth American Assembly 7–10 April 1994 (New York: Harriman, 1994).

US Navy, Office of Chief of Naval Operations, *The United States Navy in 'Desert Storm'* (Washington, DC: Department of the Navy, 1991).

Utley, Robert M., *Frontier Regulars, the United States Army and the Indian 1866–1891* (New York: Macmillan, 1973).

Vigny, Alfred de, *Servitude et Grandeur Militaires* (Paris: Calmann-Levy, 1925).

——, *The Military Condition*, trans. and notes Marguerite Barnett (London: Oxford University Press, 1964).

Wald, Kenneth D., *Religion and Politics in the United States*, 2nd edn

(Washington, DC: CQ Press, 1992).

Weigley, Russell F., *The American Way of War: A History of United States Military Strategy and Policy* (Bloomington, IN: Indiana University Press, 1977).

Weinberger, Casper, *Annual Report to Congress, Fiscal Year 1987 Budget, FY 1988: Authorization Request and FY 1987–1991 Defense Programs* (Washington, DC: Government Printing Office, 1986).

Whitehead, Fred (ed.), *Culture Wars: Opposing Viewpoints* (San Diego, CA: Greenhaven Press, 1994).

White House, *National Security Strategy of the United States* (Washington, DC: US Government Printing Office, 1993).

——, *A National Security Strategy for a New Century* (Washington, DC: US Government Printing Office, 1997).

Williams, T. Harry, *Lincoln and the Radicals* (Madison, WI: University of Wisconsin Press, 1941).

——, *Lincoln and His Generals* (New York: Alfred Knopf, 1952).

Wittkopf, Eugene R. (ed.), *The Future of American Foreign Policy* (New York: St Martin's Press, 1994).

Wolfe, Alan, *One Nation, After All: What Americans Really Think About God, Country, Family, Racism, Welfare, Immigration, Homosexuality, Work, The Right, The Left and Each Other* (New York: Viking Press, 1998).

Zeigler, David W., *War, Peace, and International Politics*, 7th edn (New York: Longman, 1997).

Index